ES — SEPT. 1925.

PACIFIC PALISADES

Where the Mountains Meet the Sea

Betty Lou Young

The beach at Pacific Palisades ca. 1926. Photograph by Clifford Clearwater

PACIFIC PALISADES

Where the Mountains Meet the Sea

Editor and Author
BETTY LOU YOUNG

Design and Photography
THOMAS R. YOUNG

PACIFIC PALISADES

HISTORICAL SOCIETY PRESS

1983

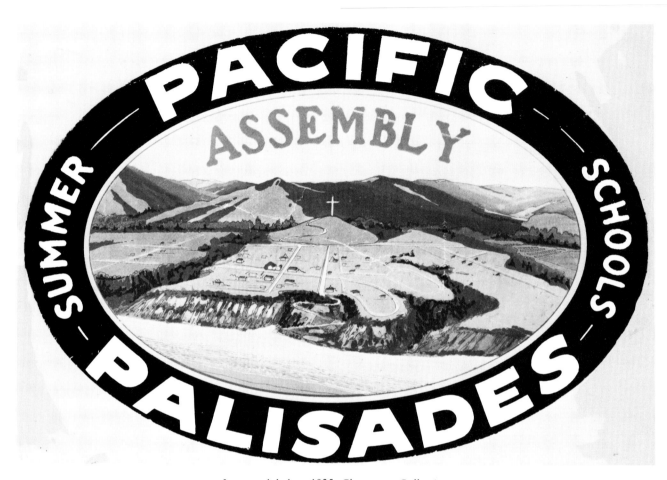

Luggage label ca. 1925. *Clearwater Collection*

Copyright 1983 Pacific Palisades Historical Society Press
Printing by Welsh Graphics
Typesetting by I/OCR Corporation
4,000 copies produced

Pacific Palisades Historical Society
Box 1299 Pacific Palisades
California 90272

Cover design: Pacific Palisades at dusk from the western rim of Temescal Canyon. The light streak in the sky above the Palos Verdes peninsula represents a plane taking off from International Airport. Photograph by Thomas R. Young

Table of Contents

Women's Christian Temperance Union booth at the Assembly grounds ca. 1923. *Clearwater Collection*

Acknowledgments

Compiling and publishing the history of Pacific Palisades has been the long-term goal of the Pacific Palisades Historical Society and was largely inspired by the Clearwater family's gift to the Society of Zola and Clifford Clearwater's collection of historical photographs, copies of *The Palisadian,* and other memorabilia.

Interest in preserving the community's past began when the Historical Society was formed on May 30, 1972, by sixteen people who shared a common interest in local history, among them eleven who are still active members: Kate and Pete Ahrens, June Blum, Zola Clearwater, Phyllis Genovese, Roberta Greenwood, Katie LaHue, Ernest Marquez, Anita Melstrom, Grace and Gordon Stuart.

The group met regularly with Katie LaHue, then reference librarian at the local library, who presided and arranged for speakers and exhibits. In July, 1973, the Society was formally incorporated, Ethel Haydon being chosen the first president under the new constitution, followed by Katie LaHue, William Burkhart, Barbara Burkhart, Betty Lou Young, Frances Brucher, Harriet Axelrad, and, currently, Bernice Park.

The decision to publish a book was made in 1980, at the instigation of Katie LaHue, who worked tirelessly for the next three years as chairman of the publications committee, spearheading every phase of the project, and writing a chapter on Thomas Ince and Inceville. Betty Lou Young served as editor and author and conducted the basic research, while Thomas R. Young signed on as photographer, a long-term commitment which included photocopying, original photography, consultation on the text, design of the book, and overall encouragement. Ernest Marquez, local historian and descendant of the Marquez and Reyes land grant families, collaborated on the design and production of the book, wrote the segment on the Rancho Boca de Santa Monica, and provided historic photographs from his extensive collection.

Dr. Richard Logan, Professor of History at UCLA, contributed a lively dissertation on the natural history of Pacific Palisades, and Roberta Greenwood, Archaeological Research Associate at the Los Angeles County Museum of Natural History gave us a colorful and informative chapter on the prehistory of the area. Dr. Edwin Carpenter, Lecturer at the Huntington Library, graciously read the completed manuscript and provided the foreword.

We were fortunate in having our own series of oral interviews which provided an unbroken chain of personal recollections from the 1890s through World War II — with such perceptive observers as Dorothy Gillis Loomis, Arthur Loomis, Angelina Marquez Olivera, Martha Ellen Scott, Zola Clearwater, Virginia Hoch Tanzola, Frances Smith Stewart, Cap Wooldridge, Martha French Patterson Wynegar, Telford and Ada Work, Jack and Mary Sauer, Ina Andrews Bitting, Rae Westenhaver, Phyllis Westenhaver Tebbe, and Marion Westenhaver McDonald. Written memoirs were received from Nancy June Robinson Evans and from the families of Francis Brunner and Beatrice Clark. Copies of valuable documents, letters, and clippings from the Santa Monica Land and Water Company Archives were provided through the courtesy of Jan and Bob Loomis and shed new light on the development of the Bay Area.

Marta Feuchtwanger and Franzi Toch Weschler graciously contributed to the chapter on the European refugees, while the segment concerning the J. Paul Getty Museum was made possible through information and pictures provided by staff members Burton Frederickson, Mitchell Hearns Bishop, Barbara Brink, and Ralph Blackburn. Recollections of Claude I. Parker were obtained from Mary Messmore and Denis Lee.

Other contributors who offered hints, anecdotes, or expertise included Sheila Thompson, Ethel Haydon, Sally Ball, Lois Flagg, Paul and Evalyn Spring, Marion Dedon, and Margaret Jane Work Pollock. A special assignment was carried out by supersleuth Jerry Myers, a former resident of Rustic Canyon, who by visiting libraries in Australia and Canada managed to track down the elusive derivation of the word "Geebungs."

Access to pictorial materials was kindly provided by Alan Jutzi of the Huntington Library, Hilda Bohem and the staff of the Special Collections Department from UCLA, June Blum of the *Palisadian-Post,* Frank and Charles Hathaway of the Los Angeles Athletic Club, the *Los Angeles Times,* California State Library, Getty Museum, and the Margaret Herrick Library of the Academy of Motion Picture Arts and Sciences. Among our many private donors were Angelina Marquez Olivera, the Scott family, Bee Clark Kottinger, Nancy June Robinson

Evans, Frances Smith Stewart, the Gabrielson family, Jack and Mary Sauer, Reuben L. Stadler, Elliott Welsh, Eleanor Moore, George and Onis Rice, Ina Andrews Bitting, Phyllis Westenhaver Tebbe, and Carolyn Patterson. All pictures were deeply appreciated and are individually credited. Special mention is due Carolyn Bartlett Farnham, who permitted us to include pictures taken by her father, the eminent Southern California photographer, Adelbert Bartlett.

There was one major omission. The kind gentleman who sent us the superb panorama of Pacific Palisades, taken in 1925, has been listed as anonymous. His name had been torn from the mailing tube, and we had no way to trace the picture's origin or to express our appreciation.

Two patient volunteers, Connie Simons and Mary Jo Sterling, served as research assistants, scanning early issues of *The Palisadian* for facts and figures. Mary Lee Greenblatt read and edited the preliminary manuscript, while selected portions of the text were reviewed by Lois Marquez, Zola Clearwater, Telford Work, Jack Sauer, Jan and Bob Loomis, John Bloch, John Pohlmann, Frank Hathaway, Marta Feuchtwanger, Lawrence Weschler, Roberta Greenwood, and June Blum. Proofreading and editing the printed galleys came under the aegis of Lea Gould, whose skillful guidance saved us from many small blunders. The index was valiantly compiled by Deborah Young.

Finally, we would like to express our appreciation to the loyal members of the Historical Society for their support, to the community-at-large for their interest and the Getty Museum for hosting a major fund-raising event on our behalf, and to William M. Garland for his promotional efforts. The day this book is published will be a happy and rewarding one for us all.

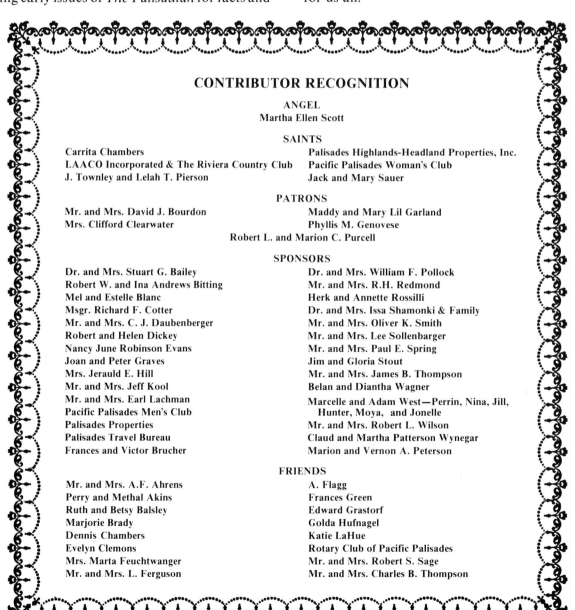

CONTRIBUTOR RECOGNITION

ANGEL
Martha Ellen Scott

SAINTS

Carrita Chambers	Palisades Highlands-Headland Properties, Inc.
LAACO Incorporated & The Riviera Country Club	Pacific Palisades Woman's Club
J. Townley and Lelah T. Pierson	Jack and Mary Sauer

PATRONS

Mr. and Mrs. David J. Bourdon	Maddy and Mary Lil Garland
Mrs. Clifford Clearwater	Phyllis M. Genovese
Robert L. and Marion C. Purcell	

SPONSORS

Dr. and Mrs. Stuart G. Bailey	Dr. and Mrs. William F. Pollock
Robert W. and Ina Andrews Bitting	Mr. and Mrs. R.H. Redmond
Mel and Estelle Blanc	Herk and Annette Rossilli
Msgr. Richard F. Cotter	Dr. and Mrs. Issa Shamonki & Family
Mr. and Mrs. C. J. Daubenberger	Mr. and Mrs. Oliver K. Smith
Robert and Helen Dickey	Mr. and Mrs. Lee Sollenbarger
Nancy June Robinson Evans	Mr. and Mrs. Paul E. Spring
Joan and Peter Graves	Jim and Gloria Stout
Mrs. Jerauld E. Hill	Mr. and Mrs. James B. Thompson
Mr. and Mrs. Jeff Kool	Belan and Diantha Wagner
Mr. and Mrs. Earl Lachman	Marcelle and Adam West—Perrin, Nina, Jill, Hunter, Moya, and Jonelle
Pacific Palisades Men's Club	Mr. and Mrs. Robert L. Wilson
Palisades Properties	Claud and Martha Patterson Wynegar
Palisades Travel Bureau	Marion and Vernon A. Peterson
Frances and Victor Brucher	

FRIENDS

Mr. and Mrs. A.F. Ahrens	A. Flagg
Perry and Methal Akins	Frances Green
Ruth and Betsy Balsley	Edward Grastorf
Marjorie Brady	Golda Hufnagel
Dennis Chambers	Katie LaHue
Evelyn Clemons	Rotary Club of Pacific Palisades
Mrs. Marta Feuchtwanger	Mr. and Mrs. Robert S. Sage
Mr. and Mrs. L. Ferguson	Mr. and Mrs. Charles B. Thompson

Foreword

Long ago at a library meeting I heard a speaker point out that the most enduring thing a local historical society can do is to publish. That was said before the time such societies became active in restoring historic structures and creating museums, but even so it seems to me still valid. A "heritage house," historic site, or museum — however well done and maintained — is by its nature fixed at one spot. Publications, on the other hand — single volumes or files of a periodical — may be found on the shelves of public or scholarly libraries all over the country, where they are of interest and use to people removed from the local scene, both in space and in time.

With this excellent history the Pacific Palisades Historical Society is now initiating a publications program. The community is to be congratulated on having so many devoted persons who in one way or another have conserved so much of its historic past. The Society is fortunate too in having members who are skilled in organizing and presenting the accumulated information and pictures.

This is, very properly, first a community history, setting forth names, dates, and references that will mean much to local residents. Who made the doughnuts for the U.S.O. canteen in World War II, or when a street name was changed, may not engross the outsider, but non-residents who peruse the book will also find much of interest and research value in it.

For example, are you concerned with the history of the movies? Here is an account of Inceville. Are you looking for bits of the ethnic mosaic? Here is a long-forgotten Japanese fishing village. Are you researching the European intellectual refugees of the Hitler period? Here are stories of those who lived and worked in Pacific Palisades and its environs. Are you interested in the history of sports in southern California? Here, again, are many references, particularly to equestrian sports. Are you studying how land was subdivided and communities built? Here are specifics of such processes: many accounts of communal enterprises (particularly of a religious nature), entrepeneurial development, real estate sales methods, and others — in relation to periods of boom, depression, and adjustment.

In addition to the refugee artists and writers, Pacific Palisades has been home or host to many other people whose names are well known in national or international circles. Those connected with motion pictures provide perhaps the most obvious example, but one will find threading through this story not only the names of many familiar Hollywood stars, but world-renowned architects, industrialists, sports personalities, educators, theologians, and scientists — even the current residents of the White House.

EDWIN H. CARPENTER

The Huntington Library
March 14, 1983

The Founder's Oaks in Temescal Canyon ca. 1915. Palisades High is to the left, just off camera. Sunset Boulevard goes from left to right just past the mound on the right. *Clearwater Collection*

Preface

Welcome to Pacific Palisades! We're not a city...a town...or even a village...and our boundaries are subject to a variety of interpretations. Nevertheless, we have our own distinct history, and Palisadians rank high in the matter of civic pride.

For the purposes of the book, we have defined Pacific Palisades as bounded on the south by the Pacific Ocean, on the west by the Los Angeles city limits, and on the north by the crest of the Santa Monica Mountains. On the east, the imaginary line extends from the beach northward along the eastern rim of Santa Monica Canyon, across the upper end of the Riviera Country Club, and northward along the western slope of Sullivan Canyon.

Most of this area coincides with the Rancho Boca de Santa Monica. It lies entirely within the city of Los Angeles, and includes all of the Pacific Palisades postal zone. Since the federal government does not respect civic boundaries, our definition of Pacific Palisades also includes lower Rustic Canyon and Santa Monica Canyon, which are part of Los Angeles but are under the jurisdiction of the Santa Monica post office, and the Getty Museum, which receives its mail via either Santa Monica or Malibu.

Confusion existed even before Pacific Palisades was founded by the Methodists in 1922, at which time the identity of the new community was already intertwined with that of its well-established neighbor, Santa Monica. A case in point concerns that book's subtitle, "Where the Mountains Meet the Sea," which had been used as a slogan by Santa Monica in the early 1900s and loosely referred to the unincorporated coastline to the west.

In 1916, however, the western mesas were annexed to the city of Los Angeles, and the dramatic strip of land between the Santa Monica Mountains and Santa Monica Bay could no longer be claimed by Santa Monica boosters. Pacific Palisades therefore adopted Santa Monica's motto for its own promotional literature — a usage which seems to have been mutually condoned.

According to *Santa Monica Evening Outlook* columnist Clara McClure, the colorful descriptive phrase was used publicly by representatives of Pacific Palisades on November 17, 1923, when they met with delegates from Santa Monica and Venice to discuss a proposed sewer trunk line along the coast — the first cooperative venture to involve the three neighboring communities. The program that evening featured Reverend Thomas Lutman of Pacific Palisades with an address bearing the title "Where the Mountains Meet the Sea," followed by Reverend Charles H. Scott and W.H. Carter who presented a two-reel movie on the same theme, dramatizing the scenic and cultural advantages of living in Pacific Palisades.

The very geographical features which had formed a barrier to early exploration and trade thus became a highly touted virtue. From its first modest plat on the flatland, Pacific Palisades rapidly grew in all directions — literally from the mountains to the sea — until it encompassed a challenging range of subdivisions and building sites, appealing to the tastes of conservative homeowners as well as to those adventuresome souls who preferred the more hazardous pleasures of canyons, bluffs, hillsides, and ridges.

Today's Palisadians are a diverse breed and have mixed allegiances. They may patronize the central business district and take part in local events, but they return home to such well-defined and distinctive neighborhoods as Castellammare, Miramar Estates, Palisades Highlands, Marquez Knolls, Huntington Palisades, Rustic Canyon, Santa Monica Canyon, and the Rivieras.

As the scope of the book grew geographically, it became necessary to focus on the early history of Pacific Palisades — the basics of land ownership and use, the role of the pioneers, and the story of the founding, and the community's progress through World War II. In addition, it became apparent that a tally of the many celebrities living in our midst, a description of the architecture, and details regarding historical sites — all must wait patiently for Volume II.

Looking ahead, a committee of the Pacific Palisades Historical Society is currently at work on a cultural survey of the community: sifting through material neighborhood by neighborhood and block by block, gathering facts, pictures — even legends — to establish a true portrait of Pacific Palisades as we know it in 1983.

Pacific Palisades in 1927, five years after its founding, showing the geographical features that make it unique . . . the sharp oceanfront cliffs, broad mesas, deep-cut canyons, and chaparral-covered mountains. The city of Santa Monica lies to the east, on the lower right hand side of the picture. Santa Monica Canyon on the lower left, appears as a wide cleft in the coastal plain, with Rustic Canyon branching off to the north. Huntington Palisades may be seen on the adjacent bluff, where newly graded roads bisect the older rows of eucalyptus trees. Immediately to the west, Potrero Canyon winds inland from the beach to what is now the business center, while Temescal Canyon, beyond, extends in a straight line to the base of the mountains. On the other side of the ridge may be seen the San Fernando Valley and distant mountain ranges. *Spence Collection/UCLA*

1

PACIFIC PALISADES
THE NATURAL SETTING

DR. RICHARD F. LOGAN

Sitting on a terrace several hundred feet above the sea, Pacific Palisades looks southward at the ocean and northward at the rugged slopes of the Santa Monica Mountains. Cooled in summer by the daily sea breeze, and moderated in winter by the proximity of the ocean, which keeps it essentially frost-free, the climate is about as favorable as one can find on earth. "The Palisades" (as we affectionately refer to the community) is fifteen miles due west of the Los Angeles Civic Center, twelve miles west of Hollywood, and three miles northwest of Santa Monica. While technically a part of Los Angeles, the community is far enough removed from the city to enjoy its benefits while avoiding many of its problems.

Pacific Palisades and the adjacent Santa Monica Mountains are underlain principally by sedimentary rocks of Pliocene to Cretaceous age, greatly folded and faulted, uplifted, and subjected to marine, fluvial and gravity erosion.

Most of the rocks originated as sediments deposited on the floor of the ocean, between 10 and 70 million years ago (not so very long ago considering the nearly 5 billion-year age of the Earth). Some were very coarse gravels, with pebbles and stones beautifully rounded by having been tumbled about by waves and streams and measuring up to a foot in diameter. When cemented together to form rock, such a deposit is called "conglomerate." The cliff on the inner side of the Coast Highway opposite the Chart House, on the tip of the point just east of Topanga Canyon, has a magnificent exposure of such material. Under other circumstances, the ocean floor was covered with sand, and sometimes shells lay on the surface or were buried in the sand. Cementation of the individual sand grains produced sandstone, which sometimes contains fossils of the original shells. At other places or at other times, thick beds of mud accumulated, to be transformed later through compression into a fairly soft rock called "shale." On the Coast Highway, about the entrance to the Getty Museum, the bluffs are composed of a fine sandstone, but along most of the stretch from Temescal Canyon to Topanga, shales predominate.

In the last ten million years, these beds have been subjected to great pressures in the Earth's crust which have slowly but inexorably folded and bent them, so that the materials which were deposited as horizontal sheets are sloping at all sorts of odd angles. This can be seen very clearly in the case of the bed of conglomerate across from the Chart House — it was originally a horizontal bed, but it is now tilted at a steep angle seawards.

This folding and tilting raised the beds from the sea to form the ancestral Santa Monica Mountains. Exposed to rain and running water, the mountains were eroded irregularly, creating rills and gullies, ridges and valleys. Later, in the last million years or so, a break in the Earth's crust (the Malibu Fault) appeared, roughly paralleling the coastline. Displacement along it raised the Santa Monica Mountains still higher; but the movement was very irregular, with no movement for tens of thousands of years, and then a period of rather rapid uplift, followed by another period of quiet. In each of the stationary periods, the waves of the sea attacked the seaward face of the mountains, eroding a flat bench backed by a seacliff into the flanks of the range. Such a bench is being eroded today — the Coast Highway runs along its inner edge at the foot of the seacliff, and the surfers ride their boards over the outer part of it. And the central part of the community of Pacific Palisades sits atop an earlier bench, raised up to its present level by this vertical movement of the Malibu Fault.

During and after its uplift to its present position, the Palisades bench received a veneer of loose material (alluvium) washed down by winter rains from the slopes of the Santa Monica Mountains, and slanting from the foot of the mountains seaward. But as the bench got higher and higher above the sea, streams began to cut channels into it, eventually eroding the canyons that cut across it, such as Santa Monica Canyon, Temescal Canyon, and Santa

Ynez Canyon. The larger of these are extensions of much larger canyons seaming the slopes of the mountains to the north; some of the smaller ones originate on the bench itself. Sunset Boulevard is able to pass around the heads of the smaller ones, but is forced to curve down into each of the larger ones.

Erosion by the waves undercuts the foot of the mountain slope, tending to produce a vertical cliff. Where the rock is a sandstone or a conglomerate, the cliff remains vertical and relatively permanent. However, where the waves attack a softer shale or a mass of alluvium, the cliff is susceptible to rapid change through landslide or mudflow. Most of these are relatively minor, but there have been some spectacular ones: the landslide that dumped the famous Bernheimer Gardens into the Coast Highway just west of the Bel-Air Bay Club; the "Killer Slide" of 1958 just west of the Sunspot Motel and Disco between Chautauqua and Temescal Canyon boulevards, which took the life of a state highway department supervisor and forced the re-routing of the Coast Highway; the massive and on-going slides of the Castellammare area; and the everthreatening

cliff that overhangs the Coast Highway at Chautauqua. The Chautauqua cliff is composed entirely of slightly consolidated alluvium; the other three slides all involved marine shales, which become extremely heavy in wet years through absorption of rain water, and simultaneously become greasy, thus lubricating a potential massive earth movement. The major part of Pacific Palisades is free of all danger from slides, but the canyon borders and sea-cliff edge present some serious stabilization problems.

The name "Pacific Palisades" is derived, incidentally, from the physical appearance of the sea-cliff when viewed from the shore. A palisade is a wall made from logs stood on end, often to create a defensive barricade around a fort. The closely spaced vertical rills and gullies eroded into the face of the cliff give the appearance of a palisade when viewed from a distance. The name is also applied to the cliffs on the west bank of the Hudson River; there a thick bed of dark lava stands in great vertical columns, appearing like a palisade when viewed from Manhattan.

Coastal Southern California has perhaps the

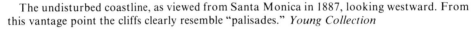

The undisturbed coastline, as viewed from Santa Monica in 1887, looking westward. From this vantage point the cliffs clearly resemble "palisades." *Young Collection*

Burning Canyon, a sharply eroded gorge west of the Bel-Air Bay Club, was a familiar sight to early Palisadians — both a geological wonder and a source of legends and myths. Smoke arose from the chasm in the daytime and a glow could be seen at night. In the 1940s the canyon was filled with earth from slides. *Clearwater Collection*

greatest variety of climates of any place of similar size on earth. It is often said that one can choose one's home climate by street address here, and that is not far from the truth.

In general, Coastal Southern California has a sub-humid Mediterranean climate: "sub-humid" in that the precipitation is in excess of the potential evaporation (when the reverse is true, the climate is considered semi-arid); Mediterranean in that virtually all of the precipitation falls in the winter half of the year, and the summers are almost totally dry. Amounts of precipitation vary greatly from place to place: Santa Monica Pier gets about 13 inches annually, while about 25 inches fall at the fire station in Topanga. Snow is virtually unknown: perhaps once a decade the firebreaks on the ridges above Pacific Palisades are whitened for a few hours. Freezing likewise very rarely occurs. Nor are high temperatures common: during Santa Anas, the hot winds from the interior, the thermometer may climb into the nineties or even exceed 100°, but this situation occurs only a few days a year, usually in September or October. The seabreeze keeps almost all parts of the Palisades in the seventies through most summer days.

Being up-wind of the urban area of greater Los Angeles, smog is of little consequence in the Palisades. Fog occurs along the coast on many summer days, its inland border varying from minute to minute: it is fairly common seaward of Sunset Boulevard, and much less so in the hills. Sequestered canyons isolated from the seabreeze have much warmer summer days and almost no fog, while the bluff-tops above the coast have strong seabreezes, much fog and cool summer days. June is the foggiest month, and September the hottest, although the hottest day of the year may come as late as November, if the Santa Ana should be strong then.

The Mediterranean climate imposes certain harsh restrictions upon the native vegetation. In most parts of the world, precipitation is either spread over most of the year, or is concentrated in the warmer months. Thus, plants are able to utilize the coincidence of warmth and moisture to achieve maximum growth. But here, the rain comes in the low-sun, colder period, and the warm season suffers from

other materials, used on one or both sides, and sometimes along the edges. Hammerstones were found in great abundance; they were used for roughening the working surfaces of the manos and to shape other stone tools. Abrading stones — used to smooth other stone or wooden articles — were found, and small rubbing stones, possibly employed to dress hides. Articles of bone or shell were very rare. There was no pottery. No direct evidence of textiles was found, although it seems unlikely that a seed-gathering economy could function without some kind of container. A thin mass of asphaltum was observed to contain an imprint of woven material, and it seems likely that the asphalt served as a waterproofing agent for a basket which has not survived.

The skeletons indicated that the people were of average stature and probably resembled the Indians of today. From comparable cultures elsewhere, it is theorized that the women may have worn a sort of apron, and the men perhaps had robes of animal skins. They may have made simple sandals for traveling on the rocky terrain. Much less is known of the socio-religious patterns of this little community than of the economic aspect of life, which is to be

Upper, typical basket mortar, 18 inches wide. The dark ring shows where basket sides were attached with asphaltum. The surface was roughened for grinding wild plants and seeds.
Lower, a pestle used for preparing grains in a mortar (similar scale).

Upper left, pitted cobble used as either anvil or hammer; *upper right,* grooved stone used as a weight in fishing. Each object is approximately 4 inches long. The third artifact is a pitted hammerstone, 6 inches long, with a small depression where the finger rested. The lower end shows wear from use.

expected in reconstructing a very old culture. From the burials there is evidence of three different forms of disposal of the dead: (1) simple inhumation with the bodies fully extended; (2) partial reburials under inverted milling stones; and (3) fractional reburials, with interment of the long leg bones only. The meagre evidence implies that the rituals were simple.

In the upper levels of the Topanga Canyon excavation and at nearby sites was evidence of a slightly later period, called Phase II because of certain evolution noted in the tools and other cultural changes. The milling stone and mano were being gradually replaced by the mortar and pestle. The flaked stone tools show both a greater refinement of technique in manufacture and more regularities in form. The Phase II burials were all in a flexed position, both with and without rock cairns. Large stone-lined fire pits may have been used for baking, roasting, or possibly ceremonial purposes. This later phase has been radiocarbon dated as 2,500 years old and is interpreted as a transitional link between the early Milling Stone and later cultural traditions in the region's prehistory.

The so-called Intermediate or Transitional Period, still poorly defined in the Los Angeles basin, dates from about 1500 B.C. to A.D. 500. Coastal populations turned increasingly to the resources of the sea: shellfish, fish, and marine mammals. Hunting increased on land as well, with the use of small, pressure-flaked projectile points which presuppose the adoption of bow and arrow. The sites contain greater quantities of bone tools and shell ornaments and indicate reliance primarily on the mortar or basket hopper mortar for processing plant foods.

The Late Prehistoric period, from A.D. 500 until historic contact, is characterized by increasing complexity in both economic and social spheres. Sites along the coast tend to be large and deep, with loose, black, and "greasy" soil; they probably represent the major, permanent village locations. The inland and upland locations are often smaller and may result from temporary, seasonal, or special purpose occupations. The exploitation of maritime resources, begun in the preceding period, reached a high level of sophistication with seaworthy boats and flourishing commerce with the Channel Islands. Social contacts and influences among groups were accelerated through trade, ceremonial, and other interactions.

Although many of the late local sites are loosely attributed to the Chumash Indians, Pacific Palisades was more likely occupied during the Late Prehistoric by those who would be called Gabrielino after the mission was established. Along the coast, the southern boundary of the Chumash is usually accepted at Malibu, or perhaps Topanga Canyon. The Santa Monica Mountains, and perhaps the Palisades, are particularly important to anthropological research precisely because of the potential for finding evidence of contacts between the Chumash and the Gabrielino, a group who ranged from Orange County through the Los Angeles basin.

The Gabrielino were Shoshonean-speakers who probably entered into southern California later than the ancestors of the Chumash. The latter were members of a group sharing eight different dialects of the Hokan linguistic family, and lands as far as northern San Luis Obispo county and the northern Channel Islands, other than Santa Barbara Island which was Gabrielino. The material culture of the two peoples was essentially similar, and the greatly oversimplified summary which follows is applicable to both.

There was a greatly increased population during the Late Prehistoric period, and an expansion of site locations into more diverse areas. The cultures were complex, prosperous, and stable, as reflected in circular framed and thatched houses often exceeding 25 feet in diameter. Each village contained at least one large *temescal*, or sweat house, used for physical and spiritual rejuvenation as well as relaxation. Plant foods were collected in their respective seasons, and the plank canoe, or *tomol*, served for fishing, hunting sea mammals, and an active trade with the island. A monetary system was based on shell beads. There were political, ceremonial, and military alliances, and highly organized rituals for dance and worship. Religious and solstice shrines were located on mountain tops, and both the Chumash and Gabrielino participated in the widespread *Chungichnish* cult which utilized *Datura* (jimson weed, a hallucinogenic plant) in special ceremonies.

Both groups had shamans (religious specialists) who obtained their power through dreams or visions and functioned mainly in curing disease through singing, using herbs, and sucking out foreign objects. The Sun and the Moon were important in the Gabrielino world view, and the Crow, Raven, Owl, and Eagle were sacred beings. The Eagle was regarded in special esteem because of the legend that a great chief, as he lay dying, told his people that he would become an eagle whose feathers were to be used in rituals. Artistry was evident in elaborate beads and ornaments made of shell, stone sculpture, superb basketry, and rock art. And lest it be thought that both the cultures and the peoples are extinct today, there are many Chumash and Gabrielino still alive and very much concerned for their Native American heritage.

Sites typical of all these periods are — or were — present in Pacific Palisades. Unfortunately, many of them were disturbed or "collected" by non-scientific methods, and none of these collections can be located for study with modern professional techniques. The Pacific Palisades *Progress* reported in 1925 that a winnowing tray or sieve made of willow branches was found in a Pulgas Canyon cave, along with numerous stone bowls, pestles, milling stones, and "talc plates" (probably soapstone comals). These were to be exhibited in community buildings. By 1927, the Pacific Palisades Association had a display at the local bank of a "large accumulation" of pestles, bowls, and other Indian "relics" discovered on local grounds. *The Palisadian* reported the discovery of a well-preserved skeleton at the location of old Inceville in 1928. The remains were stolen, but then recovered and put on display in the library with "a number of very fine specimens." Another undocumented collection which has not been traced was made during construction at the Josepho Ranch in Rustic Canyon.

A bit of local lore dating back to 1910, which is not confirmed in historical or ethnographic sources, concerns a geological phenomenon called "Burning Mountain." As described in *The Palisadian*, this canyon, apparently the small one west of the Bel-Air Bay Club, was regarded as evil by both Indians and the Mexicans. The Indians were said to conduct rituals there to confine the Evil Spirit. The same informant related that on one occasion, the son of the chief of a tribe camping at the mouth of Santa Ynez Canyon fell over the rim of the mesa into this canyon, but escaped safely after ceremonies were performed.

Of the known sites closer than Topanga Canyon, a Milling Stone location at the mouth of Santa Ynez Creek has been destroyed, and another at the junction of Sunset Boulevard and the Coast Highway was obliterated, both without study. Where the Sunset Mesa houses stand now was another site subject to only very hasty emergency salvage excavation before development; it has been radiocarbon dated as 3,000 years old. Other local sites estimated to represent Late Prehistoric occupation were lost in Temescal Canyon with the construction of Palisades High School, before current environmental laws would have mandated investigation. At least one recorded site containing human skeletal material is known in upper Temescal Canyon.

A small rock shelter in Santa Ynez Canyon was partially excavated by UCLA; the materials were interpreted as Gabrielino and dated at ca. A.D. 1500-1800. A bedrock mortar is known in Los Liones Canyon; a Milling Stone site and possible rockshelter within the proposed development at Palisades Highlands; and two additional rockshelters north of the Highlands. At least one site has been recorded at the ocean end of Santa Monica Canyon.

There is, therefore, abundant evidence that people of the past also recognized Pacific Palisades as a very favored environment. The availability of water, variety of plant foods, faunal resources of both land and sea, transportation corridors to the interior, all combined to encourage settlement from the very earliest times. Although unreplaceable cultural resources have been lost to construction since the 1920s, there are undoubtedly many sites yet to be discovered in the more remote areas which have never been archaeologically surveyed. Under current environmental regulations, new subdivisions or major land alterations will be preceded by surveys and, if necessary, scientific excavation to preserve the information which such sites contain.

The Las Pulgas Canyon cave where a winnowing tray and many other Indian artifacts were found by local residents in 1925. *Clearwater Collection*

8

3

THE RANCHO BOCA DE SANTA MONICA

ERNEST MARQUEZ

The first contact between the Indian inhabitants of the southern California coastal plain and the early Spanish explorers took place in 1542 when Juan Rodriguez Cabrillo sailed up the coast from Mexico, seeking the coveted Northwest Passage from the Pacific Ocean to the Atlantic. On October 9 two ships bearing Cabrillo and his men entered Santa Monica Bay — which they described as a large *ensenada* — and anchored for the night within sight of the shoreline before traveling northward.

For two and a half centuries after Cabrillo's visit, the great square-rigged ships, the Manila galleons, sailed down the coast each year, carrying the riches of the Orient and a few hardy passengers to Mexico. The sight of these ships — "huge houses on the sea" — became a legend with the Gabrielinos. There are also romantic but unsubstantiated tales that the galleons and the pirate ships that preyed on them sometimes anchored offshore and took on supplies of fresh water at such favorable spots as Santa Monica Canyon where there were springs and year-round streams.

The next explorer to pay an official visit to the coast was Sebastian Vizcaino in 1602. Charged with mapping the shoreline and finding a suitable location for a port to protect the Spanish ships from English pirates and provide fresh supplies for the galleons, Vizcaino bypassed Santa Monica Bay when fog obscured the mainland and recorded on his charts only the vague contours of a *Grand Ensenada.*

In 1768 rumors of Russian encroachment on her Pacific preserves and of Dutch and English ships off the Baja (Lower) California coast led Spain to move defensively for the protection of her claims to the west coast of North America. The plan was to colonize Alta (Upper) California and take possession of the land in the name of the reigning king of Spain, Charles III.

San Diego and Monterey were given approval as sites for the new colonies, accompanied by orders to establish a mission and presidio at each location. In Mexico, the Spanish Visitor-General, José de Galvez, began making elaborate preparations for the ambi-

tious venture and appointed Don Gaspar de Portolá the overall leader. Two groups were to make the journey from Baja California by land, and three ships were to sail up the coast under the command of Lieutenant Fages. All were to meet at San Diego. The first land party was led by Captain Fernando de Rivera y Moncada; Portolá and Father Junipero Serra were with the second group.

When Portolá and Father Serra reached San Diego on June 29, 1769, a scene of sickness and desolation confronted them. One ship, the San Antonio, had arrived with little delay, although the crew was suffering from scurvy; another, the San Carlos, at sea for four months, had been so devastated by scurvy and dysentery that only five members of the crew were still alive. The third ship was apparently lost at sea.

Undaunted, in mid-July, Father Serra founded the Mission San Diego de Alcala and saw a reassembled entourage of sixty-four men set off in search of Monterey Bay, guided only by copies of earlier maritime maps. The group included Portolá, Captain Rivera, Lieutenant Fages and his surviving crew, Sergeant José Ortega with his scouts, and Miguel Costansó, the engineer of the Rivera party.

On August 2 Portolá and his men reached the future site of Los Angeles and camped near the Los Angeles River, which they named *Porciúncula.* The next day they forded the stream and crossed a rich and fertile plain. Passing the asphalt beds of La Brea, they halted at the Spring of the Alders near Ballona Creek. On August 4 the procession skirted the mountains on a good road through grassy pastureland and — according to the party's official historian, Father Crespi — camped at a watering place, banked with watercress and rosebushes (a site that is known to be on the grounds of University High School today). Indians from a nearby village brought gifts of friendship — seeds, nuts, acorns, and shell beads — and received glass beads from the Spaniards in return.

At the evening campfire scouts reported that they had reached the ocean, five miles away, Ordered by

Portolá to investigate the possibility of traveling up the coastline, the scouts retraced their steps the next day, and, as Costansó wrote in his diary, "returned shortly afterwards with the news of having reached a high, steep cliff, terminating in the sea where the mountains end, absolutely cutting off the passage along the shore."*

The Portolá party therefore decided to cross the mountains by way of Sepulveda pass and camped in the San Fernando Valley near a large Indian village, before proceeding on to the north. This expedition failed because they did not recognize the harbor at Monterey from descriptions on Vizcaino's maps; instead they bypassed it and traveled as far as San Francisco Bay before turning back. A second venture, however, under Portolá's leadership resulted in the founding of a mission and presidio at Monterey in May, 1770, and the Mission San Gabriel was founded a year later, on September 8, 1771.

Thus California became a part of Spain's New World. First, missions were built, then the presidios — to house the soldiers who protected the missions. Later, *pueblos* were established to provide for the colony's agricultural needs and to accommodate the settlers who came up from Mexico. Los Angeles was one such *pueblo.*

Absolute title to all land in the new colony was vested in the Spanish Crown, which meant that direct and permanent ownership of land by an individual was prohibited. As time passed, the land laws were liberalized and permitted the allocation of land for the establishment of private ranchos in unoccupied areas outside the *pueblos.*

In 1773 some of the original soldiers who had come to Alta California as part of the original expeditions were ready to retire from active service and, rather than returning to Mexico, requested the governor of California to give them some land on which to settle and raise families. These, then, were the first Spanish land grants. Known more accurately as "permissions," they meant nothing more than grazing rights, or permission to use the land, and did not carry a clear title of ownership with them. There were no official documents of title — only the endorsement of the Spanish governor written in the margin of the applicant's petition. In most cases the petitions themselves were neither accurately recorded by the Spanish officials nor kept on file. Many were never sent back to the grantee, and of those that were, most were lost over the years. This caused considerable trouble later when the grantees had to prove ownership.

*Portolá's scouts probably reached the coast at Inspiration Point in Santa Monica and, looking northward, became the first land-based explorers to view the future site of Pacific Palisades.

Other problems arose from the customarily vague descriptions of boundary lines. Many of the huge grants were not measured at all; their agreed-upon borders were defined only by natural landmarks. This state of affairs was normally of little concern to the *rancheros,* but had to be resolved when more accurate measurements were required.

The first Spanish land grants, or "permissions," in the Los Angeles area were issued between 1784 and 1795 to a small number of Spanish army soldiers who had served for fifteen or more years and were ready to retire; wishing to settle near the *pueblo,* they asked for lands on which to establish ranchos. One such grant was issued to Francisco Reyes for the Rancho Encino in the San Fernando Valley. Aside from his ranching activities, Reyes was also a prominent man in the *pueblo:* he served as *alcalde* (mayor) from 1793 to 1795, when the population of Los Angeles had grown until it included eighty families.

In 1797 the Rancho Encino was preempted by the authorities to fill in the gap between the Buenaventura and San Gabriel missions and became the site of the Mission San Fernando Rey de España. Reyes obligingly moved his large herd of cattle and horses to temporary pasture at Santa Monica (then called San Vicente), but expressed distaste for the area when the high growth of weeds and brush made it difficult for him to keep track of his cattle.

Reyes consequently was given a rancho adjacent to La Purísima Mission near Lompoc and, in what must have been an impressive cattle drive, moved his herd north. His eldest son, Antonio, was placed in charge of the new operation. Reyes thus was not only the first *ranchero* mentioned in connection with the Santa Monica area, but it was his grandson Ysidro who later became a co-grantee of the Rancho Boca de Santa Monica, the land on which the community of Pacific Palisades is located today.

The earliest grant along the northwestern fringe of Santa Monica Bay was for the Rancho Topanga Malibu Sequit — issued to Jose Bartolomé Tapia in 1802. He built an adobe house and corrals in Malibu Canyon, an isolated spot approached only by boat or by horseback and mule train, and pastured his cattle along the grassy slopes. On the secluded beach, ships unloaded goods for his son, who was a merchant in the *pueblo,* while the remote inlets and canyons became havens for smugglers.

Mexico became an independent nation in 1822 and for a time continued the established practice of issuing provisional land grants. Soon the vast open space surrounding the *pueblo* and the missions was transformed into a network of privately owned ranchos.

In 1827 Guillermo Cota, the *alcalde* of Los Angeles, granted the land called Rancho Boca de

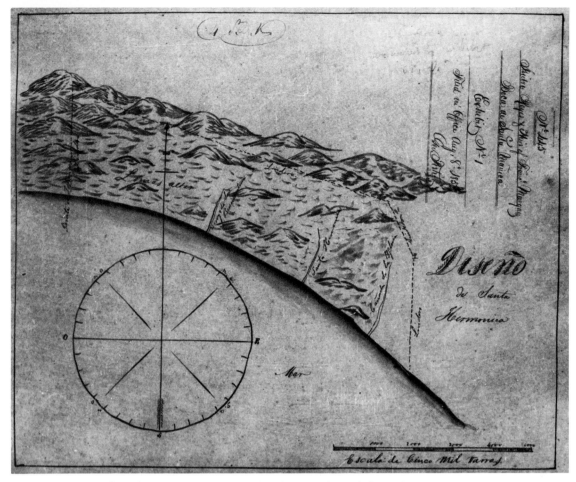

Copy of the *diseño,* or map, presented to the Land Commissioners in 1851. *Ernest Marquez Collection*

Santa Monica to Antonio Ignacio Machado and Francisco Javier Alvarado. Machado abandoned possession, but Alvarado's sons kept the grant until June 14, 1838, when they relinquished their rights to Francisco Marquez and Ysidro Reyes. Neither Machado nor Alvarado lived on the rancho. Marquez, however, had already moved there and was operating a blacksmith shop on the property even before he and Reyes obtained the grant.

Mexico revised the old land laws in 1828 and thereafter issued outright grants with title of ownership. In order to qualify, the applicant was required to be a Mexican citizen of good character and a Catholic. Furthermore, the land requested must be unoccupied territory and must not encroach on lands belonging to an Indian *rancheria,* a mission, or the *pueblo.*

On July 10, 1838, Francisco Marquez and Ysidro Reyes submitted a petition and a *diseño* for the Rancho Boca de Santa Monica to Governor Juan Alvarado in Monterey. The grant was approved the following June by acting governor Manuel Jimeno, who returned the papers to the grantees with the following message:

Whereas the citizens Francisco Marquez and Ysidro Reyes, Mexicans by birth, have claimed for their personal benefit and that of their families the tract known by the name Boca de Santa Mónica, bounded at the south by the sea, at the north by the hills, at the west by the point Topanga and at the East by the boundaries shown in the plan passing close to the cañada de Yglesia (Sullivan Canyon), all the proceedings [and] investigations in that behalf having first been gone through with . . . I have come to grant to them the aforesaid tract . . . subject to the approval of the Departmental Assembly and the following conditions:

1st   They may fence it without prejudice to the crossroads highways and rights of way; they shall enjoy it freely and exclusively, devoting it to the use or cultivation which best may suit them, but within one year they shall build a house and it shall be inhabited.

2nd   They shall petition the Magistrate who had jurisdiction to give them the juridical possession in virtue of this grant. Said Magistrate shall assign the boundaries in whose limits they shall place besides the landmarks some fruit and serviceable forest trees.

3rd   The tract in question consists of one-and-a-half range for neat cattle, a little more or less. . . . The judge who gives the possession shall cause it to be measured agreeably to ordinance and surplus that may result remaining the property of the nation for its behooving uses. [sic]

4th   If they violate these conditions they shall lose their right to the land, and it may be denounced by any other.

In compliance with these terms, the *alcalde,* Antonio Machado, came out to Santa Monica from Los Angeles on August 13, 1839, to perform the Act of Juridical Possession — a formality which included measuring the area of the grant and awarding it to the petitioners. Official cordbearers also were on

Mouth of Santa Monica Canyon as it appeared in the 1880s, showing the tents of campers from the city. *Young Collection*

hand, carrying two poles tied together with a line one hundred *varas* long. (A *vara* measured 33.3 inches, and was a unit based on the length of an average man's arm, from the back of his shoulder to his extended finger tips.)

Starting at Topanga Point (described as a *cañada* overgrown with tule), the two cordbearers, mounted on horseback, alternately rode the length of the cord until it stretched taut. The first man held his pole firmly anchored while the second man rode forward and jammed his pole into the sand, then they reversed their roles until they measured a 7,500 *vara* span along the beach, ending at the first ravine past Santa Monica Canyon (where Montana Avenue reaches the bluff).

Next they measured 4,000 *varas* from south to north, stopping at a point where a path led down into the Cañon de la Yglesia. There they found a dead mangle* and marked it with a few strokes of the cutlass. The men did not measure the northern boundary due to the mountainous nature of the terrain; instead they extended an imaginary line from the point where they stood, over the intervening ridges to Topanga Canyon. In this manner the total grant, amounting to 1½ square leagues, or 6,656 acres, was marked out, and Francisco Marquez and Ysidro Reyes took possession of the land as its first owners.

*The word "mangle" was used by 18th century Spanish explorers to describe a "mangrove-like" tree or shrub.

Francisco Marquez, whose way of life and that of his descendants was closely tied to the land, was born in Villa de Leon, Guadalajara, Mexico, in 1798 and came to Los Angeles in 1825. He settled on Main Street where he had an adobe house and a blacksmith and harness shop; as a *herrero,* or blacksmith, he traveled about, from rancho to rancho, plying his trade. In 1834 he was married at the Mission San Gabriel to Roque Valenzuela, the nineteen-year-old daughter of Manuel Valenzuela, a soldier from the Rivera party. Subsequently the couple had ten children, five of whom lived to adulthood. Francisco built the first adobe on the grant; it was located in Santa Monica Canyon on the mesa just below the flatlands of Santa Monica, where San Lorenzo Drive is today.

Ysidro Reyes was born in Los Angeles in 1813. He was the son of Jacinto Reyes and Maria Antonio Machado de Reyes, who owned the Las Virgenes Rancho near Agoura, and the grandson of Francisco Reyes, grantee of the Rancho Encino. By 1839 Ysidro Reyes was already a land owner, with thirteen acres, vineyards, and an adobe house near Fourth and Main in the *pueblo.* He also leased land at the La Brea tar pits and drove cartloads of tar to Los Angeles to be sold for roofing material.

Although Reyes's primary residence was in the *pueblo,* he built his first ranch home on the mesa west of Rustic Canyon, near the present-day intersection of Chautauqua and Sunset boulevards. Later he built a second adobe on the eastern rim of

Santa Monica Canyon, just south of Seventh Street and Adelaide Drive, and moved to that safer spot to avoid the depredations of wild animals that came down from the hills.

Herminia Reyes, who was born in 1887 and died at the age of ninety-one, told the tale of one harrowing encounter involving her grandfather, Ysidro Reyes, when he lived on the western mesa. Having lost many small animals from one of his corrals, Reyes and an Indian ranch hand decided on a nocturnal stakeout to catch the culprit in the act. Reyes went to sleep, seated by a fence post, while the Indian stood guard opposite him, near a tree. Suddenly the Indian realized that a bear had approached and was nuzzling the scarf around Reyes's neck. Afraid to shoot lest he strike the *patron,* the Indian watched breathlessly while the bear satisfied his curiosity and lumbered off.

Such face-to-face encounters may have been unusual, but the *rancheros* were justifiably proud of their skill at hunting — both to protect their animals and as sport. The canyons and mesas of the Rancho Boca de Santa Monica were rich with game, and the rugged moutains beyond were considered hunting territory by members of the Marquez family as late as the 1930s.

Life on the ranchos was simple and uncomplicated. The *ranchero's* value system was oriented to the rhythm of nature and to the present, not to the past or the future. He was not driven by ambition to acquire luxuries or riches and would often give away a prized possession simply because someone admired it. Travelers and visitors to the rancho were always sure of a place to sleep, with meals and a fresh horse to continue the journey the next day — at no cost.

The *rancheros* ran large herds of cattle and sheep on the unfenced range, generally with the help of Indian *vaqueros* and laborers, while the Indian women helped with the household tasks and care of the children. Each of the *ranchero's* animals was identified by its owner's registered brand; in the spring a series of rodeos was held at which the cattle were rounded up and segregated and the new calves were branded. These were festive events for all. Dressed in their best attire, the families gathered together for exhibitions of horsemanship, races, feasting, and dancing. The *matanza,* or slaughtering season, in the fall was also a time for celebration. Hides were an important product, as good as cash to be traded with the ship captains at San Pedro for fabrics, jewelry, and household furnishings.

Horses were an integral part of rancho life, as the *ranchero* customarily spent long days in the saddle. When a child was born, the parents and godparents immediately took the baby to the Plaza church for baptism — a round trip of some forty miles from Santa Monica Canyon — and by the age of ten, boys were expert riders. Both the Marquez and Reyes families raised race horses and held races along the top of the cliffs at Santa Monica, competing with other *rancheros* in the vicinity.

Although women also became competent riders, the general mode of transportation for women and children, as they traveled from rancho to rancho or to the *pueblo,* was by *carreta,* a bulky two-wheeled wooden cart drawn by oxen. The screeching of

View of Santa Monica Canyon in the late 1870s, looking south toward the ocean. The Pascual Marquez adobe is on the right and the ruins of the Francisco Marquez adobe is in the center of the picture. *Ernest Marquez Collection*

Francisco Marquez   Ramona Marquez   Francisca Marquez   Bonifacio Marquez   Ysidro Reyes

Registered Cattle Brands used on the Rancho Boca de Santa Monica

rough-hewn wooden wheels turning on wooden axles, lubricated only by homemade soap, was so piercing that the ever-present assemblage of dogs set up a warning howl long before the travelers came into view.

In the early days religious matters were cared for by San Gabriel Mission or at the rancho itself, where a portion of the home was set aside as a shrine for devotions. After 1822, when the Plaza church was constructed in the *pueblo,* the Plaza became the focal point for religious and social activities connected with holy days, and a trading center as well. The local *rancheros* who had town houses — Marquez, Reyes, and their neighbors, the Sepúlvedas — met there for cattle deals and bartering, as well as for the pleasures of horse races, bullfights, and card games while the women tended the children and made the rounds of the various shops.

The Sepúlvedas were a large and prestigious family whose lands adjoined the Rancho Boca de Santa Monica on the east. Their claim dated back to 1828 when grazing rights were granted to Francisco Sepúlveda for "the place called San Vicente," an expanse that extended from the Rancho La Ballona on the east to the crest of the Santa Monica Mountains on the west and north. Francisco's father, Francisco Xavier Sepúlveda, had come to California in 1781 with his wife and six children, as part of the military escort for the original colonists, and Francisco himself had served as a soldier.

In the 1830s Sepúlveda built a ranch house near the Portolá campsite at San Vicente Springs and surrounded it with orchards and vineyards. Later his three sons built their own homes on the property as well. One of the lengthiest disputes in the history of the local ranchos began in December, 1839, when Francisco Sepúlveda applied for his grant for the Rancho San Vicente and included in it portions of all three adjacent ranchos.

Two subsequent surveys placed all of the Rancho Boca de Santa Monica within the San Vicente grant, leading Sepúlveda to adopt a new name for his enlarged property — the Rancho San Vicente y Santa Monica. The dispute over the rancho boundary

lines was finally settled when Rancho Boca de Santa Monica was partitioned by the Los Angeles District Court in 1882.

Meanwhile, during the 1840s, events were taking place in California, Mexico, and in the eastern United States which would drastically affect the *rancheros'* lives. The United States coveted California, and when negotiations with Mexico collapsed over the terms of the sale, the United States went to war with Mexico and with California.

The Americans promptly took over northern California, but the south offered greater resistance. American troops marched into Los Angeles in 1846 and again in 1847, bringing about the surrender of Alta California to the United States in 1848 and heralding a drastic change in land ownership. According to the Treaty of Guadelupe Hidalgo, the United States guaranteed to the Mexican inhabitants "the free enjoyment of their liberty and property" and promised to honor "legitimate titles to every description of property, personal and real, existing in the ceded territories."

In practice, the gold rush of 1849 and its subsequent decline loosed a flood of land-hungry immigrants upon the state, putting pressure on the government to find a way to open up the lands to settlement. Aware of this sentiment, Congress passed the Land Act of 1851, which established a three-man Board of Land Commissioners, each appointed by the President of the United States, to pass on the validity of California land titles. These men neither spoke the Spanish language nor were they acquainted with Mexican laws pertaining to real estate.

The hearings began in 1851 and, except for one short session in Los Angeles, were held in San Francisco, a long and hazardous journey from the south. The owners were required to provide visual proof of their holdings, but lacked competent advice as to what to take with them. It was a heyday for unscrupulous lawyers since, without ready cash, most of the *rancheros* paid the exorbitant charges in livestock or land.

After the death of Francisco Marquez in 1850, Ysidro Reyes became the spokesman for both the

Marquez and Reyes families. He traveled to San Francisco to appear before the commissioners in November, 1852, and was fortunate in obtaining the services of an honest and public-spirited attorney, Elijah Crosby of San Francisco, to present his case.

The commissioners rendered their decision on the Rancho Boca de Santa Monica on April 14, 1854: the confirmation of an undivided one-half of the land grant to Ysidro Reyes and the denial of the other undivided one-half to Roque Valenzuela de Marquez and the children of Francisco Marquez on the technicality that no legal proof had been presented of Francisco's death.

On December 10, 1856, two years after the original hearing, the U.S. District Court reversed the ruling as it applied to the Marquez half-share, but the issuance of the patent, or final deed, was delayed until 1881. Meanwhile, Ysidro Reyes died during the smallpox epidemic of 1861 at his home in the *pueblo,* and his widow, Maria Antonia Villa, who had little interest in the rancho, gave part of her undivided one-half share to Charles Larrabee in exchange for his legal services on behalf of the rancho.

The smallpox epidemic was only one of several disasters in the early 1860s which caused drastic changes in the lives of the *rancheros,* and which, in effect, brought the region's pastoral era to an end. A fifty-inch rainfall that devastated the Los Angeles area in 1861 was followed by the great drought of 1862-64. Livestock perished by the thousands, and the remaining animals sold at prices ranging from only a few cents to little more than a dollar a head.

At this strategic time, when many of the *rancheros* were in desperate financial straits, Easterners drifting south from the depleted Sierra Nevada gold fields with cash in their pockets were able to capitalize on the *rancheros'* plight. The newcomers were quick to see the benefits of the moderate climate and attractive terrain and acquired large tracts of land at bargain prices.

Don Abel Stearns — whose youthful wife, Arcadia Bandini, was the daughter of a wealthy *ranchero* —was the largest landholder in southern California and at one time owned 177,000 acres from the shores of San Pedro Bay to San Bernardino County. Seeing his herds decimated by the drought and his debts rising, Stearns sold his land in the spring of 1868 and joined the boosters. Publicists, developers, and real estate men went into action to promote the

The rancho of Bonifacio Marquez, showing tents of campers, probably in the 1880s. *Ernest Marquez Collection*

properties. By the end of the year entire caravans of settlers were streaming into Los Angeles, while ships with "standing room only" landed their passengers at San Pedro.

In spite of the boom the plateau at the foot of the Santa Monica Mountains remained a grass-covered range where sheep and a few cattle still grazed. The name "Santa Monica" itself, referring to the area where Francisco Reyes grazed his cattle in 1797, was now commonly applied to Santa Monica Canyon, as it became a popular vacation spot — perhaps the first true resort in southern California.

According to an article in the *Los Angeles Express* in 1872, a Dr. Haywood and his family were the first vacationers to camp there under the sycamores, enjoying sole privileges from 1855 to 1867, and joined by other lucky campers thereafter. In the late sixties, school children from Los Angeles rode out from town on stagecoaches for picnics in the canyon. By the summer of 1871, several families spent vacations there; B.L. Peel put up a huge tent to accommodate up to thirty families; and on one busy Sunday, three hundred visitors stayed over for an all-night dance.

The next year a hotel opened near the mouth of the canyon, advertising: "Come and enjoy yourself. A week at the beach will add ten years to your life!"

Amusements included sailing in a skiff, surf bathing, drives and picnics along the beach and in the canyons, and dancing in the "big tent." A small grocery store nearby provided supplies for day visitors and campers, including fresh produce from the neighboring ranches.

More facilities were added, and in 1876 the urbane traveler, Ludwig Louis Salvator, archduke of Austria and son of Leopold II, wrote in glowing terms of his visit to the canyon:

On beyond is a place where carriages usually halt, called the Old Santa Monica Corral, where there are stalls for horses down underneath the alders. Not far from this stands Frank's Saloon, a large tent house or pavilion flying the American colors, which has a large rustic porch running across the front of the building. In conjunction is the stable, a large, open affair with accommodations for many horses, which is used by the stages. It is all very delightful. Under the alders on the left side of the canyon are two frames; one is a little store carrying miscellaneous goods, the other is surrounded by a cornfield. An extraordinarily beautiful clump of alders rises on the left of the brook forming a natural arbor where simple rustic seats have been erected and where, if the signs are to be believed, music is furnished at certain hours.

The Marquez family, continuing in the tradition of the *rancheros,* acted as gracious hosts, as the number of visitors to their lands grew from a small

The Pascual Marquez Bath House, a favorite spot for vacationing beachgoers (ca. 1887).
Ernest Marquez Collection

Above, Maria Antonia Villa Reyes, the widow of Ysidro Reyes, with her children, *left to right:* Margarita, Ysidro II, and Francisca Reyes. *Ernest Marquez Collection*
Lower left, Pascual Marquez with an unidentified young lady, possibly his bride. *Lower right,* Bonifacio Marquez and his son, Miguel, All, *Ernest Marquez Collection*

Pascual Marquez adobe. *Ernest Marquez Collection*

handful to many hundreds. Ludwig, in fact, commented on the romantic appearance of the native Californians, "brown as desert Arabs, carrying long canes, and [the] elegant ladies riding horseback along the cliffs." Most of the commercial enterprises were run by Anglos, though in the early 1880s Pascual Marquez built a bathhouse near the mouth of the canyon as a convenience to vacationing beach-goers.

Behind the scenes legal battles over the land continued, even while the ranchos were passing into the hands of new Yankee owners. To the north, Rancho Topanga Malibu Sequit (owned by Don Bartolo Tapia's successor, Leon Victor Prudhomme) was sold under the cloud of an imperfect title in 1857 to Matthew Keller for ten cents an acre. "Don Mateo," with more funds and perhaps better lawyers, returned to court and won clear title in 1864. Though Keller continued to reside in Los Angeles, he used the remote hillsides of "the Malibu" as grazing areas for his cattle and frequently rode on horseback up the rugged shore to his ranch house in Solstice Canyon.

The Santa Monica ranchos, on the other hand, attracted the attention of Colonel Robert S. Baker, who had been drawn to California by the gold rush and whose sizeable wealth was derived from selling supplies to the miners, as well as from cattle and sheep operations in northern California and the Tejon country near Bakersfield.

Arriving at this strategic time, Baker purchased the Rancho San Vicente y Santa Monica on September 3, 1872, paying $55,000 for over thirty thousand acres. A year later, on August 14, 1873, he bought an undivided one-half interest in the Rancho Boca de Santa Monica, without patent, for $6,000 from Maria Antonia Villa de Reyes. A small portion of the Reyes land which had been given to Charles Larrabee was sold to Baker as well. Baker was eager to take possession, but since the land was undivided, and he did not know the exact boundaries of his portion, he filed a complaint in the Los Angeles District Court in 1874 to have the grant partitioned.

The following year Colonel Baker married Arcadia Bandini de Stearns, who had been widowed in 1871. A major landholder in her own right, Arcadia was renowned as a hostess, and their apartment on the third floor of the new Baker Block on Main Street soon became the most prestigious social and political salon in Los Angeles. In later years, after Baker's death in 1894, Arcadia lived on Ocean Avenue in Santa Monica and took an active interest

Above, Manuel Marquez and Juan Carrillo, father of Leo and Ottie Carrillo. The picture was taken in Santa Monica Canyon around 1900. *Below,* Ramona Marquez, with her son, Luis. Both, *Ernest Marquez Collection*

in her business affairs until she died in 1912.

During the district court hearings there were frequent disputes involving Baker, the Marquez heirs, and the U.S. Surveyor over the exact location of the north-south boundary line between the Rancho San Vicente and the Rancho Boca de Santa Monica. Finally, in 1881, the United States patent for the entire rancho was issued and was signed by President James Garfield on July 21 of that year, nineteen days after he had been shot in the back by an assassin — a wound from which he died on September 19, 1881.

The case for the partition came before the superior court on July 6, 1882. In the meantime, Colonel Baker had sold three-quarters of his interest in the rancho to Senator John P. Jones of Nevada, and the remaining one-fourth to Arcadia, but asked that the partition be continued in his name. The three court-appointed referees were instructed to divide the rancho into fair shares for the five surviving children of Francisco Marquez and for Robert Baker. (Roque Valenzuela Marquez, the widow of Francisco, had remarried and conveyed all of her rightful portion to her children.)

William P. Reynolds, who was appointed surveyor for the partition, resurveyed the exterior boundaries

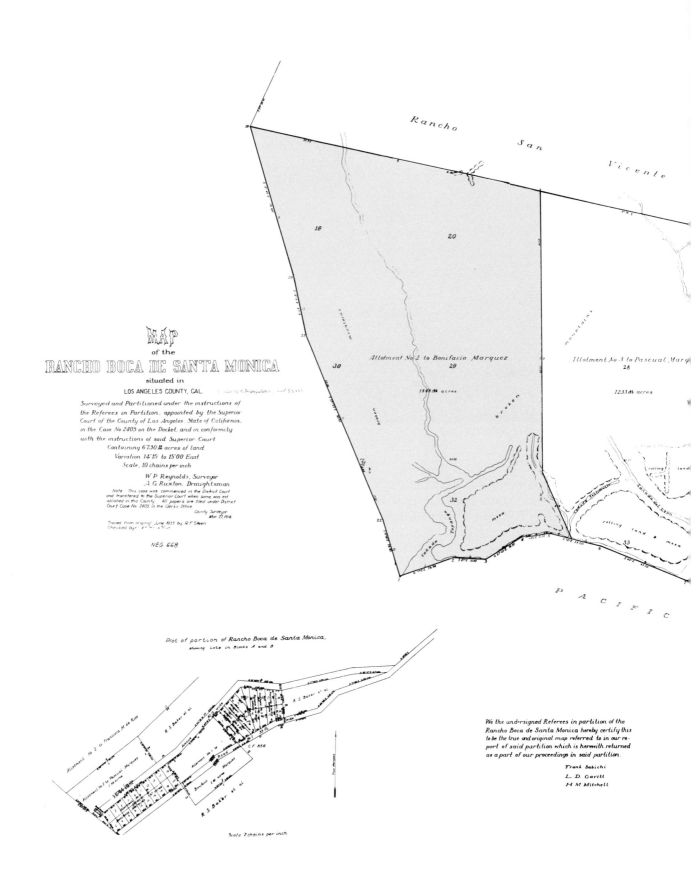

Rancho   San   Vicente

18

20

MAP
of the
RANCHO BOCA DE SANTA MONICA
situated in
LOS ANGELES COUNTY, CAL.

Surveyed and Partitioned under the instructions of
the Referees in Partition, appointed by the Superior
Court of the County of Los Angeles, State of California,
in the Case No 2405 on the Docket, and in conformity
with the instructions of said Superior Court
Containing 6730 acres of land
Variation 14°15' to 15°00' East
Scale, 10 chains per inch

W P Reynolds, Surveyor
A G Ruxton, Draughtsman

Note   This case was commenced in the District Court
and transferred to the Superior Court when same was est
ablished in this County.   All papers are filed under District
Court Case No. 2405 in the Clerks Office.
County Surveyor
Mar 17, 1916

Traced from original June 1935 by R.F. Steen
Checked by

NEG 668

Allotment No 2 to Bonifacio Marquez
29

1848 acres

Allotment No 3 to Pascual Marquez
28

1233 acres

30

32

rolling land

33

rolling land & mesa

P A C I F I C

Plot of portion of Rancho Boca de Santa Monica,
showing Lots in Blocks A and B

R S Baker et al

C F A56

R S Baker et al

Scale 2 chains per inch

We the undersigned Referees in partition of the
Rancho Boca de Santa Monica hereby certify this
to be the true and original map referred to in our report of said partition which is herewith returned
as a part of our proceedings in said partition.

Frank Sabichi
L. D. Gavitt
H. M. Mitchell

20

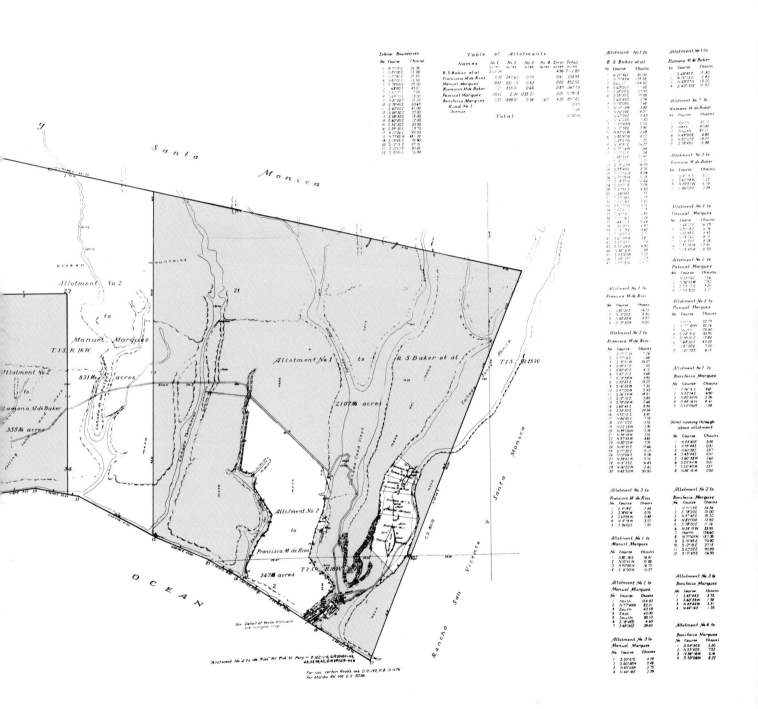

Partition map showing the allotments given to Francisco
Marquez heirs and Col. Robert Baker et al.

The Marquez family hospitality extended to descendants of the rancheros and vacationing city folk alike. This Rustic Canyon barbecue included members of the Carrillo, Lugo, Marquez and Reyes families. *Young Collection*

of the rancho, subdivided the rancho into sections as recommended by the referees, and on December 26, 1882, completed a map based on the surveys. On June 8, 1883, the decree of partition was filed with the following allotments: Francisca Marquez de Rios, 258.58 acres; Ramona Marquez de Baker, 367.73 acres; Manuel Marquez, 852.50 acres; Pascual Marquez, 1,279.18 acres; and Bonifacio Marquez, 1,857.42 acres. Robert Baker received 2,112.80 acres of land, including Rustic and Temescal canyons and the intervening mesa which would become the heart of Pacific Palisades. Subsequently these acreages were reduced by the granting of various easements and rights-of-way.

The share awarded each Marquez heir was in the form of three allotments. Pascual Marquez, for example, received his first allotment of 40.62 acres in Santa Monica Canyon where his adobe was located. His second allotment of 2.34 acres was at the mouth of the canyon, and his third allotment of 1,233.21 acres was agricultural land on the western mesas. (See the accompanying map for the location of the various allotments.)

The sale to Baker was the first of many which would erode away the sizeable landholdings of the Marquez and Reyes families. In June, 1887, Francisca Marquez and her second husband, Federico Peña, agreed to sell her Allotment No. 2 (the present site of Huntington Palisades) for $55,575 to Abbot Kinney and P. Robertson, who planned to subdivide it for residences. The property consisted of 247 acres and included rights to the water flowing over the land in Rustic Canyon.

The next major transaction took place in September, 1891, when Ramona Marquez de Reyes sold the lower 162 acres of her Allotment No. 2 to James H. Whitworth for $2,500. In 1895 Pascual Marquez sold the major portion of his Allotment No. 3 to Joseph Whitworth, retaining certain easements and two choice parcels: 17.45 acres in Santa Ynez Canyon and 17.75 acres in the Cañon de Sentimiento, where his ranch house was located.

The Whitworths were two of seven sons of a pioneering family who had arrived in the Mormon community of San Bernardino in 1856. They were successful cattlemen who owned a 125-acre ranch near Pico and La Cienega in Los Angeles and brought their herds out to the coast for summer pasture.

Bonifacio Marquez died on September 8, 1891,

Right, Perfecto Marquez (by auto) hosted large gatherings on his picnic grounds in Santa Monica Canyon. *Courtesy Angelina Marquez Olivera* *Below*, preparations for a picnic. *Ernest Marquez Collection*

Above left, Marquez family ranch house in Las Pulgas Canyon, *Ernest Marquez Collection*
Above right, Pete Badillo stands on a newly plowed field. The house in the background belonged to Mrs. Castino, second wife of Manuel Marquez. *Courtesy Angelina Marquez Olivera*

Below, the old Marquez cemetery in Santa Monica Canyon. Perfecto and Tranquilina Marquez are standing next to the grave of Pascual and Micaela Marquez. *Angelina Marquez Olivera*

Above, the Ysidro Reyes adobe, located near Seventh Street and Adelaide Drive in Santa Monica and demolished in 1906.
Below, Manuel Marquez adobe. *Young Collection*

leaving no will. His widow, Maria Antonia Olivares de Marquez was appointed administratrix by the superior court and in January, 1899, asked for authorization to sell a single, undivided parcel of land from the estate for the benefit of their children (including Bonifacio's children from a previous marriage). Accordingly, Bonifacio's Allotment No. 2, containing 1,848.01 acres, was sold to the highest bidder, E.C. Stelle, for $7,392.04. Similarly, in March, 1906, after the death of Manuel Marquez, his widow sold his 800-acre allotment for $50,000 to Robert F. Jones, brother of Senator Jones.

By the turn of the century the major portion of the Rancho Boca de Santa Monica was no longer owned by the Marquez and Reyes families. Like many other original land grant families in California who held huge expanses of land they received little monetary wealth from the sale of their acreage. The allotments located in Santa Monica Canyon were retained longer, however, as the Marquez family continued to live there and to carry on the family traditions.

The last authentic rancho-style parties were held under the oaks and the sycamores of Santa Monica Canyon in the 1890s, when the Lugos and Carrillos joined with the Marquez and Reyes families for pit-style barbecues. Later, when the older generation was gone, Pascual's son Perfecto kept the tradition of hospitality alive by maintaining picnic grounds on a portion of his property for the use of organized groups, and Bonifacio's heirs turned his handsome old barn, with its tree-shaded grounds, into a popular riding stable. Today, three direct descendants of Francisco Marquez — Angelina Marquez Olivera and Perfecto Marquez (grandchildren of Pascual) and Rosemary Miano (granddaughter of Bonifacio) — still live in Santa Monica Canyon on portions of the old land grant, and Pascual's grandson, Forrest Freed, has retained a strip of land along the creek. Each spring, too, Canyon School stages a fiesta with appropriate songs, dances, and games in memory of the canyon's rich heritage.

Part of S. P. Mammoth Wharf and Santa Monica Canyon. H.F. Rile. Photo.

The mouth of Santa Monica Canyon in 1895, when the Long Wharf was at its prime. Note the tug *Collis* offshore, the Southern Pacific train on the trestle, Dillon's Saloon (with the cupola), the Miguel Marquez (later Romero) barn, and the water tank on top of the hill. *Young Collection*

4

PORT LOS ANGELES "THE LONG WHARF"

As indicated in the preceding chapter, the first Americans to own land along the northern fringe of Santa Monica Bay were Matthew Keller, who purchased the Rancho Malibu in 1857, and Colonel Baker, who acquired the Rancho San Vicente y Santa Monica in 1879 and added a half interest in the Rancho Boca de Santa Monica the following year — using his vast domain primarily as range land for his herds.

In 1897 a wealthy young Harvard graduate, Frederick Hastings Rindge, succeeded Keller as owner of "the Malibu." With more than a trace of romance in his blood, Rindge had come west with his twenty-two-year-old bride, May Knight Rindge, seeking the fulfillment of a dream: " . . . a farm near the ocean and under the lee of the mountains . . . a troutbrook, wild trees, a lake, good soil, and excellent climate, one not too cool in summer."

Malibu Canyon proved a perfect choice. Selecting it as his homesite, Rindge went on the construct the first coastal road — a crude trail, parts of which were passable only at low tide. From this time on, the couple's love of the Malibu and their passionate dedication to the land played a major role in the fate of the northbound highway and the development of such future coastal communities as Pacific Palisades.

Meanwhile, growth and progress were overdue. In September, 1874, the dynamic senator from Nevada, John Percival Jones, arrived on the peaceful Santa Monica scene and promptly set in motion a series of ambitious plans. He was even then well known as a man of action and a formidable speaker who held audiences spellbound with his rapid-fire delivery, colorful sense of humor, and command of mining camp lingo. English by birth, Jones had struck it rich — first at the mines of Nevada's Comstock Lode and later at the Panamint silver mines in California. Now he hoped to build a railroad of his own to carry Panamint ore from the Owens Valley to the sea.

Such a plan patently interfered with the impending stranglehold of the Southern Pacific on local commerce. Nevertheless, the senator was ready to risk his immense fortune and to use his considerable influence in Washington to achieve his goal. The transcontinental railroad had reached San Francisco in 1869, but all passengers and freight bound for Los Angeles still had to make the final leg of the journey by ship or tedious overland travel. To close the gap, the Southern Pacific had begun extending its tracks southward from San Francisco through the San Joaquin Valley and had struck a deal with Los Angeles to include that city on its main line.

By coincidence, a group of Los Angeles business leaders had already begun planning their own railroad line from Independence, in the Owens Valley, to Los Angeles. When Jones arrived he joined the group, put up the major part of the funds required, and began looking for a route over which the line could be extended to a suitable port. His inquiries led to a meeting with Colonel Baker on the Santa Monica bluffs, where Jones ascertained that not only did Baker own the surrounding land, he also held a franchise for a narrow-gauge railroad to the coast. Baker had planned to link Los Angeles with a new town to be named Truxton after the son of General E.F. Beale, his partner in the Tejon country, and proposed placing the terminus of the railroad in the vicinity of the old Shoo-Fly Landing.

The prospects for Truxton passed into limbo on January 4, 1875, when the sale of three-fourths of Baker's landholdings to Senator Jones was officially recorded and articles of incorporation for the Los Angeles & Independence Railroad were filed. Shortly thereafter, Baker deeded the remaining portion of his property to his wife, Arcadia. Collis Huntington and Leland Stanford, who dominated the Southern Pacific, were outraged at Jones's actions, but they accepted the challenge, and the Southern Pacific Railroad moved into fierce competition and a track-building contest with the fledgling Los Angeles & Independence line.

Senator Jones immediately began work on a new wharf near Shoo-Fly Landing and rushed plans to

The middle mesa of the Forestry Station, as viewed from the west, around 1890. The Edmond ranch house and the Uplifter clubhouse would be built in later years just out of the picture on the left. *Courtesy Lawrence Kamber*

the drawing board for an adjacent town, to be named Santa Monica. The opening day for the sale of lots was scheduled for July 15, 1875. Crowds arrived in festive mood, not only in horsedrawn carriages from Los Angeles, but by ship from San Francisco. The fluent and persuasive orator, Tom Fitch, also came down from the north to preside over the occasion, and before the day ended, Santa Monica had been born.

Nine months later the town had a thousand residents, a school district, a church, and a newspaper. Two trains a day were delivering prospective property buyers, as well as vacationers, to the beach. Behind the scenes, however, the wave of growth had crested. Banks in both San Francisco and Los Angeles were collapsing and Comstock shares were tumbling. By September 5, 1876, when the Southern Pacific completed its line over the Tehachapi Mountains and its trains rolled into Los Angeles, hopes for the Los Angeles & Independence Railroad had dwindled. The disastrous drought of 1877 caused a decline in population throughout the Southland and a corresponding drop in real estate values. The Los Angeles & Independence line to Santa Monica fell into disrepair, and work on the section to Independence came to a halt after only a mile or two of track had been laid.

As Comstock securities continued to plunge

downward and the rich Panamint mines' most productive veins were exhausted, Senator Jones watched his fortune fade away. In a move prompted by political fence-mending, Collis P. Huntington paid Jones a token $250,000 for the beleaguered railroad — one-fourth of its cost.

The ever-resilient Jones, who kept his seat in the United States Senate for thirty years, managed to recoup his wealth and built an imposing summer home on Ocean Avenue in Santa Monica. Santa Monica also staged a remarkable recovery, evolving into a residential and resort community rather than a shipping center. Within a decade the great boom of 1887 had revived real estate speculation, and new dreams of glory were on the rise.

It was at this time that another visionary, Abbot Kinney, produced the first plans for developing a portion of what is now Pacific Palisades. Kinney was a man of many accomplishments — distinguished scholar, tobacco millionaire, world traveler, and an idealist with a knack for the practical. He had come to California from the East in 1880 and settled in Sierra Madre, where he planted a large orchard and earned a reputation as a horticulturalist. A few years later he moved to Santa Monica for the benefits of the sea air and was appointed to the newly organized state Board of Forestry.

In 1887 Kinney took steps to turn his recently

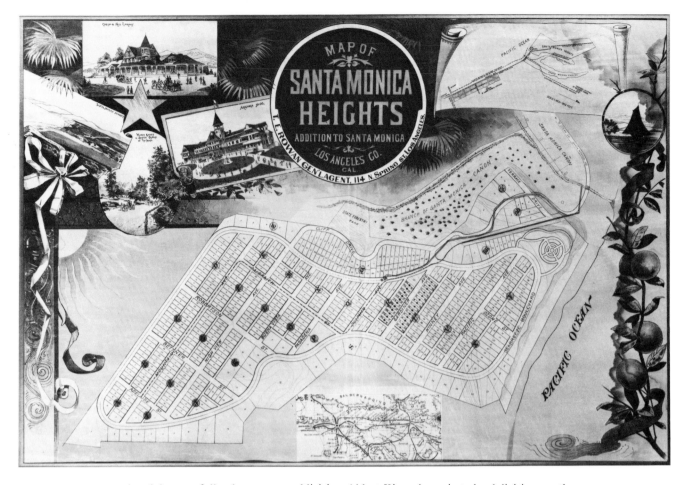

An elaborate, full-color poster publicizing Abbot Kinney's projected subdivision on the eastern fringe of what is today Huntington Palisades. *Young Collection*

purchased property on the bluffs west of Santa Monica Canyon into a fashionable residential area. Maps were drawn, trees planted, and the Santa Monica Outlook Railway organized (with Kinney as president) for the purpose of building a steam road from the new Southern Pacific depot in Santa Monica, along the base of the bluffs, and up the side of Rustic Canyon to "Santa Monica Heights."

Kinney also persuaded Senator Jones and Arcadia Bandini de Baker to donate six acres of land (later increased to twenty acres) in Rustic Canyon to the State of California for the nation's first experimental forestry station. The primary research project involved a scientific study of various strains of eucalyptus trees — newly introduced from Australia and the object of widespread horticultural interest. The theory was that large-scale plantings of eucalypts could provide not only timber, but such other useful and marketable products as medicinal oils. Their landscaping value was of secondary interest.

Hopes for the successful commercial use of eucalypts proved disappointing, but the large specimens planted by Kinney near the bluffs in Huntington Palisades remain today as a graceful legacy of his enterprise, and the forestry station

grove in Rustic Canyon with its impressive stand of eucalypts and other exotic trees was accorded official state historical landmark status in 1971. As for Kinney, he abandoned his subdivision plans — perhaps as a result of the depression of 1888 — and sold his entire property on the mesa to Collis P. Huntington.

Huntington's reputation for ruthless business dealings had preceded him. Years before, during the gold rush, he had set up shop as a hardware dealer in Sacramento and acquired a sizeable fortune by selling necessities to miners at cutthroat prices. Later, aided by generous government assistance, he parlayed his railroad holdings into domination of the mighty Southern Pacific network.

Once competition from the Los Angeles & Independence Railroad had been squelched, Huntington moved to reinforce a Southern Pacific Railroad monopoly in the area. The Los Angeles & Independence terminal at Los Angeles was torn down; an excuse was found to demolish the wharf at Santa Monica; and rates on the Southern Pacific's San Pedro line were raised to an exorbitant level. In his book, *Port Los Angeles*, Ernest Marquez observes that moving freight from Los Angeles to San

29

Activity on the Southern Pacific wharf at Port Los Angeles on May 13, 1893, two days after the steamer *San Mateo* arrived — the first ship to use the new facilities. The coal bunker was still under construction; coal was being unloaded; and visitors apparently were free to wander at will. *Ernest Marquez Collection*

Pedro became as costly as shipping it from San Pedro to Hong Kong.

San Pedro had already received some federal funds for development of its harbor, and even though shippers resented being at the mercy of the Southern Pacific, the location did seem feasible for a deep-water port. The Los Angeles Chamber of Commerce led the way in attempts to improve the facility, conducting influential personages on tours of the harbor and using Southern Pacific trains for the purpose. In October, 1889, the Chamber rolled out the red carpet for United States Senator William B. Frye, chairman of the Senate Commerce Committee, who visited the site with several committee members, only to be taken aback when Frye openly scoffed at any prospect of San Pedro's becoming the official deep-water port for Los Angeles.

The next day, in fact, Frye visited Senator Jones at the latter's Ocean Avenue home and, looking out over the water, remarked pointedly and for publication that Santa Monica Bay would be a more suitable choice. This statement caught the attention of Collis Huntington, who was already apprehensive over the port facilities recently installed by the Atchison, Topeka & Santa Fe Railroad at Redondo Beach, as well as the acquisition by the Terminal Land Company of property adjacent to the San Pedro inner harbor, possibly on behalf of the Union Pacific Railroad. Quietly, Huntington decided to build his own harbor at Santa Monica and made the first move in April, 1890, when he succeeded Leland Stanford as president of the Southern Pacific.

Huntington applied for a wharf franchise, purchased a one-half interest in Senator Jones's landholdings for $125,000, and directed his agents to continue buying up real estate in the immediate area. In the process, Bonifacio and Pascual Marquez were persuaded to grant to the Pacific Improvement Company (a Southern Pacific subsidiary) a right-of-way along the ocean front at Santa Monica Canyon in return for the customary "sum of $1 plus benefits" that would accrue from the operation of the Southern Pacific over their property — benefits that were never realized. Meanwhile, Huntington made plans to establish a private estate on the bluffs above Santa Monica Canyon, from which point he could watch ships from all over the world heading into the great seaport he envisioned at the mouth of Potrero Canyon.

Congress was responsible for approving and appropriating funds for construction of major United States seaports, and in late 1891 the Mendell Board, a group of Army engineers appointed by Congress, submitted their final report, recommending San Pedro as the preferred site for a Los Angeles facility. Huntington, confident of the Southern Pacific's formidable political influence, chose to ignore the verdict and proceeded with the construction of his ambitious Santa Monica project.

By April, 1892, tracks from Los Angeles had been laid, and the Southern Pacific announced its plans for the new wharf, extending 4,720 feet out into the ocean, with huge coal bunkers and other port facilities at its outer end. A breakwater was to be built and the inner harbor area filled with earth taken from the hills, thus providing land for mills, lumberyards, and other industries appropriate to a major seaport. As construction progressed, Huntington provided special tours for city officials and business leaders. These privileged visitors boarded railroad cars which were pushed out onto the wharf by Southern Pacific engines, there to be impressed by the pier's increasing length and the spectacular views it provided.

In December, 1892, another set of Army engineers appointed by Congress, the Craighill Board, issued a report unanimously favoring San Pedro over Santa Monica as a harbor site. Again the official recommendation had little local effect. By this time, a roundhouse with turntable, coal bunker, and water tank had been erected at the entrance to Potrero Canyon, together with several cabins that served as housing for the men working on the wharf. The Southern Pacific also extended its tracks to the north as far as Temescal Canyon, where earth was obtained for ballast, and claimed a right-of-way on up the coast, hinting that such an easement might become part of a line to Ventura.

On April 29, 1893, Huntington officially named the new wharf "Port Los Angeles," and two weeks later the first ship arrived — the collier *San Mateo,* bearing passengers as well as freight. Special trains carried crowds of spectators from Los Angeles to witness the event. The Santa Monica band played rousing tunes, and a few exuberant onlookers tossed bouquets of flowers at the rusty old ship to create a holiday atmosphere. The following October, dignitaries gathered to celebrate the completion of the Long Wharf and to inaugurate the new restaurant at its outer end. Thousands of visitors subsequently came to Port Los Angeles to watch the ships, dine in style, or try their luck at fishing. During its first year of operation, the port handled more than three hundred vessels, effectively diverting trade from both San Pedro and Redondo Beach, and saving several hours in travel time from San Francisco to Los Angeles.

Federal legislation being part and parcel of the development of important American rivers and harbors, the national press spoke out on the controversial port issue, and individual newspapers lined up on opposing sides. The appointment of Senator Jones to the Commerce Committee and his support for Santa Monica quickly drew fire. One New York

By the turn of the century the time was rapidly approaching when sailing ships would discontinue their stops at the long wharf and local residents would no longer be employed there loading and unloading vessels. Posing on the ship *Lucipara* from Glasgow, November 28, 1900, are: Top row, 3rd from left, Roman Marquez; 5th, Chucuraco Rivas; 7th, Joe Mariscal; 8th, Leandro Duron; 9th, Mike Duron. Standing in middle row, 2nd from left, Emilio Lesama; 5th, Frank Garcia; 6th, Frank Marquez; 7th, Estevan de la Pena; 10th, Vincent Rivera. *Ernest Marquez Collection*

The long, curving shape of the pier, which extended 4,720 feet out into the bay, was a thrilling site when viewed from the bluffs. *Ernest Marquez Collection*

publication noted that his backing of Collis Huntington's plan was predictable, since he and Arcadia Bandini de Baker owned three-fourths of the land affected by the Santa Monica project, and the remainder was already in the possession of Huntington's representative, Frank Davis.

Senator Frye continued his vigorous campaign on behalf of Port Los Angeles and was prepared to bestow upon it the $3 million cost of the breakwater. The Los Angeles Chamber of Commerce, which had backed San Pedro, began to waver. Most Angelenos, however, in company with the *Los Angeles Times,* the Free Harbor League, the Santa Fe Railroad, and Senator Stephen M. White of California (a committee member) cast their lot solidly in favor of San Pedro.

At the crucial moment in the dispute, when the Rivers and Harbors Committee appropriations bill reached the Senate floor, Senator White resolved the issue by introducing an amendment to the bill and, in a burst of brilliant oratory, prevailed upon his Senate colleagues to approve entrusting the final decision to a third commission of geodetic and coastal engineering professionals, the Walker Board. In March 1897, the Walker Board gave the go-ahead to San Pedro, thus sealing the future fate of Port Los Angeles.

The Long Wharf stayed in business for some years thereafter and acquired a new dimension in 1899, when Japanese fishermen founded a village on the beach to the west, using the workmen's shacks as a nucleus. The first resident of this little beach community was Hatsuje Sano of Japan who had become discouraged in his attempt to cultivate abalone on the Mendocino coast north of San Francisco and had moved to Los Angeles. On land leased from the Southern Pacific, a row of new homes, a church, and hotels for Japanese vacationers from Los Angeles sprang up, and the number of permanent residents eventually reached three hundred (including a few Russians), all dependent on commercial fishing. Their catches, which ran up to thirty tons per day, were unloaded at the Long Wharf for hauling to market by Southern Pacific trains.

The various operations at Port Los Angeles changed the character of Santa Monica Canyon, where shacks and modest homes housed many of the workmen, and taverns such as Dillon's popular saloon provided comforts and amusement for sailors on shore leave. By 1894 enough families with children lived in the area to warrant the opening of Canyon School on Sycamore Road under the aegis of the Santa Monica School Board. Its student body —made up of descendants of the *Californios,* Japanese and Russian children, together with a few stray Anglos — was a League of Nations in microcosm.

Following the Walker Board's decision of 1897, however, Port Los Angeles lost its momentum, and the era came to an end with the death of Collis P. Huntington on August 13, 1900. E.H. Harriman — rather than Collis's nephew and protégé, Henry Huntington — seized control of the Southern Pacific and assumed the presidency in 1902. Harriman had little interest in the Long Wharf. By this time the immense structure was not only aging and costly to maintain, but industrial conversion from coal to oil was rendering its huge bunkers obsolete, and more and more ships were using the San Pedro facilities.

Henry Huntington, meanwhile, began acquiring a network of electric rail lines in competition with

Movie making at the fishing village about 1914. Japanese movies were made in the Los Angeles area by a local Japanese company and then sent to Japan. Sessue Hayakawa was one of several stars who appeared in these early films. Ince even had full time Japanese actors living in the village. *Ernest Marquez Collection*

Above, the mouth of Santa Monica Canyon was a bustling vacation spot in 1916, when the Long Wharf and the Bundy Bath House were favorite tourist attractions. Note the set for Thomas Ince's great motion picture *Civilization* on the distant hilltop. Ince's studio at Inceville was located in Santa Ynez Canyon, immediately beyond. *Ernest Marquez Collection*

Below, a Japanese fishing village housing some three hundred residents extended along the beach to the west of the pier. After the decline of Port Los Angeles, the buildings fell into disrepair and were demolished in 1920. *Ernest Marquez Collection*

Pioneer developer Robert C. Gillis, in front of the family home on the corner of Fourth Street and Adelaide Drive in Santa Monica. *Courtesy Adelaide Gillis McCormick*

the steam railroads. In 1906 Harriman, acting for the Southern Pacific, caught Huntington off guard and purchased the Los Angeles Pacific Railroad from its founders, General Moses H. Sherman and Eli P. Clark. Two years later, the Los Angeles Pacific leased the Long Wharf and made it a feature of its Balloon Route Trolley trips. Using the old Los Angeles & Independence line, regular trolley service was extended from downtown Los Angeles to the end of the pier, trains running hourly from Santa Monica to the wharf at a bargain fare of ten cents each way.

The Southern Pacific went on to acquire Huntington's half-interest in the Pacific Electric Railway and other railway holdings in 1910, merging them all into a single system which operated under the Pacific Electric name. In 1913 the new owners removed the bunkers and 1,600 feet at the far end of the wharf. During the ensuing years a series of landslides covered the tracks below the bluff with dirt, hampering access, and a costly fire seriously

damaged the Japanese village. Gradually the Japanese fishermen and their families moved to a new location on Terminal Island.

On July 9, 1920, the Pacific Electric Railway ordered the dismantling of the pier and other structures, citing as cause the financial losses incurred by the rail line and the cost of maintenance. The Japanese village was doomed as well when health authorities declared that an expensive sewer system must be installed to make it habitable. Demolition began at once, and by December it was completed.

The Pacific Electric continued to provide trolley service as far as Santa Monica Canyon until August 22, 1933. After that it removed all track, poles, and materials, leveled the raised area at the mouth of the canyon, and dismantled the trestle. Today the rock-ribbed point of land from which the wharf once extended and an official state landmark plaque nearby remain the only evidences of the ambitious structure's existence.

5

PRELUDE TO PROGRESS

The arrival of an energetic young Canadian, Robert C. Gillis, in Santa Monica in the mid-1880s marked the beginning of a new epoch in the development of the Santa Monica Bay area. Once launched on his career, Gillis's large-scale purchases of land and his association with the Santa Monica Land and Water Company set the pattern for subdivisions from Westwood to Pacific Palisades.

Gillis was born in Moncton, New Brunswick, and grew up in Nova Scotia, where he trained as a chemist and studied briefly for the ministry. His family were devout Scotch Presbyterians who dedicated their Sundays to church services and Bible readings, laying the foundation for Robert Gillis's life-long interest in philosophy and religion.

As a newcomer to Santa Monica, Gillis stayed with his brother, William, and was employed by him at the local drug store. His brief professional career was interrupted, however, when he met Frances Lindsey, a young lady who had come from Maine with her brother Charles Lindsey, Santa Monica's first dentist. In 1888 Frances and Robert Gillis were married.

The young couple went east on their honeymoon to visit their families, remained there on business, and in 1892 returned to Santa Monica with their two-year-old daughter, Adelaide. For a time the brothers ran the pharmacy together, but Robert Gillis soon saw a more promising career in real estate and began investing in land. By then the Long Wharf was under construction and the surrounding area seemed destined for rapid growth.

In 1898 Gillis began acquiring stock in the Santa Monica Land and Water Company, founded the preceding year by Senator John P. Jones and Arcadia Bandini de Baker, who had transferred 30,000 acres of their Rancho Boca de Santa Monica and Rancho San Vicente y Santa Monica landholdings to form the new company. This area included the heart of today's Pacific Palisades and the mountains beyond, as well as major portions of Santa Monica, Santa Monica Canyon, Rustic Canyon, Bel-Air, and Brentwood.

Anticipating the course of westside development, Gillis and a group of investors bought 625 acres of the Wolfskill ranch in West Los Angeles in 1903 and two years later subdivided portions of it as the Sawtelle and Westgate tracts.* At the same time Gillis and his associates began subdividing properties in Brentwood and along San Vicente Boulevard. He envisioned a model community in the Brentwood area that would include landscaped boulevards, restricted residential construction, rail service, and a modern hotel located in an adjacent canyon. The property was sold before development began, but the new owners adopted many of these concepts, and Gillis arranged to have a branch of the Los Angeles Pacific trolley line built along San Vicente to the sea.

On Christmas Day in 1904, the *Los Angeles Times* announced that the vast Santa Monica Land and Water Company tract had been sold by its founders to a syndicate of capitalists. Included in the list of directors were R.C. Gillis, H.M. Gorham, C.L. Bundy, J.J. Davis, and John D. Pope. By 1906 Gillis had acquired all of the outstanding shares in the corporation, and from that time until his death in 1947, he functioned as the managing head of the company, giving him control of thousands of acres of prime westside property. Also, by 1911, Gillis, through one or another of the ownerships which he controlled, had acquired a major portion of the Pacific Palisades coastline — from Topanga to Santa Monica Canyon.

The Gillis family made their home in Santa Monica until 1901. Adelaide's younger sister, Dorothy, was born there in 1895, and both girls attended the local grammar school, as did Dorothy and Gregory Jones who lived nearby. Occasionally, Dorothy Gillis Loomis recalls, their friends' eminent grandfather, Senator Jones, would send his carriage, drawn by a pair of handsome gray horses, to convey

*Both tracts also included some Santa Monica Land and Water Company property.

37

the Jones and Gillis children to school in style.

Even after the Gillis family moved to Los Angeles, they spent summers in Santa Monica at their vacation home on the corner of Fourth and Adelaide. From this base the girls set out on excursions to the beach, met vessels arriving at Port Los Angeles, and rode on horseback up the canyons. The Long Wharf was also a favorite fishing spot for the Gillises' Chinese cook, Charlie King. Charlie, who kept an immaculate kitchen, shared his domain with the family poodle, Tinker Bell, and the two of them often went fishing together, bringing home a fine, fresh catch for the evening meal. Closer to home, the enterprising Charlie made a few extra pennies by catching skunks in the fields, skinning them, and selling their sacs to the local Chinese herbalist.

A favorite weekend retreat for the Gillises was nearby Rustic Canyon, where their relatives, the Edmonds, owned a small ranch. George Edmond was a geology professor from Johns Hopkins University who had come to California for his health, and his wife, Katherine Clark Edmond, was a cousin of Mrs. Gillis's from Maine. In 1895 the Edmonds purchased land adjacent to the Forestry Station from Senator Jones and Arcadia Bandini de Baker and camped with their daughter, Betty, in a tent under an oak tree until their rambling ranch house was completed. For the next twenty-five years the Edmonds' only neighbors were the couples who managed the station, and their private life combined the rigors of pioneering with the pleasures of books and music.

As children, Betty and her cousin Adelaide learned to put up with snakes and lizards and played house down by the stream, digging holes in a clay bank to make imaginary rooms. Later, young friends from Santa Monica came out by tally-ho to picnic under the oaks and walk in the meadows, which were carpeted each spring with brodiaea, yellow violets, and mariposa lilies.

The life style at the ranch changed when Katherine died and George married a family friend, Julia Boynton, who was a Stanford graduate and an avid scholar. The couple became more seclusive, cherishing the peace and quiet of their canyon home and discouraging trespassers. Betty left to attend Throop Institute in Pasadena (the forerunner of the California Institute of Technology), where she majored in art, and went on to Paris for training in sculpture.

Even though Robert Gillis maintained an active interest in the Santa Monica Bay area throughout his lifetime, his overall career was of broader scope. He was retiring by nature and deliberately avoided publicity, yet he was involved in extensive land and mining ventures with the great entrepreneurs of the day. He was also credited with negotiating the complex sale of the Los Angeles Pacific Railway system to E. H. Harriman while the two men were on a trip to Japan in 1905 — a major financial coup. The transaction was concluded the following year.

Gillis's financial ingenuity and zest for action were combined with respect for the land and enthusiasm for its constructive use. He discovered the virtues of lima beans at a fair in Ventura and thereafter grew them successfully on his undeveloped westside property. He also planted a lemon orchard

George and Katherine Clark Edmond, in their ranch house in Rustic Canyon. Their only neighbors were the families who cared for the adjacent Forestry Station. *Courtesy Melzar Lindsey*

on the Riviera (where he planned eventually to build a home) and maintained a packing plant in Santa Monica that processed his lemons under the "Sawtelle" label.

Due in part to lack of an adequate water supply, the coastal area west of Santa Monica Canyon remained rural and sparsely populated until after World War I. The Santa Monica Land and Water Company leased portions of its land to tenant farmers, such as Henry Bowers, whose modest farmhouse was located near today's Pacific Palisades business district. He planted fields of oat and barley hay and lima beans, kept a couple of cows, several horses, a pen full of pigs, and enough turkeys for holiday entertaining. Francis Brunner, who later operated bus lines to Pacific Palisades, described Thanksgiving dinners in the Bowers home in the early 1900s as a special treat for Francis and the other Brunner children. Nearby, in lower Temescal Canyon, Ed Smale raised pigs and fine horses and fought a running battle with coyotes, bobcats, mountain lions, and rattlesnakes.

Farther west, on land in Las Pulgas Canyon owned by saloonkeeper Henry Sexton, Al Straszacker had a cottage, truck garden, and grain fields. The mouth of Santa Ynez Canyon was occupied by Inceville, part of a site leased to moviemaker Thomas Ince by the Santa Monica Land Company to accommodate Ince's extensive sets and to provide back-country for his Westerns. The intervening fields were for the most part cultivated by members of the Marquez family.

After the death of Collis Huntington in 1900, the

Above, one of the groups of young people who came over from Santa Monica to picnic with Betty Edmond in Rustic Canyon. *Courtesy Melzar Lindsey*

Below, a 1915 view of Al Straszacker's cottage in the east arm of Las Pulgas Canyon. Straszacker farmed the flat land and raised stock on the surrounding hills with the help of his ranch hand, "One-Armed Joe" Olivares. *Clearwater Collection*

mesa later known as Huntington Palisades was held in the name of his widow, Arabella. This included a sixteen-acre subdivision named Santa Monica Heights, which had been laid out in 1887 by Abbot Kinney. The only structures on the Huntington property, however, were small summer cabins — many with no sanitary facilities — scattered along the bluff and occupied periodically by vacationing city dwellers who had no formal claim to the sites. There was also a cottage halfway up the Chautauqua hill, opposite Vance Place, on a handsome natural plateau which, according to Dorothy Gillis Loomis, had been won in a poker game by her father, R.C. Gillis, at the expense of a luckless sea captain whose ship had docked at the Long Wharf.

Access to the western mesas was still rough and circuitous. The only coastal route was along the beach at low tide. Otherwise, the road from Santa Monica to Santa Monica Canyon crossed the plateau, descended where Seventh Street is today, and climbed up the western wall of the canyon at a tangent from the coast. Marquez Road, as this portion was called, was little more than a path which continued on across the mesas, over a rude wooden bridge at Temescal Canyon, and back to the coast at Santa Ynez.

From there the road hugged the shoreline, past Haystack Rock and Castle Rock, and through Arch Rock, before turning inland at Topanga Canyon. A narrow wagon trail crossed the mountains to Calabasas, serving the homesteaders who had ranches high up in the hills. Beyond Topanga Canyon, the seaward slope of the mountains remained unspoiled, largely due to the Rindge family's resistance to change. It was they who for many years kept the railroad and any other trade route from being extended to the west and north.

The Rindges had a home on Ocean Avenue in Santa Monica, and Frederick Rindge was active in both civic and Methodist church affairs. The family's real love, however, was their Malibu ranch, where they planted gardens with exotic trees and shrubs, raised fruit and field crops, improved the roads, and extended their cattle operations. In Rindge's book entitled *Happy Days in Southern California,* he wrote: "Here in these almost holy hills, in this calm and sweet retreat, protected from the wearing haste of city life — here time flies. . . . The ennobling stillness makes the mind ascend to heaven."

Pastoral scene on the mesas that are today Pacific Palisades, showing the land virtually unchanged since the days of the *rancheros.* This and subsequent pictures were taken in 1915 by the real estate firm of Wright, Callender and Andrews in connection with a planned subdivision to be named "Santa Monica Highlands" and were used in a brochure. These prints were made from Zola Clearwater's original glass negatives.

Above, a 1915 view looking seaward across the mesas and Las Pulgas Canyon, with a glimpse of the Long Wharf shortly before the coal bunkers and its "working end" were removed. The vantage point is near the intersection of Sunset Boulevard and Las Casas Avenue. *Clearwater Collection.*

Below, Rustic Canyon from the same series, looking across the plateau which became the Uplifters' polo field and is today bounded by Greentree Road. Visible in the distance, across the creek, is the Edmond ranch house. *Clearwater Collection*

Above, a view looking southeastward from the old coast road, showing Castle Rock, *left,* and Haystack Rock, *right,* two prominent landmarks between Santa Ynez and Topanga canyons. Haystack Rock broke up long ago, and Castle Rock was removed by stages as a hazard to bathers and a hindrance to traffic.

Below, Arch Rock, near the mouth of Topanga Canyon. In the early days, such obstructions prohibited travel along the coast road except at low tide. This famous tourist attraction was allegedly blasted away one dark and stormy night in 1906 by Rindge employees to permit threshing machines and other heavy machinery to reach the Rindge ranch. *Both, Ernest Marquez Collection*

The Wharf and Landing Malibu Railroad

Above, the Rindges' Malibu wharf and a portion of the Malibu Railway, both under construction. *Below,* the famous Malibu gate that carried a warning to visitors, "Malibu Rancho — Trespassers Strictly Prohibited," thereby discouraging travel north along the coast from Pacific Palisades. *Both, Ernest Marquez Collection*

Although Rindge was a romantic, he was not a purist. He envisioned some commercial development for his land as indicated by his remarks: "This coast offers inducements for the building of a road well-nigh equal to Italy's famous Cornice Road; if Ocean Avenue were extended from Santa Monica to Hueneme, the days of coaching would come back."

For Rindge himself, such plans were not to be. In 1903 a great fire, perhaps started by campers, swept the Malibu. Within two hours the Rindge home in Malibu Canyon burned to the ground. The family moved to Los Angeles, and two years later, after a short illness, Frederick Rindge died.

May Knight Rindge was determined to keep the ranch and to carry out her husband's wishes. Suspecting the Southern Pacific of seeking a right-of-way up the coast, she built the Hueneme & Malibu & Port Los Angeles Railroad along the shoreline of the Malibu and used it to ship grain and hides to market, thereby satisfying the requirements of the Interstate Commerce Commission and thwarting the plans of the railroad giants. With equal dedication she fought attempts by the state to put a highway through her property — a battle that began in 1908 and lasted until 1925.

As time passed, May K. Rindge found that increasing vigilance was required to keep the Malibu safe from vandalizing homeowners, livestock rustlers, and other intruders. In 1917 she declared all of the ranch roads closed to the public and backed up her decision with fences, gates, and armed guards. For nearly a decade thereafter, the only available access to the north along the beach was at low tide, and May K. Rindge herself became a symbol of dogged resistance.

Meanwhile, in 1912, the Santa Monica Land Company — owned by Robert C. Gillis, Robert P. Sherman, and Joseph J. Davis — filed a subdivision tract plan for lower Rustic Canyon (part of the former Senator Jones and Arcadia Bandini de Baker holdings) and by 1913 most of Santa Monica Canyon (which had been bought piecemeal from members of the Marquez family) was platted. Roads and walkways were built, and the first homes were offered for sale — many by developer Frank E. Bundy.

Simultaneously, Canyon School was moved from county-owned property in the 400-block of Sycamore Road to a new site on Channel Road which was donated to the county for that purpose by Pascual Marquez, and the original site was subdivided into six lots by the land company. In 1925, when Santa Monica Canyon became part of the city of Los Angeles, ownership of the Channel Road property was transferred to the Los Angeles Unified School District.

Canyon School as it appeared on October 29, 1894, when it was located on Sycamore Road. The group includes several members of the Marquez and Reyes families. *Young Collection*

Private Watkins of Inceville. *Courtesy Angelina Marquez Olivera*

Canyonites William Marquez, Castulo Pascual "Dunnie" Marquez, Emilio Monyier, "Red" Webb, and Pat Galgani — all were called to the colors and served in France. Even Inceville sent one of its own, a Mr. Watkins who mailed back a picture of himself — tall and distinguished, nattily dressed in his field uniform.

There were tragedies. Pat Galgani died in battle, and Dunnie Marquez, who had fought with the American forces in every major battle in France, suffered the lingering effects of gas warfare and died of lung cancer in 1928 at the age of thirty-three, leaving two children, Theresa and author-historian Ernest Marquez.

The Edmond family too mourned an untimely loss. Betty, who had returned to California in 1914, volunteered to go overseas with the Red Cross as an interpreter. Preliminary medical procedures for her departure required her to undergo a tonsillectomy and, while still under the anesthetic, she died of complications. Shortly thereafter her father also died, leaving the widowed Julia Edmond the sole occupant of the Rustic Canyon ranch.

Dunnie Marquez with the armed forces in Germany. *Ernest Marquez Collection*

Prospects for development took a new turn in 1915, when the real estate firm of Wright, Callender and Andrews purchased the Santa Monica Land and Water Company property which would one day become the center of Pacific Palisades. Their plans were given a welcome boost on June 6, 1916, when local voters overwhelmingly approved annexation of the surrounding Westgate tract to the city of Los Angeles in return for a guaranteed water supply — a promise promptly fulfilled by the installation of a twenty-inch water main from Stone Canyon to Pacific Palisades along what is now Albright Street. With this addition of 43.67 square miles to its territory, not only was the West Side given assurance of future growth, but Los Angeles became the largest city in area in the nation.

The benefits of this potential bonanza were delayed until after World War I, which froze real estate activity and dramatically affected many segments of the sparse local population. Santa Monica

6

THOMAS INCE AND THE MAGIC OF INCEVILLE

KATHERINE LA HUE

The dream and the promise of Port Los Angeles as a major factor in West Coast shipping had for the most part ceased to exist by 1911 when pioneer moviemaker Thomas Ince launched a very different, but equally significant, venture in a remote area that one day would be part of Pacific Palisades.

Transplanted from New York to Southern California, the art of the cinema grew, flourished, and came of age in the years between 1911 and 1919 — the era of the great studios, the first of which was Inceville. There, at the mouth of Santa Ynez Canyon, in a complex of buildings and stage sets, Ince produced hundreds of movies, issued under such diverse names as 101 Ranch, Kay-Bee, Bronco, Bison, Domino, and Triangle.

The first home of the fledgling film industry was New York, where movies had been produced since 1895. In 1909 inventor Thomas Alva Edison, owner of the basic patents, merged his interests with Biograph, Vitagraph, and several other studios to form the Motion Picture Patents Company, hoping thereby to eliminate the independents. All of the member companies pooled their patent claims, and each was licensed to manufacture films.

Instead of discouraging competition, however, the Patent Company engendered more. By 1912 a host of "outlaw" independent companies had been formed, including IMP (Independent Motion Pictures), Bison, Fox, Keystone, and the New York Motion Picture Company. It was a cutthroat business all around. As the independents defied the Patent Trust, open violence and guerilla warfare raged — a conflict which lasted for five years while legal battles were fought in the courts.

Independent directors and actors began moving west in large numbers to escape the oppression of the Patent Company and to enjoy the advantages of California's temperate climate. The Mexican border also offered an escape route should the Patent Trust extend its violence to the West Coast. Thus it was that Ince came to Los Angeles in 1911, a year after three future film greats — D.W. Griffith, Mary

Pickford, and Mack Sennett — had made their first pioneering trip to the land of sunshine for the purpose of film-making.

Thomas Ince was born into a theatrical family in Newport, Rhode Island, on November 6, 1882. His parents both acted on the legitimate stage and, like Ince, his two brothers, John and Ralph, became directors in the days of silent films. In 1907 Thomas Ince married actress Elinor Kershaw, his one and only marriage. Before moving west Ince tried his hand at acting, first on the stage, then in the movies, playing a "heavy" in the American Biograph film, *His New Lid*. The same year, 1910, he wrote and directed his first film for IMP.

In 1911 Ince and Mary Pickford sailed to Cuba to escape the Patent Trust and to make films; it was there that Mary Pickford learned much of her style under Ince's direction. Returning to New York, Ince went to work for Kessel and Bauman, who set up a joint venture with the New York Motion Picture Company. Together the group decided to establish a West Coast studio in Santa Ynez Canyon, which had been used as a location for film making since 1909.

In October, 1911, Ince leased approximately 18,000 acres of picturesque land, extending from the ocean front up Santa Ynez Canyon and into the Santa Monica Mountains for a distance of 7½ miles. This provided a natural setting for seashore, mountain, and desert locations — according to Ince, the best place in the world to make "Western" movies and an ideal spot for motion pictures in general.

Today Ince is credited with creating the best early dramas with authentic cowboy and Indian characters and is known as the "father of the Western." Even as he was building the first frame structures in Santa Ynez Canyon, Ince hired the entire 101 Ranch Wildwest Show, complete with a Sioux Indian tribe, and began turning out Westerns.

Thomas Ince was not the first nor the only movie maker to discover the merits of the Santa Monica

Thomas Ince editing his films, a process he never delegated but continued to perform throughout his producing career. *Courtesy Katherine La Hue*

area. The first feature film made in the West was *The Count of Monte Cristo,* produced in 1907 by William Selig. After completing the interior scenes in his Chicago studio, Selig decided to come west to film the outdoor scenes and used the beach at the foot of the palisades as one of his locations.

Between 1910 and 1912 three major studios set up facilities in Santa Monica proper. Kalem took over the old Southern Pacific depot in the 1600-block of Ocean Avenue; Essanay moved into the old Boehme house on the corner of Santa Monica Boulevard and Ocean; and the Vitagraph Company used an outdoor stage at the rear of the old City Hall, facing the ocean.

Inceville, however, was the most ambitious studio in the area and the only independent, Thomas Ince at the time being vice-president and manager of the New York Motion Picture Company. Significantly, one of the last battles involving the Patent Trust was fought on the old coast road in 1912. Henchmen for the trust had actually destroyed the Keystone Studio at Edendale, near Glendale, and were coming down the coast road toward Inceville, when Ince opened fire on them with the cannon from his Civil War location. Not knowing whether the cannon were real or props, but hearing the boom, the agents of the Patent Trust turned tail and made their last retreat.

Descriptions of Inceville in 1913 told of a wonderland in the wilderness, a municipality of seven hundred people with its own post office — all dedicated to the making of movies. To this end, Ince had invested $35,000 in buildings, stages, and sets — a bit of Switzerland, a Puritan settlement, a Japanese village, and many more. Beyond the breakers an ancient brigantine weighed anchor, cutlassed men swarming over the sides of the ship, while on the shore performing cowboys galloped about, twirling their lassoos in pursuit of errant cattle. The main herds were kept in the hills, where Ince also raised feed and garden produce. Supplies of every sort were needed to house and feed a veritable army of actors, directors, and subordinates.

Ince was a master at recognizing and developing new talent. He brought William S. Hart into films in 1912 to play two-reel Westerns; later Hart played in *The Bargain,* the first feature-length Western written as an original screen play. Ince also introduced the Japanese film star, Sessue Hayakawa, and employed Jean Hersholt, a recent arrival from Denmark.

Under Ince's guidance, Charles Ray, Enid Markey, Douglas Fairbanks, and Billie Burke became stars, and, although never on Ince's payroll, Charles Chaplin and Mabel Normand appeared in pictures made by Sennett on Inceville locations. In fact, according to a 1927 fan magazine, it was at Inceville that the world's favorite clown first put on his famous derby hat, flexible cane, abbreviated moustache, ill-fitting trousers, and big shoes — the outfit that became Chaplin's trademark — and went down to the Venice beach to appear in *The Kid's Auto Races.*

Above, the Keystone Kops and their unruly Hupmobile on the Huntington Palisades cliff, with the Bundy Bath House below. *Courtesy Katie LaHue*

Below, the filming of *Evangeline* by Castle Rock. *Ernest Marquez Collection*

Inceville reached its apogee, and the art of the cinema came of age under Thomas Ince in 1915. Each of the great directors who emerged at this time supplemented the techniques developed by D.W. Griffith, using devices and styles of his own; of all these men, Ince enjoyed the highest reputation. He brought discipline and organization to storytelling, while Maurice Jacques Tourneau contributed pictorial imagination and Mack Sennett introduced his popular brand of slapstick comedy.

Five to six hundred people worked at Inceville during this period, and the average monthly payroll ranged from $75,000 to $85,000. Robert Duncan wrote: "To watch them at their tasks is like visiting a beehive. Everyone busily engaged about his or her work, and all working to one end — to make good pictures." Everything was systematized and each person knew what to do.

At the top of the administrative pyramid was Ince — inscrutable and dynamic, the "enigma of picture drama." Essentially a businessman and organizer, he conducted himself and his film-making in an efficient fashion and his "lot" was noted for its discipline. Ince appeared on the sets in workmanlike garb, wearing a nondescript cap and sweater and holding a stumpy cigar in his mouth. His attitude and methods were far removed from the happy-go-lucky spirit which generally prevailed in the industry.

The physical layout of Inceville reflected Ince's attention to detail. In one or another of the departments everything necessary for his gigantic productions was provided. According to Duncan, the stages, administration buildings, and workshops covered the flat area of the canyon, while sets and locations were built on the seven surrounding hills.

There were five stages, the main one being a glass stage 300 by 100 feet in size, while the auxiliary stages measured 75 by 50 feet. Two hundred dressing rooms bordered the stages, and at either end of each stage were docks with five hundred distinct sets kept in readiness for instant use.

The administration buildings were set up to handle routine business and the workers' daily schedules. Also in the main complex was the commissary where hundreds of workers ate their noonday meal, and where many had dinner as well. Other basic facilities included a power house and reservoir, a saddlery and corral, stables for more than three hundred horses, and an arsenal where firearms, boxes of ammunition, and explosives were kept.

A wardrobe building contained row after row of

The Inceville Studios — sets, stages, and offices — at the mouth of Santa Ynez Canyon. Note the stream running through the property. Adelbert Bartlett, photographer. *Courtesy Carolyn Bartlett Farnham*

Thomas Ince, center, with William S. Hart to the right and Chief Eagleshirt to the left. Ince and Eagleshirt became blood brothers because of Ince's generosity toward the Indians. *Marc Wanamaker/ Bison Archive*

costumes — many of them designed for actors playing Indian, Western, or military roles. The dressmaking and tailoring shops were immense plants in which American and European styles of every vintage were studied and suitable replicas created.

In another shop three hundred carpenters worked at preparing sets and fixing odds-and-ends. A special crew of men was in charge of lights and props on each of the stages. The art department turned out portraits, mural decorations, and the decorated subtitles necessary for silent movies, while a technical shop handled the printing, toning, tinting, and editing of the film itself. Finally, a special music department employed the talented and versatile Victor Shertzinger and a half-dozen other composers to write music for every picture produced by the studio.

By 1916 eight directors were working at Inceville under the personal supervision of producer Ince. The most famous was William S. Hart, the only director who also acted in his own movies. Known as "Two-Gun Hart" by his co-workers, he was described as the best-loved man in Inceville.

Ince was one of the first producer-directors to recognize the importance of the scenario — one reason his movies were better than those of the vast majority of producers. C. Gardner Sullivan, Ince's premier scenarist, and a platoon of assistants turned out "whacking" good plays according to Ince's formula — dramatic plots with a compelling theme and a moral. Ince chose the story, carefully scrutinized the resulting scenario, and handed it to the director marked, "Shoot as is."

Most of the cowboys, Indians, and assorted workmen lived at Inceville. Actors, on the other hand, came out from Los Angeles and other communities as needed, taking the red trolley cars to the Long Wharf, where buckboards waited to carry them the rest of the way. Some commuters rode on horses or ponies, and a few, including Ince, drove their cars on one of the two narrow dirt roads that reached the canyon.

When extras were needed for crowd scenes, Ince advertised "a grand free movie fiesta and barbecue." Santa Monicans and others came by the hundreds, lined up for a free lunch, and obligingly donned Western costumes provided by Ince.

Arthur Loomis, a pioneer resident of Santa Monica and husband of Dorothy Gillis Loomis, liked to tell the story of his own acting debut at Inceville. Loomis, who died in 1979, recalled that as a high school student he was eager to earn five dollars and answered the call for extras. He borrowed Dorothy's horse and appeared in a cowboy-Indian scene, riding at top speed over a hill and down into the Jones Bowl area, where — to his chagrin and the cameraman's delight — he fell off into the dirt. Offered ten dollars to repeat his gymnastic performance the next day, the young stunt man prudently declined.

Above, in this rare photograph can be seen the *Civilization* set in the upper left, the cowboy ranch lower left and the Indian village far right. The studio was at its zenith at this time in 1916.
Courtesy Marc Wanamaker/Bison Archive

Below, the Scottish village was the set for the film *Peggy. Clearwater Collection*

Twenty-five thousand extras — the largest number ever assembled by Ince — took part in the mob scene for Ince's 1916 "peace" extravaganza, *Civilization*. The set for the mythical city stood in dramatic solitude on the open mesa east of Inceville, where Marquez School is now located. It was built by sixty carpenters over a period of three months at a cost of $80,000 and was used for only one hundred feet of film, a segment requiring 1 3/4 minutes to view.

Civilization was one of the most ambitious anti-war films ever produced, taking nine months to film and three months to assemble. Many movie historians consider it Ince's masterpiece; certainly it was a high point in his career. Running for reelection on a "peace platform," President Woodrow Wilson invited Thomas Ince to the White House for a showing of *Civilization*. Later the film was given at least partial credit for Wilson's victory.

By the spring of 1917 the United States was at war, and showings of *Civilization* were cancelled, at a great financial loss to Ince. His film, however, fared better than that of his competitor, D.W. Griffith, whose appeal for peace in the epic film *Intolerance* was completed even later and was out of step with the mood of the times. It failed so disastrously that Griffith's career was irreparably damaged.

In 1915-16 the average cost of an Inceville film was $40,000, and one five-reel picture was released each week, for a total outlay of $2,080,000 a year. Commenting on his mounting budgets, Ince is supposed to have said, "The salaries paid stars are as lofty as the seven hills on which stands Inceville."

The popularity of the more expensive feature films (five reels or more in length) and the decline of "shorts" (two-reelers) revolutionized the industry. Costs rose out of sight and many companies succumbed. In the fight for survival, Ince pooled his resources with friends and former antagonists alike to obtain sufficient capital to assure exhibition and distribution of his films.

On July 20, 1915, the leading motion picture geniuses of the day combined under the name "Triangle Films" — Thomas Ince, D.W. Griffith, and

Thomas Ince at the wheel of his car, surrounded by the buildings of Inceville. *Courtesy Katherine LaHue*

Above, the Pacific Palisades shoreline, with Thomas Ince's monumental set for *Civilization* on the distant hilltop. The Inceville studio was located in Santa Ynez Canyon, immediately beyond. *Clearwater Collection*

Below, a closeup of the *Civilization* set, near the present site of Marquez School. *Courtesy Katherine LaHue*

Mack Sennett entering into an uneasy coalition with financier Harry M. Aitken. Each director produced movies in his own studio, as Mutual combined with Kessel and Bauman to finance and distribute films under the Triangle label.

Ince forged ahead and built a new half-million-dollar studio on Washington Boulevard in Culver City to use for indoor movies, or "society films," while retaining Inceville for outdoor locations and Westerns. On December 31, 1915, he opened the new studio (which also served as headquarters for Triangle Films) with an elaborate reception and grand ball.

The event was symbolic. For four brief years, from 1911 to 1915, Inceville was part of an era in which directors made short films and two-reelers on a low budget, with a sweep and dash that reflected the energy of the people who made them. It was a time when moviemaking was fun, more a group sport than an art, and it passed rapidly.

By 1915 Ince was producing feature films with all the elements he had developed at Inceville: the complete studio; the director-producer relationship; the fully developed scenario; the "star" system; sharp editing of the final film; authentic sets, costumes, and locations. Ince did not initiate all of these elements, but he influenced the entire industry with his systematized method of moviemaking. Truly, Inceville lived up to its epithet, "the cradle of modern filmdom."

On January 12, 1916, only a few days after the gala opening of the Culver City studio, a major fire broke out at Inceville — the first of many which would eventually destroy all of the dry frame buildings. The 1916 blaze resulted in a $100,000 property loss, the destruction of the administration building, and injuries to Ince and a dozen of his workers who were trapped in the second-story cutting room, the men miraculously escaping death when seven tanks of waste film exploded. The fire was confined to a single structure thanks to the efforts of the cowboys and Indians who lived at the studio and manned the fire fighting equipment. Fortunately, Ince's completed films had been moved to Culver City a few days previously, and losses were limited to films in progress.

Both studios operated full-tilt in 1916, with Inceville serving as home base, and a fleet of automobiles shuttling back and forth between the two studios. Most players had their favorite dressing rooms at Inceville and preferred riding over on horses or ponies if shooting schedules and the nature of their costumes permitted. Actual filming generally ended at 3:00 P.M., when the natural light began to "yellow." Forty-five minutes later, autos and ponies began to arrive from Culver City, and a steady stream of people poured in for the next half-hour.

As early as October 14, 1916, news items indicated that Triangle Films was about to fall apart. "I

understand it is rumored out here that Triangle is about to disband," Ince announced to the press. "I cannot imagine from where such twaddle came, for Triangle has never been in better financial condition."

By 1917 the demise of Triangle seemed imminent. William S. Hart and his long-time mentor, Ince, became estranged, and Hart left Triangle. Mack Sennett relinquished his studio's name, Keystone, to Triangle and left to join Paramount. Rumors were circulated that Ince had signed up with the newly formed Artcraft Film Company, as had D.W. Griffith, Cecil B. DeMille, Mary Pickford, and Hart.

Santa Monica city officials tried to persuade Ince to return to that area, hoping to make Santa Monica the movie capital of the world, with the attendant financial benefits to that city. However, Ince neither returned to Santa Monica, nor did he join Artcraft. Film historian Lewis Jacobs observes, "After the war, at the height of his career, he inexplicably disappeared from the forefront of the movie world after his company, Triangle Films, finally collapsed in 1919."

Ince moved out of Triangle and into a new studio of his own just down the street. Its elegant facade and homelike appearance — reminiscent of a Southern plantation — concealed utilitarian structures and a lot. Here he worked as an independent and distributed through Paramount; later he joined Metro, and finally he allied himself with Associated

Producers. One of the film classics he made during this period was *Anna Christie,* starring Blanche Sweet, issued in December, 1923.

The last headlines involving Thomas Ince were concerned not with make-believe drama, but with the final tragic drama of his life — Ince's mysterious death on November 19, 1924. Today, fifty-eight years later, new versions of the incident and new answers to the questions raised by the circumstances of his death continue to make news.

It all began when Ince entered into negotiations with William Randolph Hearst, Ince seeking to obtain stories from Hearst's *Cosmopolitan* magazine to use in making pictures, and Hearst urging Ince to take over production of Marion Davies movies. Both Thomas Ince and his wife were invited by Hearst to celebrate Ince's forty-third birthday on Hearst's yacht, *Oneida,* in San Diego Bay, and while there the men were to finalize their business agreement. Instead, Mrs. Ince stayed in Los Angeles to care for one of their sons, who was ill. Ince alone took the train to San Diego on November 18 — his birthday — and boarded the 280-foot yacht. There he joined Hearst, Marion Davies, Charlie Chaplin, and others who remain unnamed, for an evening of festivities.

What happened next has been clouded by rumor and conflicting newspaper reports. According to the officially accepted version, Hearst's physician, Dr. Goodman, arrived at the yacht the morning after the

Four-page panorama of the Inceville "regulars" — cowboys, Indians, cavalrymen, Pilgrims, and Revolutionary War soldiers — as well as some of the horses and livestock used by Ince in his Westerns. Adelbert Bartlett, photographer. *Courtesy Carolyn Bartlett Farnham*

party to find Ince suffering from indigestion. Ince was known to have ulcers and had been drinking. Goodman helped his patient ashore and accompanied him on the train, bound for Los Angeles. By the time they reached Del Mar, Ince's condition was worse. Goodman took Ince to an inn, summoned a local doctor, and called Mrs. Ince, telling her to come at once.

Mrs. Ince arrived by car — accompanied by her eldest son, Bill, and Ince's physician, Dr. Glasgow — and took Ince back to their home in Los Angeles, where he was attended by Dr. Glasgow. Later on November 19, Ince had a heart attack and died. At the request of the widow the body was cremated, and funeral services were held two days later at Hollywood Cemetery.

The San Diego district attorney did not begin an investigation until mid-December, and by that time there was little firm evidence — certainly none could be obtained from an examination of the body. In addition, of all the guests aboard the yacht, the district attorney interviewed only Dr. Goodman, who was Hearst's private physician and head of Hearst's Cosmopolitan Studios. Goodman and the Del Mar physician agreed on the foregoing story in their testimony, and in essence it tallied with the later version given by Mrs. Ince to George Pratt, curator of Eastman House and an authority on Ince films, in a letter written to Pratt shortly before her death in 1971.

From the outset, however, there was confusion and cause for suspicion. According to the *Los Angeles Times* of November 20, 1924, Ince died "from heart disease superinduced by indigestion at his home in Benedict Canyon." At the same time it was rumored that he had been struck by a bullet fired by Hearst. Each story, with variations, was stoutly defended.

Hearst's own paper, the *Los Angeles Herald Express,* ran the Ince story on the same date under the headline, "Special Car Rushes Stricken Man Home from the Ranch." It stated that Ince and his family were visiting Hearst at the publisher's San Simeon ranch when Ince became ill. Unconscious, Ince was placed in a special car, with specialists and nurses in attendance, and taken to his home, where he died in the presence of his wife and members of his family.

On November 21, the *New York Times* reported that Ince's illness began on the way to San Diego, and the *Los Angeles Times* maintained that his attack of indigestion occurred "while he was a member of a yachting party in San Diego," no name being given, either of the yacht or its owner.

The story generally accepted by the motion picture industry and retold in the November 4, 1981, issue of *Los Angeles* magazine, was that Ince's birthday had turned into a drinking bout. Hearst discovered Marion Davies and Charlie Chaplin in an intimate embrace, flew into a jealous rage, and ran for the only gun aboard. In the resulting confusion he mistook Ince for Chaplin and shot the wrong man. A second set of rumors conjectured that Hearst might have gone after Ince, a man who was

Above, directors and stars at Inceville. Studio manager E.H. Allen is in the top row, on the far left, Charles Ray, top row, 5th from the right, and William Desmond Taylor, 2nd row, 3rd from the right. Adelbert Bartlett, photographer. *Courtesy Carolyn Bartlett Farnham*

The church set on the beach front which escaped the big Inceville fire of 1922. It remained there as a symbol of past glories until the 1930s. *Courtesy Elliott Welsh*

known for his flagrant womanizing and might have been involved in a dalliance with Marion Davies.

A third solution is offered in the same issue of *Los Angeles* magazine by Patte Barham, daughter of editor Frank Barham of the *Herald Express* and a reporter in her own right. She suggests that Hearst quarreled with Marion Davies over Marion's drinking and flirtations and that Marion retreated to her cabin, returned a short time later with gun in hand and announced she was going to end it all. Ince tried to take the gun away from her. Everyone thought it was a blank pistol until the gun was fired, wounding Ince.

Since none of the major characters in the drama is living today, there seems little hope that the controversy can ever be put to rest. Ironically, the scandal of Ince's death has done more to keep the image of Ince alive than the genius of his work.

Following Ince's death, a new studio, Metro-Goldwyn-Mayer, was organized, with Louis B. Mayer, Samuel Goldwyn, and Irving Thalberg taking over Ince's Culver City lot and using many of the methods pioneered by Ince at Inceville.

In retrospect, the rise and fall of Ince's motion picture career closely paralleled the rise and fall of Inceville itself. Ince renewed his lease on the canyon property in 1917 and planned to continue movie-making at both studios. At about the same time, William S. Hart quarreled with Ince over salary and

left Triangle. Without his old star, and with the decline in popularity of Western films, the buildings at Inceville were gradually abandoned.

The place was virtually a ghost town when the last remnants of Inceville were burned on the Fourth of July in 1922 — a runaway fire that tested the mettle of the newly organized Pacific Palisades volunteer fire department. The only survivor was a weather-worn old church, which stood sentinel over the charred ruins. By 1924, the year of Thomas Ince's death, the glories of Inceville had virtually faded into memory.

Today, film historians honor the contributions of Ince and his work at Inceville to the development of the film industry. Film historian Kenneth Macgowan writes: "If D. W. Griffith was film's first real director, Thomas Ince was film's first important producer, instituting a system that uncomfortably divides the artists' responsibility between two men. Ince showed future studio heads how to run a studio."

Students of cinema arts have staged revival showings of Ince films on campuses. According to Lewis Jacobs, Ince's most notable movies were *Civilization, The Battle of Gettysburg, The Coward, Viva la France, Behind the Door, Extravagance, The Italian, 23½ Hours of Leave,* and two William S. Hart Westerns, *The Two-Gun Man* and *Hell's Hinges.* The majority of these were produced in the picturesque canyon hideaway at Inceville.

7

THE SPIRIT OF UPLIFT

Memories of World War I were slow to fade, but by 1919 the mood of optimism had returned and business was again on the upswing. Real estate agents in the Santa Monica Bay area dusted off their "For Sale" signs and led prospective investors to newly available tracts of land. One of the most appealing was the tree-shaded plateau in Rustic Canyon where the Edmond ranch and the Forestry Station were both being offered for sale. The widowed Julia Edmond had decided to move to Pasadena, and the University of California was giving up its research facilities, putting the two adjacent pieces of property on the market.

Among the first clients to express an interest were the Methodists, who were looking for a site for their Assembly campground, an offshoot of the popular Chautauqua movement. Close on their heels were the Uplifters, a fun-loving group of business and professional men from the Los Angeles Athletic Club who were seeking a parklike spot where they could establish a "country home," similar to two prestigious San Francisco area retreats — the Bohemian Club Grove on the Russian River and the Family Club Farm on the Peninsula.

The local Methodist-sponsored Chautauqua gatherings were lineal descendants of the first Chautauqua Assembly, which was held in 1874 in New York — the brainchild of Dr. John Heyl Vincent, a Methodist minister from Illinois, and Lewis Miller, an Akron mill owner who provided the financial backing. Vincent deplored the highly emotional atmosphere of religious camp meetings, believing that serious religious education should begin with the children and that their teachers should be well trained. He also believed that young people should be out-of-doors where they could appreciate and enjoy "God's Temple." A world traveler himself, Vincent held all-day classes outside during the summer, staking out a map of the Holy Land and leading the group from point-to-point for lectures.

The two men chose an abandoned camp site at Lake Chautauqua in western New York state for their first two-week program, which attracted teacher-participants from all over the world. It opened with the singing of "Nearer, My God, to Thee," and before the season was over, almost fifteen thousand people had come for the sessions, slogging through the rain to temporary quarters in tents or finding rooms in nearby towns.

Miller and Vincent both brought their families to Chautauqua, building rustic cottages, half tent and half chalet. A roofed amphitheater was constructed, as was an elaborate hotel. Music, dramatic interpretation, lectures, and oratory were offered on a non-denominational basis — the best cultural and educational talent, together with good food, fun, and fireworks — all for a modest price. To reach those in the hinterlands they provided correspondence courses in history, science, and literature.

The movement was resoundingly successful, although psychologist William James criticized the offerings as superficial: "This order is too tame, this culture too second-rate, this goodness is too uninspiring. This human drama without a villain or a pang; this community so refined that ice-cream soda-water is the utmost offering it can make to the brute animal in man . . . I cannot abide with them."

More than two hundred offshoots of the original Chautauqua sprang up from coast to coast — pavilions in groves of trees or beside bodies of water — based on the concept of vacation with study. Most of them operated with Bishop Vincent's official approval, but in 1903, two promoters latched onto the idea and organized the first tent Chautauquas, using the name without authorization. They provided tents and sold a packaged succession of performers to small towns across the nation. Thus, while evangelist Billy Sunday or educator Booker T. Washington might find himself on the same program as a Swiss bell-ringer or a trained seal, the expanded Chautauqua plan evolved into a separate and useful booking medium for lecturers, celebrities, and artists, serving Main Street audiences

61

Dr. Charles Holmes Scott, founder of Pacific Palisades. *Courtesy of the Scott Family*

across the country.

In Southern California the origin of the Pacific Palisades group could be traced back to the first Methodist camp meeting, which was held in the 1870s in a eucalyptus grove near Compton, close to the banks of the Los Angeles River. Subsequently the Southern California Methodist Conference was given a site for their gatherings at Arroyo Grande, near San Luis Obispo, and a statewide center was established at Pacific Grove — both at a considerable distance from the Los Angeles area.

In 1883 the Conference obtained a more convenient location when the developers of Long Beach set aside a plot of land for public use. It was offered to the local ministerial association, who built a tabernacle and chapel specifically for camp meetings and the Methodist church. Eventually the entire facility was turned over to the Southern California Conference of the Methodist Episcopal

Church as a site for the Annual Methodist Assembly and the new Chautauqua programs.

Religious and cultural activities of this sort provided a popular summer attraction for a resort town such as Long Beach. The spirit was that of a vacation — of country folk in early summer when the chores were done — combined with the warmth of a neighborhood gathering and the zeal of a revival meeting. Such events met a particular need in the Southland where newcomers sought new friends and new roots.

As Long Beach began to grow and prosper, the rumor was circulated that the Methodists would soon be forced out and that a part of the site had already been sold for a subdivision. The Conference therefore accepted from the new settlement at Huntington Beach a $60,000 tract of land and a donation of $5,000 toward a new tabernacle. They called the camp Arbramar, "the Grove by the Sea," named for the sheltering eucalyptus trees. The dedication was held in 1905, the first camp meeting in 1906, and a Chautauqua the following year.

The Conference was already considering future expansion and had begun a systematic study of other church-oriented communities when the discovery of oil in 1919 and the growing boomtown flavor of Huntington Beach led to the decision that an immediate move was necessary. Following the Annual Conference in October, Bishop Adna W. Leonard of San Francisco appointed a search committee and designated Reverend Charles Holmes Scott of Pasadena to supervise the overall project. The original quest for a simple camp site now included the planning of a whole religious community under the auspices of the Methodist Episcopal Church.

Reverend Scott brought a combination of scholarship and idealism to the new assignment. He was born of New England stock in La Peer, Michigan, on August 28, 1877, and came to Los Angeles at the age of six, his parents and their eight children settling in the Bunker Hill area. He was graduated from the University of Southern California in 1905 and received his master's degree at that institution three years later. While still at USC, he met and married Anna Elizabeth Maurer, a deeply religious young lady and a USC graduate. In 1925 Charles Scott received an honorary doctor of divinity degree from his alma mater.

As is the fate of young ministers, the Scotts were moved from one town and one parish to another. Their first assignment was the Methodist Church in Ventura, where Warren, the eldest of their six children, was born, then Lincoln Avenue Methodist Church in Pasadena, where Martha and Wesley were born. Wayne and Wendell arrived during the family's stay in Ontario, and Mary while they were in South Pasadena. Martha Scott still remembers vividly that with each move they would be met by members of the Ladies' Aid who would cluck their tongues over the size of the family and count out the required number of bowls. Enough basic furnishings and hand-me-downs would be provided to give the newcomers a fresh start.

Scott lost no time in seeking a site for the new community, as indicated by documents recently found in the Santa Monica Land and Water Company archives. He set up headquarters in the Wright and Callender Building in downtown Los Angeles and began canvassing southern and central California for prospective locations and contacting key men of influence throughout the area.

A letter written to Frank Lee of the Santa Monica Land and Water Company in 1919 suggests that Scott even then looked with favor on the Santa Monica area as a result of his meetings with the company's president, Robert C. Gillis. He thanked Gillis for his advice and made a prophetic reference to their mutual interest in purchasing the Huntington property, known today as Huntington Palisades — already seeing it as an essential part of the overall plan.

Scott also took a trip to visit church-sponsored communities in the East to gather ideas and wrote a more specific letter to Gillis on March 5, 1920. In it he stated that the Methodist Church planned to acquire a site of several hundred acres and to build a major resort city which would accommodate the various religious and educational activities of the Southwest, mentioning similar developments at Bay View, Michigan; Lakeside, Ohio; and Ocean Grove, New Jersey as being the most successful. In each instance the organizers had subdivided the land and had sold renewable ninety-nine year leases to pay for an auditorium and other public facilities. Scott noted enthusiastically that the Ocean Grove auditorium held ten thousand people and that their events attracted half a million people in 1919.

Scott believed that the local development could be twice as large, considering the advantages of the year-round climate, superior location, and the variety of local support groups. He projected a demand for permanent homes, as well as accommodations for thousands of tourists in winter and for people from the hot interior during the summer. The thirty-five periodicals published by the church and their twenty thousand ministers around the country could act as publicity agents to spread the word to the church's 4,250,000 members. Scott emphasized that the facilities would serve "all religious and educational bodies and that no individual would profit from the enterprise." Although the Long Beach Chamber of Commerce had tried to make a suitable site available, Scott preferred a location within the boundaries of Los Angeles so the new venture could participate in that city's progress.

As part of the selection procedure, Scott brought a delegation of Methodist ministers and laymen to the Santa Monica area. They seem to have been impressed. In 1920 they put their money down on 16.6 acres of Julia Edmond's Rustic Canyon property and 11.80 acres of adjacent Forestry Station land and announced that the 1921 summer camp meeting would be held there in the grove.

For the site of the town itself they chose the level mesa land to the west—just in time. The real estate firm of Wright, Callender and Andrews was already preparing a subdivision of its own on the very land being considered by the Methodists — between Potrero and Santa Ynez canyons — and had issued promotional brochures calling it "Santa Monica

Highlands." Aerial photographs taken at the time show road tracings with dead-end streets and cul-de-sacs which were obliterated when the new grading began.

Dr. Merle Smith of the First Methodist Church of Pasadena is credited with coining the name when he stood with the group on the bluffs, looked out over the ocean, and exclaimed, "This is indeed Pacific Palisades." Later, the committee decided to move the permanent Assembly site from Rustic Canyon to more spacious grounds in Temescal Canyon, adjacent to the residential district.

Actually, the name "Palisades" — referring to the spectacular oceanfront cliffs — had originally been applied to "the Palisades" tract in Santa Monica, developed between 1905 and 1908 by the Alta Santa Monica Land Company. Billed as the most scenic subdivision in Southern California, it extended from Seventh Street to Ocean Avenue, and from the rim of Santa Monica Canyon to Montana Avenue. By 1921–22, ownership had passed to Robert Gillis and the Santa Monica Land and Water Company who advertised it as "Santa Monica Palisades." Thus, for many years, "the Palisades" (now a popular nickname for Pacific Palisades) was used only in speaking of the Santa Monica tract.

At the annual meeting of the Southern California Conference of the Methodist Episcopal Church in October, 1920, the Pacific Palisades Association was established to implement the plans. The corporation negotiated the purchase of 1,068 acres at $618 an acre from the Wright and Callender Company of Los Angeles on May 19, 1921, to be financed by the sale of $1,000 promissory notes to investors throughout the Southland. These Founders' Certificates, as they were called, served as a bond; they were redeemable within a year, bore 6% interest, and were deductible from the price of a ninety-nine-year renewable lease on a lot — patterned after leases used at Ocean Grove, New Jersey and Lake Chautauqua, New York. Through leaseholds instead of outright property sales, the Association sought to control the quality of the community and determine the nature of its residents. To obtain immediate operating funds, 1,750 Convertible Investment Notes at $100 each were also offered for sale. These bore 6% interest and were to be repaid in three years. Note-holders were entitled to use this amount, plus a bonus of 10%, as a down-payment on a leasehold.

The Association functioned through its president and board of trustees, most of whom were Methodist ministers or laymen. However, members of other Protestant denominations and several prominent businessmen also served. These included Robert C. Gillis, who had a wide variety of business interests and was nominally a Presbyterian; Andrew Chaffey, an Episcopalian and founder of the California Bank; C.C. Chapman of Fullerton, pioneer citrus

Founders Certificate

This Certificate entitles ___Leonard A. Warrell___
the undersigned, Founder of Pacific Palisades Association, to a leasehold interest of the appraised value of one thousand dollars in property acquired under contract, by the Huntington Beach Methodist Assembly, consisting of approximately 1068 acres, situate on the Ocean front near Santa Monica, Los Angeles County, California, to be conveyed to a corporation to be formed for the purpose of founding thereon a religious and educational center similar to that at Lake Chautauqua, New York.

It is understood that this land is being acquired under the authority of the Southern California Conference of the Methodist Episcopal Church, which proposes to merge the Huntington Beach Methodist Assembly into this project, and that said land will be subdivided into lots which will be leased for a renewable ninety-nine year term upon substantially uniform conditions, the form of lease to be modeled after the leases issued at Lake Chautauqua, New York, and Ocean Grove, New Jersey.

As soon as the land shall have been platted and appraised by the corporation to be formed, said corporation shall appoint a day upon which the certificate holder may make selection of lot and shall notify said certificate holder at the address given on this certificate. Should more than one certificate holder select the same lot, the Board of Trustees of said corporation shall decide who shall have said lot in any impartial manner adopted by it. After said Founders' Day holders of certificates may select any unleased lots in the order in which they may make application. Provided however that if the certificate holder does not select a lot within one year he may thereafter surrender this certificate and upon ninety days notice in writing shall be repaid the sum of one thousand dollars with interest at the rate of six per cent per annum from this date.

IN WITNESS WHEREOF the Huntington Beach Methodist Assembly has caused these presents to be executed in duplicate by its Superintendent and its corporate seal to be affixed, and the Founder has hereunto set his hand this __31st__ day of ___August___, 1921.

By ___Leonard A. Warrell___ Founder.
___Chas H Scott___ Superintendent.

.SEAL

Address
227 South Pacific Avenue
San Pedro, California

APPLIED ON LOT No. 546
APR 6 1922

Above, Leonard A. Warrell's founders certificate. *Ernest Marquez Collection*
Below, panorama of Methodist ministers at the 1921 camp meeting in Rustic Canyon, with Reverend Scott pictured in the center of the top row. *Gabrielson Collection*

grower and founder of Chapman College; George I. Cochran, founder and president of the Pacific Mutual Life Insurance Company; and Clarence Matson, a resident of Pacific Palisades who headed the trade department of the Los Angeles Chamber of Commerce and was instrumental in promoting and developing Los Angeles Harbor.

It is important to note that the Association and its properties were controlled by its board of trustees; at no time did the bondholders have a voice in the management. The board was specifically empowered by the Articles of Incorporation to purchase property for the benefit of the institution and to "convey, sell, mortgage, lease, improve, subdivide, plot, or otherwise use and dispose of the property of the corporation" as they saw fit.

Throughout their Rustic Canyon negotiations the Methodists had sharp competition from the Uplifters Club. This spirited group of Angelenos had purchased its own forty-acre share of the Edmond property in 1920 and had designs on the rest. The club itself had been organized as an offshoot of the Los Angeles Athletic Club in 1913, with Harry Haldeman, a plumbing company executive who had recently arrived from Chicago, as founder and Grand Muscle (president) and L. Frank Baum, author of the Oz books, as the creative genius.

Uplifter symbol adopted when the club was formed in 1913. Later the "LAAC" was omitted. *Young Collection*

The name "Uplifters" had no spiritual significance per se, referring instead to the uplifting of the arts and the hoisting of a cocktail, which, in the puritanical mood of the day, was considered quite shocking. The Uplifters had a dual purpose: they sponsored professional artists and included them as members, and at the same time each Uplifter was urged to participate in some creative artistic fashion. Even those with no previous training organized their own choruses, band, and orchestra, and staged elaborate plays and operettas, combining amateur and professional talent. Such prominent artists as Harold Lloyd, Charles Wakefield Cadman, Hal

In May, 1921, the Uplifters arrived to inspect the grounds of their newly puchased Country Home and followed Grand Muscle Harry Haldeman on a tour of the premises. *Courtesy UCLA Special Collections*

Roach, and Baum wrote, composed, coached, and performed for their various productions.

The climax of each year's series of events was the Annual Outing, a stag event held each summer or fall at some mountain or seaside resort. The search for a permanent site for these retreats — to be known as the Uplifters Ranch or Uplifters Country Home — ended at Rustic Canyon. Some agreement must have been reached with the Methodists, since the Uplifters purchased the Forestry Station parcel from them in June and acquired the remaining Edmond property in the fall. Meanwhile, the Uplifters scheduled their own opening celebration for May 28, 1921, on the expanded acreage.

Under threatening skies, Haldeman led a motorcade out from the city for the dedication ceremonies, followed by a barbecue and an evening of song and entertainment around the Campfire Circle. The program concluded with an inspirational allegory, a "Woodland Fantasy," with an all-star cast. The most dramatic performance was given by dancer Ted Shawn, the Spirit of the Dance, who performed a "wild, weird, fantastic waltz . . . with barbaric abandon." Finally, the Spirit of Uplift, played by Shakespearean actor Frederick Warde, called on Inspiration and brought forth smoke and flame. Sending messengers out into the world to spread the

Above, dedication ceremonies in the Campfire Circle included possession of the Uplifter Ranch by the Chief of the Washatoes and his Indian braves. *Courtesy George and Onis Rice*
Below, the Edmond ranch house was kept for use as a clubhouse by the Uplifters on the advice of Harry Haldeman, seated second from the left. *Courtesy UCLA Special Collections*

tidings of the Uplifter creed, he exited majestically "into misty nothingness with the woods aglow in variegated colors."

That was a hard act to follow. The Uplifters spent the rest of the summer preparing for the first formal Outing to be held in the premises in the fall. Under Haldeman's supervision, workmen converted and enlarged the Edmond home for use as a clubhouse, built dormitories, and started work on tennis courts and a swimming pool. Howard Latimer laid out the roads and stone walls and built the first house, appropriately located on "Latimer Road." Each member who purchased four shares in the Country Home at $250 a share was permitted to lease a lot and to build a weekend cottage or vacation home.

At the same time the Methodists were busy installing a tent city of their own at the Forestry Station a few yards away. They brought in utilities, set up 225 tents, and raised a temporary tabernacle seating two thousand people. The first occupants were members of the Southern California Veterans' Association, who held a ten-day encampment there early in August.

The Methodists themselves occupied the Rustic Canyon camp site from August 14 through 28, attendance averaging a thousand on week days and capacity crowds on weekends. Religious programs featured the noted evangelist Dr. Easley Naftzer and his party of "singers and players," while Dr. Grieves led the daily prayer meetings. Plans for the new community were also announced, and on August 30, 1921, the *Santa Monica Outlook* stated that almost

all of the 250 "holders" certificates, at $1,000 each, had been subscribed, and that "the last ten would be gone before sunset."

In mid-September the Association further announced that they had retained landscape architect Clarence Day of Pasadena to draw up a physical plan. He had engineered famous showplaces in Santa Barbara and Pasadena and looked forward to shaping a new community from such a beautiful expanse of raw land. Having previously lived near another large Methodist enterprise at Asbury Park, New Jersey, he stated that he was familiar with the concepts involved.

A committee of eight, led by Day and a second landscape architect, Aurele Vermeulen, was appointed to decide on the first plat. Their presentation was to be an artistic one, showing such features as a civic center, eighteen-hole golf course, tennis courts, baseball diamond, and, on the ocean front, a pleasure pier and plunge. Meanwhile, Day's men began work on a headquarters building and planted their surveyors' stakes in long rows across the hay fields.

Before the year ended, 275 certificates had been sold. Those who held notes were designated "Founders" and were given first choice of building lots. A date was set for the opening, and a Founders' Handbook was issued which referred to Pacific Palisades in idyllic terms: " . . . a private park providing a relaxed atmosphere where people would be able to devote their entire energies to religious and cultural pursuits."

Above, elaborate pageantry at the Uplifters Outing in 1922. *Courtesy Los Angeles City Department of Recreation and Parks*

Below, Harry Haldeman, *left,* and Sim Crabill, *right,* were instrumental in planning the layout of the Uplifters Ranch. *Courtesy UCLA Special Collections*

Idealized plan for Pacific Palisades, drawn by A.E. Mitchell in 1921. On the highest hill stands the Temple of Peace, with Via de la Paz extending from there to the shoreline, where provisions were made for a hotel and recreational facilities. *Clearwater Collection*

8

PACIFIC PALISADES THE FOUNDING

For the new community of Pacific Palisades, the choice of an opening date — January 14, 1922 — seemed an auspicious one. It was an unusually beautiful day, with a clear blue sky, warm sunshine, and rolling hills carpeted in green. Reverend Charles Scott himself described the event two years later in the *Pacific Palisades Progress:*

By nine o'clock in the morning the people began to arrive, and by ten-thirty the mesa was dotted with groups of Founders and members of their families, selecting first, second, and third choices among the lots which had been staked out by surveyors. Rivalry was keen, but with a very few exceptions, most friendly, and sometimes it was jolly.

Armed with maps, participants drove their cars from one end of the property to the other over hastily cleared streets, leaving plumes and trails of dust. Selection continued until one o'clock, when the dust-covered group gathered around the construction office for coffee and sandwiches while representatives of the Association checked over the lists to find duplications. At two o'clock, under Founders' Oaks, the drawings took place. The names of the rivals were placed in a hat, two at a time, as Reverend Scott's daughter Martha drew the lucky slips and the winners were announced. By two-thirty the drawings were complete and the assembled company lined up for the official photograph.

According to the site plan drawn by Clarence Day, the original offering gave prospective leaseholders a choice of two subdivisions, Founders Tracts I and II — both officially part of Los Angeles County tract number 9300. The former, lying north of Beverly Boulevard,* was laid out by Day in a conventional rectangular plan. It provided relatively small lots on narrow streets where retired ministers and missionaries could build modest homes and live economically and comfortably.

Founders Tract II was designed more artistically

as the focal point of the community. The mesa was outlined by curving avenues to achieve a maximum number of lots with an ocean or canyon view. A broad thoroughfare, Via de la Paz (Avenue of Peace), led up the center of the tract from the bluffs to the base of Peace Hill, where an imposing domed Hall of Nations, or Temple of Peace, was to be constructed, funded by a million one-dollar contributions from all over the world. This was to be a meeting place, with a seating capacity of ten thousand, where people of every nation could gather together and exchange ideas in an atmosphere of peace and Christian brotherhood.

Four square blocks near the junction of Beverly Boulevard and Via de la Paz were set aside for commercial enterprises, and a few lots were reserved for rental units. The broad, oak-shaded floor of Temescal Canyon was planned for the Assembly Camp; a portion of the western rim was set aside for "Church Vacation Homes;" and the rest of the canyon was designated park land. Other features included an extension of Bridge Street (now Bowdoin) over Potrero Canyon by means of a bridge, a branch of the Pacific Electric railway line up Potrero Canyon, and an Alpine Village on the northern slope of Temescal Canyon — none of which materialized.

Leasehold contracts offered by the Pacific Palisades Association specified the price to be paid for each lot, the type of structure to be permitted, and the minimum cost, with plans to be approved by an architectural review board. Leaseholders were required to pay one percent of the price of the lot each year for maintenance of the institutional facilities in Temescal Canyon and received certain benefits, such as access to the grounds and free programs, in return. Only Caucasians were permitted to own property, and the sale of tobacco and alcoholic beverages was strictly forbidden — the latter provision being in accord not only with the Founders' philosophy, but with the Eighteenth Amendment, which had been adopted two years

*Originally "Marquez Road." Later the name "Beverly" Boulevard was changed to "Sunset," as it remains today.

previously.

By January 21, a total of 257 Founders' lots had been selected, at a total valuation of $348,975, or an average of $1,358 per lot. Work on private homes and on street improvements began in the early spring, as soon as the heaviest rains were over. In his role as construction engineer, Clarence Day brought in his own crews, which were independent of the Association and were quartered at the grading camp along Radcliffe Avenue, just south of De Pauw Street. Their first task was to carve out the long, straight stretch of Via de la Paz.

A second grading camp was set up at Bestor Boulevard and McKendree Street under the supervision of Dick Pendergrass of Calexico. His crew, brought from the Imperial Valley, included ninety head of mules and the accompanying skinners, plow holders, corral bucks, and cooks. Day's outfit was responsible for cutting the streets south of Beverly Boulevard, while Pendergrass handled those to the north. Both crews used large railroad plows to cut into the heavy adobe soil and "four-up fresnos" (earth graders with four spans of mules) to clear the new roadways.

The main construction office was located in the first new building, which stood for many years at 15340 Sunset Boulevard (today the site of Gelson's Market). This housed the office of construction superintendent Clark Standiford, the sales division under William J. Moore, and such departments as purchasing, engineering, and payroll. Subsequently the structure was revamped and named "The Bishop's Cottage," in honor of the bishop who stayed there when he came to visit or to preside over the Assembly. In the thirties it was transformed into the White Gate (later the Kettle Drum) Tea Room.

In mid-May construction began on the various Assembly buildings in Temescal Canyon. The old ranch barn was turned into a warehouse and a long shed into a mess hall. The workmen, most of whom were Mexican, occupied tents along the canyon edge, while the area around Founders' Oaks became a family camp, providing temporary homes for the Standifords, Clifford Clearwaters, and Reuben L. Stadlers. Farther up the canyon were the August Hochs and the Robert E. Norrises.

Zola Clearwater, who still lives in Pacific Palisades, recalls that she came to Temescal Canyon in 1922 as a bride; it was Memorial Day, and her husband, Cliff, had taken a job as timekeeper on the

On January 14, 1922, Pacific Palisades officially came into being when a group of the Founders, led by the Association president, Reverend Charles H. Scott, gathered under the oaks in Temescal Canyon and drew lots for their choice of homesites. *Clearwater Collection*

Above, surveyors and engineers at work in Temescal Canyon. Reverend Scott is on the extreme right, with chief construction engineer Clarence P. Day at his side. *Below,* the first tents for the resident staff were pitched under Founders' Oaks. Later, a row of cottages, *center rear,* provided more comfortable accommodations. *Both, Clearwater Collection*

project. Arriving in a truck with their furniture and clothing, the young couple were assigned to a wooden platform under an oak tree and directed to the warehouse where they were issued a tent. Toilet facilities, they were told, were located over the hill, just below the site now occupied by the Woman's Club, and water was obtained from a centrally located faucet. Pure, clear water for drinking, however, was carried up from the creek. The main pipeline, constructed in 1916 and never used, was full of sediment, making the tap water unpalatable. Other amenities were equally sparse — a kerosene lamp and two-burner cookstove, provided by the Clearwaters.

All efforts were turned toward preparations for the first summer session, which was only weeks away. Workmen began at once, installing roads and utility systems. In the lower canyon they built an outdoor amphitheater, dining hall, and an athletic field with tennis courts. North of Beverly Boulevard they constructed a tabernacle (auditorium), cafeteria, thirty-five small cabins, and some two hundred tent frames. Between the two locations they installed a picnic area and an outdoor auditorium, and at the beach, a small bath house and picnic pavilion.

Above, view down Fiske Street, with the Pendergrass grading camp in the foreground. *Below,* grading Swarthmore Avenue in May, 1922, using teams of mules and "fresnos" (graders). *Both, Clearwater Collection*

Above, Clarence P. Day's grading camp near the present intersection of Radcliffe and De Pauw streets. *Lower left,* Clark Standiford, superintendent of construction from 1922 to 1925. *Lower right,* the $9,000 rock crusher, as it stood crumpled after the blast. *All, Clearwater Collection*

Every phase of the operation was managed by the Pacific Palisades Association. To provide rock and gravel for the roadways, crews installed a rock crusher on a ledge along the western slope of Temescal Canyon and turned a portion of the hill behind it into a quarry as a source of raw materials. The Association even had its own lumber yard and mill, much of the wood being sugar pine from the Lake Almanor region in Lassen County. In addition to more conventional products, the mill also produced green slabs with the bark attached to yield the popular rustic effect.

The rock crusher caused some extra-curricular excitement one day when a deluge of rocks released by a blast came sliding down the hill, hit the underpinnings, and toppled the apparatus. Thereafter, the rock crusher was placed in a safer location on the canyon floor. The quality of the rock lent a special patina to the sidewalks. Some of the hard clay remained in chunks and when incorporated in the paving, washed away, leaving a spattering of small holes which, to the children's distress, played hob with their roller skating.

The success of the effort was largely due to the energy and drive of Clark Standiford, an Imperial Valley rancher and a prominent member of the Methodist Church. Cliff Clearwater described him as "a tall, loosely-hooked-together man who never was seen to walk leisurely but always strode with a gait that could be told a mile away." He routed the men out of bed in the early morning and drove himself and those around him relentlessly, "encouraging, lashing, cajoling, denouncing and praising with equal vigor." Cliff knew this well, since it was his task to ride around on horseback, checking on progress at the various sites.

It was little short of miraculous when, on June 29, registrants at the Southern California Holiness Association Camp Meeting and the Christian Church Young People's Conference arrived and found the basic accommodations ready for them. The tents and "casitas" ("little houses" — actually bark-faced log cabins) were equipped with cots and a washstand, a bowl and pitcher. Some units provided housekeeping facilities, which included an oil stove, a supply of oil, dishes and cooking utensils. Rents were reasonable, a tent for two costing only six dollars for seven days.

Two shops had opened to supply the essentials —Carl Hoss's grocery store and Leonard A. Warrell's meat market. Shortly thereafter, Robert E. Norris established a plumbing shop on the corner of Temescal Canyon Road and Beverly Boulevard. His wife, Clarissa, was Charles Scott's sister, and Norris himself had helped to set up the 1921 Methodist campground in Rustic Canyon. The shop later became Norris Hardware, which today ranks as the community's oldest business and is operated by the

The first new building on the property housed the main construction office and was located where Gelson's Market is today. *Clearwater Collection*

The view looking east from the quarry, with the administration building in the center of the picture. The Assembly Camp, catering to adults, was north of Beverly Boulevard in Temescal Canyon, *on the left,* and the Institute Camp, with facilities for young people, was south of the road, *on the right. Clearwater Collection*

Norrises' son Charles. The first post office was installed in a freestanding set of pigeon holes in the Clearwaters' tent; Zola sorted the mail and Cliff delivered it twice a day on horseback to the various tents and dwellings.

The first Chautauqua and Summer Assembly began on Tuesday, July 11, 1922, and lasted for two weeks. The major events were held in the new auditorium, designed to seat 1,600, and the schedule was maintained in brisk order by having a large bell rung on the hour and half-hour. After Reverend Scott's opening welcome, each day was full, from devotions at nine o'clock in the morning to the last concert at eight in the evening. Time was allowed for meals in the cafeteria and for late afternoon recreation.

Programs and lectures were offered in several categories, including religious studies with Dr. William C. Isett and a course in the educational value of play by William La Porte of USC. Bertha Coler conducted workshops on the decorative arts; Robert Clark gave sessions on such practical aspects of music as gospel singing and hymnology; and Eleanor Miller's Department of Expression included instruction on plays and pageantry, Chautauqua reading, pianologues, and story telling.

Dr. Isett of the Association and impresario L.E. Behymer arranged the special events. Highlight of the first season was a performance by the world's greatest contralto, Madame Schumann-Heinck, making her only concert appearance of the year on the Pacific Coast. Other celebrities included Dr. Rufus B. von Klein Smid of USC speaking on Latin-American affairs, poet-philosopher James W. Foley offering tidbits of wisdom, Charles Wakefield Cadman's trio presenting his famous American Indian ballads, and a young baritone named Lawrence Tibbett, who thrilled the capacity crowd with operatic arias.

By fall, many of the tent families living in Temescal Canyon had moved into cottages, conveniently located along the main entrance road. The Clearwaters occupied one of these units, as did the Scott family. Martha Scott recalls that her father hastily drew up a floor plan for their permanent home over breakfast one morning as her mother looked on apprehensively.

The first private house, that of Emory Welton at 819 Hartzell Street in Founders Tract I, was completed that summer. Soon there was a sprinkling of homes in both tracts, including the attractive two-story house provided by the Association for Dr.

Above, the Assembly Camp office in June, 1922, with Professor Earle of Pasadena in charge. *Below,* the first "business district" in the new community. *On the left,* Mr. and Mrs. Leonard A. Warrell in front of their meat market. *On the right,* Mr. and Mrs. Carl Hoss on the porch of the grocery store. The boys seated on the right of the bench are Wendell and Wesley Scott, sons of Reverend Scott. *Both, Clearwater Collection*

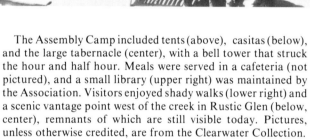

The Assembly Camp included tents (above), casitas (below), and the large tabernacle (center), with a bell tower that struck the hour and half hour. Meals were served in a cafeteria (not pictured), and a small library (upper right) was maintained by the Association. Visitors enjoyed shady walks (lower right) and a scenic vantage point west of the creek in Rustic Glen (below, center), remnants of which are still visible today. Pictures, unless otherwise credited, are from the Clearwater Collection.

Gabrielson Collection

THE ASSEMBLY CAMP

THE INSTITUTE CAMP

Registration for the Institute Camp in June, 1922, was held in a tent (left), and the first public transportation was provided by an open-air Reo bus (above). For many years, large gatherings were held at the outdoor amphitheater (below), and festive meals, such as Thanksgiving dinners, were served in the dining hall (lower left). The Lodge was located to the right. In another area, six hundred Boy Scouts could be accommodated at campouts (upper left). All pictures, *Clearwater Collection*

Aerial photograph taken early in 1923, showing Founders' Tract I at the top, the future business district at the left (3), Beverly (Sunset) Boulevard (5), an unidentified barn (2), and a movie set stockade (1) on the future site of Huntington Palisades. *Clearwater Collection*

Scott and his family on Via de la Paz midway between the commercial center and the ocean front. It was so spacious as compared with most pastoral dwellings, in fact, that it was the object of outspoken envy on the part of visiting clergymen.

The first church services and grammar school classes were held in the cafeteria, which was heated in winter time by a pot-bellied stove. Martha recalls that most of the children came from the construction camp and spoke little English. The teacher was a portly lady, unimaginative in her methods, and ill-prepared for the challenge. It was a temptation for Martha and some of the other students to play truant and find more interesting pursuits in the out-of-doors. The older children were bused to Lincoln Junior High School in Santa Monica and to Warren G. Harding High School (later renamed University High in honor of UCLA) in West Los Angeles.

By mid-September it was apparent that the budding community was a success. Sales of real estate were going well; the response to the summer session had been enthusiastic; and the needs of the permanent residents were being met. It was also time for a new period of planning and growth. Scott and the board for some reason bypassed Day; instead they made an arrangement with another local construction engineer, H.T. Cory, and through him with the Olmsted Brothers of Brookline, Massachusetts, nationally known landscape architects and community planners whom Scott had contacted in 1920 while on his Eastern tour.

Frederick L. Olmsted, Jr., the elder of the two brothers, had prepared a plan for the South Bay city of Torrance in 1911 and the preliminary plan for Palos Verdes in 1914. The latter project was delayed by World War I, but in 1921 efforts to obtain new financing began and by October, 1922, the firm had established an office in Redondo Beach and was ready to begin work. Scott may thus have been aware that Pacific Palisades could negotiate a more reasonable fee by sharing the Olmsteds' services with the ongoing Palos Verdes development.

According to letters in the Olmsted Brothers archive in the Library of Congress, Frederick L. Olmsted, Jr., sent Cory a well researched, comprehensive proposal for Pacific Palisades on September 15, 1922. A basic contract at $1,500 a month for ten months was agreed upon, which included bimonthly visits by Frederick Olmsted, or four visits a month by his representatives, and which placed Cory in charge of design and construction.

The semi-covert nature of the new arrangement was revealed in a letter written by Scott to Robert C. Gillis on October 21, 1922. Day had apparently aroused Scott's suspicion by leasing five acres of strategically located Huntington property for a nursery and landscape business and was planning a trip to the East, where, Scott feared, Day might meet with Henry Huntington, whom he knew socially and for whom he had worked.

Mr. Day knows too much about the progress of our enterprise and about how important the Huntington land is to it. It would be a strong temptation for him to say something indiscreet which might stand in the way of our securing it, especially in view of our having secured the Olmsted Brothers to take his place.

Scott went on to plead the desirability of extending the Association plan from Rustic Canyon to the western city limits and of acquiring the Huntington property and the Jones-Rindge ranch* (between Temescal and Las Pulgas canyons) as soon as possible.

Within the month Scott announced the Olmsted appointment to the Southern California Methodist Conference at their annual meeting and assigned top priority to revising and completing the original tracts. Scott also noted the demand for additional top-quality lots. To provide these, he urged Olmsted to subdivide the land along Chautauqua Boulevard and to lay out Chautauqua Heights on the ridge to the north prior to the first anniversary of Founders' Day in January, 1923.

The work was carried out by means of a four-way correspondence between Scott, Olmsted, Cory, and Clark Standiford, who was responsible for the actual grading and paving. One of Standiford's first concerns was for the welfare of his men. Calling Scott's attention to the dismal plight of the thirty

Early promotional brochure. *Clearwater Collection*

unmarried laborers who lived in tents and had no congenial place to spend their evenings, he obtained the board's permission to construct a recreation building with a bowling alley and other facilities for the use of the men and the resident families.

On November 23, the Pacific Palisades Association announced that a million dollars' worth of property had been sold, and on December 17, offered the Chautauqua lots, which had been meticulously tailored to suit the steep terrain, to the leaseholders. On January 14, 1923, right on schedule, the tract was opened to the public. Olmsted next drew up a comprehensive landscaping plan for the original subdivision, obtained several hundred choice plants — including *Cocos plumosa* trees for Via de la Paz and *Magnolia grandiflora* for Monument Street — and sent a list of specifications for establishing an on-the-site nursery.

*The major portion of the Jones-Rindge Ranch was owned by Robert F. Jones, brother of Senator John P. Jones. Only a narrow, 6.09-acre strip, a right-of-way for the Malibu railroad, was listed on the tax rolls in the Rindge name.

In April the Association negotiated the purchase of the Jones-Rindge ranch, 831 acres for $850,000, and in June finished off the original tract with the purchase of a thirty-acre coastal strip from Robert C. Gillis and Arthur Fleming for $150,000, the Association paying $75,000 for the land and the remaining amount being given as a donation.

Olmsted's original timetable was interrupted at this point when Scott asked him to prepare plans for the Jones-Rindge property in time for the second Founders' Day celebration in January, 1924. The firm thus worked simultaneously on plans for the Community Center and for the Church Vacation Homes area on Bowdoin Street, as well as the layout for the Temescal and Temescal Heights tracts north of Beverly Boulevard, the Las Pulgas tract to the south, and the Jones Bowl tract on the slope between the Las Pulgas tract and the coast.

Like Founders' Tract II, the new Las Pulgas tract was situated on an oceanfront plateau bordered by canyons and cliffs. Olmsted therefore laid it out with curving streets, lots oriented toward the views, and street intersections with small islands to create "pocket parks." The Almar Plaza complex, for example, had four islands and was designated a mini-commercial center where quaint shops would add a note of charm and provide necessities for the neighborhood — a development that did not take place due to zoning provisions imposed by the city in 1928.

The Association moved the grading camp to Las Pulgas Canyon to be closer to the project and built a handsome new two-story tract office on the western mesa, overlooking Temescal Canyon. Known as Harmony Hall because it accommodated music classes, it was opened to the public in August, 1924, and served as a reception center for individual visitors and busloads of prospective clients.

Suddenly, at the height of the planning process, the involvement of the Olmsteds came to an end. On December 19, 1923, perhaps as a result of a belt-tightening board meeting, Scott wrote a terse letter to Olmsted stating that the original contract period had passed; he requested that all designs and plans be turned over to the Association and notified Olmsted that his services, although much appreciated, would be terminated at the end of the year.

Olmsted defended his firm's record with a list of the 150 plans and studies that had been completed, reminded Scott of the extra time spent on the Jones-Rindge project, and pointed out that the fees charged had been less than budgeted. Furthermore,

View of Harmony Hall from Founders' Oaks. *Clearwater Collection*

GUIDE MAP
PACIFIC PALISADES

A visitors' guide map to Pacific Palisades, prepared by Jack Sauer in 1927, listing various trails, roads, and scenic vantage points and giving the basic layout of the community.

he refused to turn over any plans to the Association until they met their unpaid bill of $6,635.43 for the Olmsteds' services.

Distressed over abandoning the development midway, Olmsted obtained a three-month extension from the Association board to complete those projects which were in progress. He and the staff finished platting the thirty-acre Jones Bowl subdivision, which included a controversial access road winding down the slide-prone slope to the coast, where Scott had envisioned a hotel and recreational complex. They also drew designs for a complete subdivision in upper Las Pulgas Canyon with shops, an aviary, a small park, and clusters of view lots.

Visions of developing a comprehensive general plan for the entire community faded away. Olmsted had hoped to design landscaping for the new tracts, to subdivide suitable portions of the mountains, provide for the care of the canyons and other scenic areas, develop a network of parks, analyze restrictions and zoning, and establish a system of maintenance.

A major omission was an overall plan for Temescal Canyon. Olmsted and Scott referred to the upper canyon as Temescal Park and considered it as a

A group of soloists that included the famous baritone, Lawrence Tibbett, *second from left. Courtesy Frances Smith Stewart*

Pageant at a makeshift stage in the canyon. *Gabrielson Collection*

community park, as well as an assembly grounds. They planned to landscape it with native plants and to add a swimming pool for adults and a wading pool for children. As it developed, this area became the Assembly Camp and was used primarily by adults. Its facilities were booked the year round by such large groups as the Southern California Veterans' Encampment, YMCA Regional Conferences, and the Southern California Holiness Association (popularly known as "Holy Rollers").

A six-week period each summer was reserved for the Chautauqua, or Summer Assembly, which attracted thousands of participants from all over the Southwest. Visiting artists included Alice Gentle, Olga Steeb, and Lawrence Tibbett, as well as guest speakers Ilya Tolstoi, David Starr Jordan, Elbert Russell, Reverend Ralph W. Sockman, and Bishop Charles Wesley Burns. Many were entertained by the Scotts and became good friends — particularly Madame Schumann-Heinck, who enjoyed conversing in German with the Scotts, and Lawrence Tibbett, who came as a soloist and member of a quartet the first summer and as musical director in 1923 and 1924. On the latter occasions, he lived in a tent on the Assembly Grounds with his wife and twin sons and established the tradition of closing each session with a performance of the *Messiah*. Moving on from his Chautauqua experiences, Tibbett appeared at the Hollywood Bowl and subsequently sang in starring roles at the Metropolitan Opera Company in New York.

By 1924 Eleanor Miller's young drama students were ready to perform, using a small stage in a

The beachside auto camp facilities were used by a variety of religious groups, such as the Baptists' Young People's Union whose outdoor barbecue was pictured in *Pictorial California*. *Swarzwald/Patterson Collection*

Entrance to the Auto Camp from the coast highway. *Clearwater Collection*

canyon near the Tabernacle, cleared and readied for that purpose. The event was an international festival, combining culture and education. Frances Smith Stewart recalls that it was her role to come running down the hill in the glare of the spotlight and to pause in the middle of the stage, arms outstretched, and recite in a clear voice: "I am the Panama Canal."

As it developed, the lower canyon was designated the Institute Camp and catered to young people. The facilities included an outdoor amphitheater for large gatherings; several small classrooms; and The Lodge, which housed visiting dignitaries, group leaders, and vacationers. A large dining hall served meals to groups and accommodated the Sunday interdenominational church services. The recreational area, which was open to all, included a quarter-mile track, tennis and basketball courts, a baseball diamond, a gymnasium and bowling alley, showers and dressing rooms. Field days, held during the year, brought families together for races and games, fun and foolishness.

Hikers, swimmers, and sun bathers found their own amusement. A favorite trail led down Temescal Canyon to the ocean, winding through a wonderland of sycamores, live oaks, shrubs, and ferns, kept lush the whole year round by the same running springs that today bedevil the broad paved access road. Newcomers to the area were warned to steer clear of the poison oak and blackberry brambles.

Near the base of the trail, the Temescal Auto Camp provided forty tents, lunch and ice cream stands, and public picnic tables, making a thrifty beach vacation possible for economy-minded families. There was also a modest bathhouse, built near the water's edge at the foot of Via de la Paz. When it was destroyed by a storm in February, 1926, the *Progress* observed candidly: "Those with any eye for the aesthetic cannot regard its destruction as an unmitigated disaster." Plans for a more ambitious replacement were turned over to Thomas P. Barber, the official Association architect.

Property sales moved ahead briskly, as the number of homes reached one hundred by the end of 1924. The most famous name to be added to the roster was that of William Jennings Bryan, whose Cross of Gold speech and compelling presence had made him the outstanding attraction on the Chautauqua circuit. He purchased two lots near Inspiration Point and announced that he would make this his permanent home — a plan that was interrupted by his death on July 25, 1925, a few days after the conclusion of the famous Scopes trial, in which the fundamentalist Bryan matched oratorical skills with Clarence Darrow over the issue of evolution.

Coincidentally, the Chautauqua movement followed a similar course. A record twelve thousand towns and villages in America staged fiftieth anniversary Chautauquas in 1924, with thirty million patrons in attendance. The following summer it was all over. The system had become hopelessly mired in administrative problems, and even the "Mother" Chautauqua in New York failed to open. It was a sad day. The movement had brought learning and culture to the West and to Pacific Palisades, which still had vigor and vitality and kept the dream alive a little longer.

The community took a solid step forward in September, 1924, when a small local news sheet appeared, bearing the nebulous title, *"Pacific Palisades ?____?"* and carrying an article, "Name the Baby." Thereafter, the *"Pacific Palisades Progress"* was published monthly by the Association, with Thomas R. Gettys as its first editor. It carried local church and social items and the latest statistics on the real estate venture. As sales began to lag in the mid-twenties, the Association published brochures with views of the community enticingly captioned "Where the Mountains Meet the Sea" and offered to make "creative financing" available for prospective leaseholders. Profits from sales, they hastened to add, would be turned back into the community for the benefit of all.

The first business block also appeared in 1924, occupying a wedge-shaped piece of land between streets then known as Beverly Boulevard, Hillcrest Road, and Park Place — previously a duck pond with cattails. According to the Olmsted plan it was to have been part of a civic center complex that included a large public square, a hotel, administration building, library, and auditorium, all suitably landscaped and bounded on the north by a park with a lake and concert grove.

The Association reserved several rooms for its various departments and rented space to a variety of commercial tenants — Nelson's grocery, Warrell's meat market, Norris's plumbing and hardware, James Neville's electric shop, E.N. Lundy's cleaners and dyers, Bertha Coler's decorating studio and gift shop, Mrs. L.F. Peckham's dry goods establishment,

Field day rides, *Gabrielson Collection*

Panoramic view of the Athletic Field in lower Temescal Canyon, with Harmony Hall on the hill and the bowling alley below. The occasion was the Field Day program on June 23, 1928. Identified in the picture are: Jimmy Rogers, *at the left,* on the white-faced pony; Will Rogers, Jr., with the white shirt, standing in the center with two other men; and Snowy Baker, back to the camera, at the right, dressed in white. *Clearwater Collection*

Sack races, *Clearwater Collection*

Above, the movie set in Las Pulgas Canyon, which was constructed in 1923 for *King of the Wild Horses,* and thereafter used for other pictures. It became a favorite picnic spot for Palisadians and the site of a memorable Halloween celebration. *Courtesy Bee Clark Kottinger* *Below,* the Business Block under construction. *Clearwater Collection*

and Sylvia Morrison's drug store.

Several professional men, including Dr. Richard J. Morrison, moved in after the building was completed, and on April 1, 1926, the California Bank opened a branch in a choice corner room, formerly occupied by the Association land office. Doubtless, A.M. Chaffey's dual role as treasurer of the Association and president of the California Bank made this new convenience possible. J. Howard Steensen was appointed manager and Fred H. Tichenor assistant manager.

The dedication of the Business Block, which was held on Saturday, November 15, 1924, was a modest affair. Reverend Scott delivered the benediction and reviewed the parade — the band riding in a bus and twenty automobiles following in single file. A second ceremony was held on Founders' Day, January 14, 1925, when the shops held an official open house and a small park surrounding Founders' Oaks was dedicated in honor of the first families. Sighting storm clouds and fearing rain, the residents moved their picnic lunches into the auditorium and congratulated each other on winning third place in Class A in the Pasadena Rose Parade — welcome publicity for the new community.

As work progressed, landscaping continued to be an integral part of the overall plan. Jesse R. Vore, who had been in charge of Pasadena's street trees, was named superintendent and carried out his task with devotion. He set up nurseries at the northwest corner of Via de la Paz and Beverly Boulevard and in the eastern arm of Las Pulgas Canyon and raised over 50,000 plants. Criticizing some of Olmsted's choices as unsuitable, Vore used many varieties of native shrubs and trees, as well as hardy exotics.

Half of these plants were used on Via de la Paz; it was literally banked with shrubbery and equipped with a watering system to create and maintain the impressive appearance of the avenue.

Most of Pacific Palisades was still agricultural, with fields of hay, lima beans, and peas. Japanese families tilled small garden plots on a portion of the Huntington property, raised ducks, and sold flowers at a roadside stand. Las Pulgas Canyon continued in the rural tradition with a riding academy which rented horses to budding equestrians at sixty cents an hour. It also accommodated Sid Herndon's apiary and a goat farm operated by two Greeks, Sam Kocotis and Peter Kiriakos, the latter pasturing his goats on the hillside and delivering goats' milk to the community in his Model T Ford. A sign over the entrance to their domain read "Land of Milk and Honey." As the town grew, the goats were transported to Saugus and the bees to Little Sycamore Canyon, farther north in the Santa Monica Mountains.

Elsewhere in Las Pulgas Canyon was a Western-style movie set which was constructed for the film, *King of Wild Horses,* and thereafter became a favorite picnic spot. Nearby was the base of an ancient trail, presumably used by Indians and early settlers to cross the mountains. It was cleared by the Association and formally opened on February 28, 1925. A hundred-odd hikers met at the pseudo-hacienda, wearing their boots and carrying their canteens, and climbed to the top of the ridge. At the junction with the Split Rock trail they reassembled and formed a club, electing R.S. Stadler president and Cliff Clearwater photographer.

A small group of golfers also laid out a nine-hole

Dedication of the Business Block on November 15, 1924, with the band playing and John Stadler raising the flag. *Clearwater Collection*

93

Panorama of Pacific Palisades in 1925, when the community boasted one hundred homes. Temescal Canyon appears on the far right; Via de la Paz extends from the photographer's vantage point to the sea, with Monument Street at an angle to the left. The Business Block and Founders' Tract II are on the right, Founders' Tract I on the left. *Courtesy of an anonymous donor*

Deer grazing on the lawn of a McKendree Street home (as seen in the panorama above). *Clearwater Collection*

The completed Business Block, as seen from Swarthmore Avenue. *Clearwater Collection*

First class in the new elementary school on Via de la Paz.
Courtesy Frances Smith Stewart

Dr. Edwards at the beach with an early morning nature study class. *Courtesy Bee Clark Kottinger*

course on the mesa northwest of Temescal Canyon. Using Harmony Hall as a clubhouse, they installed fairways, tee-frames, and sand boxes. Sponsors paid two dollars for memberships, named L.C. Willey as president, and chose gold and blue as the club's colors. When hopes for a real course languished — due in part to local religious sanctions against Sunday play — the venture died.

Street names came into the news, as the *Progress* sponsored a contest to replace the temporary street designations on the tract map. The Women's Forum and Dr. Waite were instant winners, using the names of distinguished religious leaders, in alphabetical order, for Founders' Tract I. Chautauqua, on the east, was to have an extension called Vincent Street, and Monument Street was to have been named after Dr. Louis Miller. South of Beverly Boulevard, streets were named for American Christian colleges. A different theme was chosen for the Las Pulgas tract — Indian names suggested by C.D. Clearwater and Spanish names by Mrs. Odessa Vasquez. The city engineering department made the final decision, taking citywide duplications into account, and jettisoned several front-runners, including Vincent, Miller, Luther, Esmeralda, and Matilija.

Prospects for more rapid civic growth were enhanced when Los Angeles voters by a wide margin passed a million-dollar bond issue to finance the extension of Beverly Boulevard from the western edge of Beverly Hills to the sea, the vote in Pacific Palisades being 181 to 1. Residents also turned out en masse on August 18, 1925, to watch the completion of grading, as a steam shovel working along the western side of Rustic Canyon removed the last load of dirt from the roadway. Appropriate ceremonies ensued with Dr. Scott presiding.

The same year, May K. Rindge's costly battle to keep her land inviolate reached the Supreme Court. The State of California won the case under the law of eminent domain and began construction of the two-lane Roosevelt Highway to Ventura. Anticipating change, developers had already opened several Malibu areas for subdivision. No longer was Pacific Palisades an end-of-the-line appendage to the urban area.

Spirits rose still higher when Dr. Scott was selected chairman of a committee to plan a three hundred-acre Los Angeles campus for the University of California; working with him were representatives of the Chambers of Commerce of the southwestern area of the city. Thanks in part to Dr. Scott's able presentation, the regents chose the Westwood site. Ground was broken in 1927 and the official "Moving Day" held on May 31, 1929 — a gala occasion when the entire student body paraded from the old school on Vermont Avenue to the new campus at Westwood.

At the same time, Occidental College and Loyola University both announced plans for Westside campuses. Palisadians were ecstatic. The community's widely publicized slogan, "Bring the Children Here," took on new meaning: the colleges were seen both as a resource for local young people and as a means of bringing cultured and learned residents to Pacific Palisades.

Only a few of the first settlers were actually families with children — the Scotts, Norrises, and Hochs among them. Mrs. Hoch was delayed in the East, caring for a gravely ill sister, so it was fourteen-year-old Virginia who took charge of the family and kept house in a makeshift cabin. Later she worked part-time in Nelson's Market in the Business Block and for many years spent her summers presiding over the order desk and keeping the books.

Gradually, as more young people arrived, grammar school classes grew in size and improved in quality. The school itself moved to the construction center after the first year, then in 1925 to four frame bungalows on a site provided by the Los Angeles City Board of Education at Via de la Paz and Bowdoin Street. By then, there were ninety-two students and three teachers, with Laura Hollingshead as principal. To supplement the work of the school, the Association organized a small library on the Assembly Grounds and initiated field trips under the leadership of Dr. Charles Lincoln Edwards of the Los Angeles City Schools to acquaint the children with the wonders of nature which so bountifully surrounded them.

Scott family portrait with (left to right) Mary, Martha, Warren, Wesley, Wayne—and Wendell sitting between Dr. and Mrs. Scott. *Courtesy Scott Family*

Soon, too, there were the new babies. The first was Elizabeth Corr, born to the Ray T. Corrs on December 22, 1922. Corr was an Imperial Valley rancher who operated the Association's filling station and later became the community's first postmaster. On March 10, 1923, the first boy, Louis Laird, was born to the Clifford Clearwaters.

The whole community — united in their beliefs and sense of moral values — lived, worked, and played together with the warmth and enthusiasm of an extended family. Holidays were festivals for all. According to the *Progress*, Halloween was celebrated with a special flair at the old movie set in Las Pulgas Canyon in 1924:

The old Spanish ranch house with its courtyard, well, outdoor oven, and servants' quarters, a spooky affair after dark at any time, was appropriately decorated with lighted jack-o-lanterns and other Hallowe'en symbols. The interior of the house was fitted with the various devices in imitation of a "run house" [sic], and a continuous procession of young and old continually made their way through it.

Several hundred celebrants in masks and homemade costumes crowded into the servants' quarters for games and filed around the grounds in a dress parade. Later they returned to Temescal Canyon for a bonfire, band music, and Dr. Scott's dramatic rendition of a James Whitcomb Riley poem. Finally, everyone unmasked amidst squeals of surprise and delight, and lined up for the barbecue.

Thanksgiving brought the community together in true pioneer fashion for several years. In 1924, nine hundred residents and guests met in the outdoor amphitheater for a special Thanksgiving religious service conducted by Dr. Oren B. Waite, pastor of the community church. Music was provided by the choir and orchestra under the direction of Nancy Kendall-Robinson.

After the final anthem, the crowd trooped down through the trees to the dining hall where volunteers assisted in the preparation and serving of the meal. It was a traditional Thanksgiving repast, with large helpings of turkey and mashed potatoes, wedges of pie, and bowls of fruit and nuts. All the while, lively tunes were played by the band, most of whom were members of the Williams family. Norwegian-born Alfred Gunderson Williams was the bandmaster, and each of his sons played an instrument: Norman, the trumpet; Alfred, the French horn; Bill and his father, the bass horn.

The Easter sunrise service, a tradition since 1922, was held on Peace Hill, below a giant lighted cross. Each year the crowd grew larger, until in 1926, over six thousand people wended their way up the hill. From above it was an impressive sight, the lamps of the cars shining brightly as they moved up Via de la Paz toward the cross in the pre-dawn darkness.

It was a spine-tingling moment when the crowd, waiting in hushed silence, heard trumpet calls from the top of the hill heralding the dawn. The program that year included a series of anthems played by the band, basso profundo solos by Captain C.D. Wooldridge, and Van Dyke's "God of the Open Air" performed by the choir under Mrs. Robinson's direction. At the end the band played "Onward, Christian Soldiers." This was the signal for the congregation to come forward, pick up lilies from jars set in the ground in front of the speakers' platform, and march in procession down the hill, singing the rousing chorus.

In the early days, religion and music — both sacred and secular — were at the heart of the community, even though it was the sale of real estate and the financial health of the organization that made it possible. The wholesome way of life, with its simple pleasures, evokes memories of Andy Hardy, Booth Tarkington's *Seventeen,* even Mark Twain. It was the age of innocence, with picnics and flagwaving and an accepted set of values.

Martha Scott still remembers Pacific Palisades in the twenties as a special place and time to be young. Living in the Scott household was an adventure in itself. For both Dr. and Mrs. Scott, religion provided a deep-seated faith, a special buoyancy of body and mind. Both were physical culture enthusiasts, exercising each morning and allowing the children a bedtime romp through the house — in the buff — to be sure they would sleep soundly. They believed in

The Pacific Palisades band in front of Harmony Hall. *Front row, left to right:* Bill Williams, William Balsley, Norman Williams, Harrison Reno, Benjamin Norris, Alex Douglas, Robert E. Norris, Merrill Baird. *Back row,* Alf Williams, Frank Parr, A.G. Williams (leader), Ray Vore, —————. *Clearwater Collection*

Above, first Easter celebration on Peace Hill, in 1922 — looking down Via de la Paz toward the ocean. *Clearwater Collection*

Lower left, the service itself. *Lower right,* the procession down the hill, with members of the congregation carrying lilies. *Gabrielson Collection*

the nutritional value of vegetables and coarse-grain cereals from the grist mill. Mrs. Scott even wrote an article for Bernarr Macfadden's magazine, espousing the cause of wholesome food. Included in the magazine article were pictures of the family and of Mrs. Scott, pregnant with her sixth child and dressed in a black bloomer outfit.

The Scotts had family devotions at breakfast time, followed by Bible readings. Community religious services in which they participated were fundamentalist and reminiscent of the old-time camp meetings. Martha recalls that most evangelical services ended with the congregation singing "Just As I Am," which brought tears to her eyes and led many of the young people to go forward, kneel down, and profess their dedication to a Christian way of life.

Dr. Scott's personal philosophy found expression in the Summer Assemblies, which continued in the same vein as the Chautauquas. Top-flight speakers on a wide variety of topics were recruited from the colleges, and a full summer school program, from kindergarten through high school, was provided for young people. There were classes in music, drama, home decorating, and the arts, with the best available

instruction, and a busy schedule of special events. For all this, the charge was ten dollars, excluding only one or two concerts or lectures of remarkable caliber.

Although the community remained essentially homogeneous, new migrants were attracted from all over the country and abroad. Illinois, Ohio, and Iowa shared top billing with England and Canada. Most of the new residents were Methodists, but other Protestant denominations were represented, even on the board of trustees, and the church itself was interdenominational. By 1923 the congregation had grown so large that Dr. Oren B. Waite was assigned to Pacific Palisades as pastor of the church and program chairman for the Association.

The first service and social organizations were associated with the church — the Women's Missionary Society, Epworth League, Women's Council, and Ladies' Aid Society. On February 5, 1925, the first meeting of "The Forum" was held, with ninety-six women and men in attendance. The idea of such a group had been suggested by Mrs. Lillian T. Taylor who was elected its first president. In subsequent years, the Women's Forum, as it came to be known, provided the distaff side of Pacific Pali-

Methodist juniors at the beach with their teachers. The picture was taken on the old Long Wharf jetty. *First row, left to right:* Robert Anglemeyer, Telford Work, Violet Christianson, Ina Andrews, _____, Jean Little. *Second row,* Bill Keller, _____, Miss Ida Townsend, Mrs. Lillian Taylor, Jean Barnbrock, Judy Marks, Margaret Jane Work, Bonnie Buckner. *Third row,* Dorothy Meiser, Beatrice Clark, _____Hunting, Vivia Meiser, Jeanette Waite, Phyllis Maurer, Ruth Barnbrock, Betty Norris. *Top row,* Jean Anglemeyer, Eva Christianson.

sades with an opportunity for study, sociability, and service, and today, as the Woman's Club, it still holds a prominent place in the community.

The children developed their own camaraderie. For them, even the daily bus ride was a joyous occasion. Handsome Captain Wooldridge, the bass soloist, doubled as bus driver and gave each rider individual attention. One of the girls was good for a laugh each morning as she was chronically late. She would come running down the street, trailing her lunch and school books, or pulling the curlers out of her hair, as "Cap" beeped insistently on the horn.

For teenagers, the beach and the mountains were close at hand and events of all sorts brought them together. Martha Scott recalls that the twenties were "flapper" years for the girls and that boys had a craze for "strip-downs." Young fellows of high school age would put a car together from the junk yard — "two seats to sit in and back of that a gas tank, and four wheels, and a little bit of motor and maybe a windshield, and maybe not."

One Sunday Bob Smallman, son of choir director John Smallman, came by for Martha in his strip-down and together they stopped to pick up Fern Buckner, who played the violin. Martha was sitting precariously on the gas tank when they turned the corner. The wheels slipped on the gravel surface of the street and Martha fell off. "Instead of letting go, my friend hung onto me, so to this day I have scarred-up knees, clear down to the bone."

Music was woven into the fabric of the whole

Nancy Kendall Robinson. *Courtesy Nancy June Robinson Evans*

community, just as it had provided the strength of the Chautauqua movement. In *We Called It Culture,* Robert Case observed that when the music failed, Main Street began to doubt Chautauqua. Later, the nationwide circuit was criticized for "too many saxophone solos, too many shrill girlish trios recruited from the next county, too much of the bird whistlers and bell ringers and piano monologues in costume, and singers who drew cartoons and modeled in clay. Everybody laughed at the novelty musical instruments, but they really wanted the best in the world."

Pacific Palisades provided quality — not sophistication, perhaps, but quality. After the Chautauqua disbanded, the importance of music continued to grow. John Smallman, leader of the famous a cappella choir that bore his name and a highly respected teacher, directed the music department at the Summer Assembly and coordinated classes in theory and technique, as well as in group performance.

Sharing and later taking over teaching and program responsibilities was Pacific Palisades' own Nancy Kendall Robinson, who had come to the United States from England after World War I, with a degree in music from the Victoria College School of Music in London and a teaching credential from St. Margaret's College in Yorkshire. During the war she lead the recreational and musical activities of

Captain Wooldridge in uniform, with his beloved dog. *Courtesy Nancy June Robinson Evans*

101

Children in costume for one of Nancy Kendall Robinson's concerts. *Back row, left to right,* Josephine Crawford, Margaret Jane Work, Madeline Koenig, Dorcus Jones, Margaret Bornhauser, Marcia Carde, Jean Anglemeyer, Marie Jones, Jean Little, Margaret Monk, Tom Kinsley. *Front row,* Jeanette Waite, Phyllis Maurer, Miriam Kinsley. *Courtesy Bee Clark Kottinger*

nine thousand girls employed at a munitions factory in Scotland. In 1917 she performed for the King and Queen of England when they visited the factory and was presented to them.

She was married in 1919 to William Kendall Robinson, whom she had known since childhood, and emigrated with him to Porterville in the San Joaquin Valley the following year. A trained automotive engineer, he was placed in charge of equipment and machinery at Fairfield Farms.

The couple met Captain Charles Douglas Wooldridge through the Porterville First Methodist Church, where Mrs. Robinson was director of music. "Cap," as he was affectionately called, was also from England and was a talented musician with a thrilling bass voice. He had begun singing at Winchester Cathedral as a small boy, attended Oxford University, and served with the British Army in India and Egypt. During World War I, he fought in Gallipoli and in the trenches of France and Belgium, suffering severe wounds from which he never fully recovered. In 1921, attracted by ads for citrus and grape ranches in the San Joaquin Valley, he came to California, the land of sunshine and opportunity.

Years of drought persuaded the trio to come to Pacific Palisades in 1924. William Robinson opened an auto repair shop in Santa Monica, while Cap drove the local red buses back and forth to Santa Monica and took the children to school. Most of all, he was in demand for his voice, as a member of the choir and as a soloist. Later he appeared in motion pictures.

Mrs. Robinson became musical director for the Association and gave private instruction in piano and voice as well. Soon her pupils were winning major awards in local competition. In 1925 her Pacific Palisades Methodist Church choir took first place in the Southern California Eisteddfod Music Festival Competition, held at the Philharmonic Auditorium. It created quite a stir when an unknown group, under a woman director, finished ahead of many famous and well-established choral groups.

The following year, the local church orchestra, with nineteen members, reached the finals where it vanquished a twenty-seven-member orchestra and earned the highest number of points awarded to any musical group in any category. Cap Wooldridge missed first place in the individual competition by only two points, no mean feat since the music he was given was too high for his voice and had to be transposed.

Cap was the star of every musical event. One year, at Eastertime, he had taken the music home with him and overslept. He was utterly chagrined when a messenger from the choir ran down to the canyon and awakened him. In front of all the spectators, Cap had to clamber up Peace Hill and give his performance.

For her part, Mrs. Robinson was a demanding taskmaster. Her very appearance, with her blue eyes and white hair, was compelling. At choir practice or when giving a piano lesson, she would say, "Hit it!" with great vigor to emphasize a dramatic point. Beyond that, she was tireless in giving her time and her energies for the benefit of her students.

SHOWTIME
IN THE
PALISADES

Upper left, the well-known choir director and music teacher, John Smallman. *Upper right,* a rousing gypsy gala. *Both, courtesy Frances Smith Stewart*

Below, Nancy Kendall Robinson, *standing,* with the orchestra and chorus. Violinist Fern Buckner is seated in the front, *on the left. Courtesy Nancy June Robinson Evans*

Uplifters in costume for the Circus Parade at the 1922 Annual Outing in Rustic Canyon. The gentleman on the right is writer Irvin S. Cobb. *Courtesy George and Onis Rice*

9

FLOWERING OF THE DREAM

No sooner had the Methodists abandoned their Forestry Station campsite in Rustic Canyon in 1921 than the Uplifters purchased the additional acreage and held their first official Outing there in October, renovating the Edmond ranch house for use as a clubhouse and occupying the adjacent grove. Staid businessmen drove out from town for the festivities, donned outlandish costumes, and quaffed their own brand of spirits on the very spot where evangelists had inveighed against the Devil's ways.

The men slept in tents and hastily-built dormitories and relaxed out under the oaks and sycamores. After dinner, they brought out their "Hymnals" and gathered around the campfire to sing such old favorites as "Susan Doozan," "Mary's Pousse Cafe," and "Oh, By Jingo." Before long they were creating their own ballads in praise of their new-found paradise. The Saturday night High Jinks play, "The Will of Manitou," written by James W. Foley, featured attorney Lloyd Moultrie, dressed in Indian garb, paddling a canoe down the shallow waters of Rustic Creek to take possession of the Ranch for the Uplifters.

The original, makeshift clubhouse was destroyed by fire at Christmastime in 1922, and was replaced by a new Spanish-style building designed by architect William Dodd, with a large dining room and an auditorium complete with pipe organ. By 1925 many rustic-style homes had been built, some of logs or log-faced, others of simple shingle or clapboard design.

Under Harry Haldeman's leadership, the organization grew until it included most of the up-and-coming business and professional men from Los Angeles. Some spent weekends and summers on the Ranch; a few became full-time residents. Recreation of every sort was provided — swimming, tennis, and most of all, equestrian sports. Banker Marco Hellman donated a riding arena and gave the original impetus to the riding club. His own spacious log cabin was a mecca for groups of friends who rode out from the city to enjoy the hospitality for which Hellman was famous.

As the interest of horse fanciers became more sophisticated, the mesa west of the stream was purchased for a race track, where member-owned horses competed, ridden either by their owners or by designated member-riders. Then came polo, an even more luxurious sport. A full-fledged polo facility, with stands and stables, was installed in 1927-28 and became one of the stops on the international polo circuit. The Pedleys and other nationally ranked players were frequent visitors, with such local bigwigs as Hal Roach, Big Boy Williams, Jack Holt, and Will Rogers on hand almost every weekend.

Reginald "Snowy" Baker came out from the Los Angeles Athletic Club to serve as manager of

Everybody's favorite — Snowy Baker. *Brunson/Pringle Collection*

Above, Marco Hellman's home was originally part of a movie set and was reconstructed out of whole logs on the Uplifter Ranch. *Courtesy Peter and Fern Quenzer*

Below, a window in the bar was painted with a cartoon by Woodrow Faulkner depicting "Half of Hellman's dirty dozen." *Courtesy Kathy and Larry Keating*

equestrian sports. Snowy was an import from Australia and a legend in his own time. He was an Olympic athlete who had competed in twenty-nine different sports and had won world championships in several. As a boy, he had worked on a cattle station and became a daredevil horseman; later, as a silent film star, he had made a series of adventure pictures and, with his rugged good looks, became a popular screen idol. His dedication to amateur sports was intense. He dreamed of involving every man, woman, and child in some sort of meaningful athletic program, and the Uplifters Club was ready-made for his talents. Snowy played on the polo team and joined the men at the Outings; he gave riding lessons and organized equestrian activities for every age group.

An equally enthusiastic claque pursued the arts. Famous singers, actors, dancers, musicians, and other entertainers from the stage, movies, and the Chautauqua circuit appeared regularly. In warm weather, events were held in a huge amphitheater by the creek or on a small stage near the campfire circle. At other times the spacious indoor auditorium was used. Musical and dramatic performances by the Uplifters and their families were also encouraged.

After the old clubhouse burned in December, 1922, the Uplifters built a new Spanish-style clubhouse, which was dedicated at the Annual Outing in September, 1923. Today this facility is part of Rustic Canyon Park. *Courtesy George and Onis Rice*

The orchestra had grown and by now was semi-professional; singing groups abounded; and fine plays with both amateurs and professionals, Uplifters and guests, were considered regular fare. Many of the productions used the picturesque setting of woods, hills, and stream to heighten the dramatic effect.

The highlight of each year's social calendar was the Annual Outing, expanded from a long weekend to a full week. Several events became traditions, such as the midweek shirt contest, the Friday night Low Jinks, the Saturday night High Jinks, and a repeat performance of the specially written High Jinks light opera on Sunday for the families. The Outing itself remained resolutely stag: women and children retired to their homes in the city for the duration.

The easygoing atmosphere of the Uplifters Ranch doubtless was the object of concern among the Methodists on the hill above, and perhaps the subliminal envy of many of John Wesley's rigidly oriented followers. Residents of the two communities seldom mixed socially, but rumors of the Uplifters' bucolic shenanigans flew. One pioneer resident of Pacific Palisades recalls that a large group of

Palisadians stood in a solemn row along the rim of the mesa during one of the more raucous outings and held hands, singing hymns and praying for the misguided souls in the canyon below.

Indeed, Prohibition was no barrier to Uplifter camaraderie. The club itself had a bar, and most homes were rigged to have bars hidden behind moveable walls or tucked away in basements. Top-level law enforcement officers who attended many of the festivities could be relied on to look the other way. The social climate of Los Angeles was still puritanical and the very notion of illicit tippling provided as much of the fun and laughter as the drinking itself.

Except for the Outings, social events were family-oriented and wholesome. There were classes in swimming, riding excursions into the hills, and the famous barbecues. Appropriately prepared meals could be served to members and guests in the dining room, at the cottages, or beside stone fireplaces along the creek.

A palm branch of sorts was extended to the more conservative folk in Pacific Palisades when the Uplifter polo field went into operation. It was a favorite weekend pastime for residents and passers-

The Pacific Palisades coastline as it appeared in 1923, with Las Pulgas Canyon (above, center), Temescal Canyon (right), road grading for the new Las Pulgas subdivision on the intervening mesa, and the Jones Bowl road (lower right).

The streets of Founders' Tract I (center left) and Founders' Tract II (lower left) were as yet unpaved, but the first few homes had been built, and Via de la Paz extended in a straight line from Peace Hill to the bluff, then in an S-curve to the beach. The original bath house, which later washed away, is located on the shoreline below. To the right is Potrero Canyon and the stub of the Long Wharf. On the eastern mesa is the future site of Huntington Palisades, with Abbot Kinney's orderly rows of eucalyptus trees. Above, and in the center, is Rustic Canyon and the Uplifters Ranch. On the far right is Santa Monica Canyon, and beyond, the city of Santa Monica. Panorama from the *Clearwater Collection.*

"Pikers' Peak," along upper Chautauqua Boulevard, where local residents had a clear and comfortable view of events on the Uplifter polo field — without paying admission fees.
Swarzwald-Patterson Collection

by to line up on "Pikers' Peak" and watch the games free of charge. Jedd Fuller wrote in *The Palisadian,* "The hillside setters have as much fun as though they were down among the Uplifters, and it don't cost them nothin' either." Later, the Uplifters planted a row of eucalyptus trees along the fringe of the highway to obstruct the freeloaders' view.

By 1926 the booster spirit had thoroughly infected the Southland, including Pacific Palisades. New land developments from San Diego to Ventura were announced weekly in the newspapers, each with its own set of inducements, tailored to the clientele. Some provided variety shows and barbecues, while others offered deed restrictions and dignity. Pacific Palisades, with its leasehold policies, had never entered the open market and was new to the game.

It was in this optimistic mood that the Association proudly announced the purchase of the 226-acre Huntington property from the Huntington family's estate in New York for $1,650,000 and launched a handsome new subdivision, appropriately named Huntington Palisades. The deal was a complicated one, involving Robert C. Gillis, Dr. Scott, and Gillis's associate, Arthur H. Fleming of Pasadena. Fleming was a wealthy lumberman, a major contributor to the California Institute of Technology, and president of that school's board of trustees.

The use of the prestigious Huntington name was suggested by Andrew Chaffey, treasurer of the Association and a resident of nearby Brentwood, who deemed it appropriate to honor the former owner of the land, Collis Huntington, and his attempts to develop a major harbor at Port Los Angeles on the coastline below. When Collis died in 1900, his widow, Arabella, inherited the property and in 1913 married Collis's nephew, Henry. Arabella, in turn, died in New York in 1924, and left the property to her son, Archer. At this point Palisadians feared that when Henry Huntington also died, the land in question would not be developed to their liking and were convinced that it represented "a dagger pointed at the heart of Pacific Palisades."

By acquiring this buffer zone — a move Scott and Gillis had always viewed as imperative — the Association hoped to protect the quality of the community and make a profit as well. The design of the tract reflected the high standards set by Scott and Gillis and included elements characteristic of the Olmsteds. As in Founders' Tract II and the Las Pulgas Tract, curving streets and view lots outlined the periphery. Within this boundary, concentric semi-circular drives surrounded an open park area (bounded by El Cerco Place) and intersected a broad entry street with landscaped central parkways (Pampas Ricas).

Lots were varied in size to accommodate large homes on the choicest sites — at intersections and along the mesa rim. Underground utilities were installed and ornamental light fixtures were provided, costing four times the normal amount for such services. A forty-acre plot adjacent to Potrero Canyon and Beverly Boulevard was designated for commercial use, as was a strip along the coast highway. In contrast to property in the earlier tracts, which changed hands under leasehold, lots in Huntington Palisades were advertised openly and sold under long-lasting deed restrictions.

Mark Daniels was retained to direct the landscaping and beautification phase of the development, while W.W. Williams was placed in charge of engineering and construction. Most of the old eucalyptus trees planted by Abbot Kinney were carefully preserved, though the new streets cut across their even rows. Street names were chosen by Williams in honor of his lady friend, a singer and dancer from Mexico. Thus, Alma Real was named for the lady herself, and the remaining streets after famous places in Mexico. The street trees were selected by Dorothy Gillis Loomis and included the flowering eucalyptus which was the favorite of her father, R.C. Gillis.

The first step in the improvement of Huntington Palisades was the removal of the row of summer cabins from the edge of the bluff. Four were purchased at $200 each by Perfecto Marquez for

Above, some of the more than fifty squatters' shacks which formed semicircle around the bluffs before Huntington Palisades was developed. Those pictured were along the edge of Potrero Canyon and had a panoramic view of the coastline. *Clearwater Collection*

Below, the Lighthouse was built on the point of land which had provided the base for the Long Wharf. The new landmark contained a restaurant and dressing rooms for bathers. On the cliff was one of the signs promoting Huntington Palisades, and beside it, the tract office which had been put together out of two of the shacks. *Ernest Marquez Collection*

rental units and were transported to his property in Santa Monica Canyon, adjacent to Canyon School. Two other cabins which were located on the rim of the mesa near the mouth of Potrero Canyon were converted into a sales office for the convenience of guests and visitors. Colonel Percy Rairden of the Santa Monica Land and Water Company was placed in charge of sales for Huntington Palisades and agreed with the Methodist ownership that no selling would be permitted on Sundays.

One small frame dwelling on the Rustic Canyon fringe of Huntington Palisades antedated the elaborate planning process and remains there today — outside the tract. It was built in 1923 by Ethel Rollins Shanks, a nationally known business executive, who later purchased three large lots on Chautauqua Boulevard to insure her right of access. Even as impressive homes were built around her, she successfully circumvented the new restrictions and for many years maintained her business headquarters in what appeared to be a complex of greenhouses and a series of vacant lots.

Development of the Huntington tract was an expensive undertaking. Cost of the raw land alone stood at $7,500 an acre and improvements at $3,500, for a total cost of $12,000 an acre, including finance charges — a record high price in 1926. The Santa Monica Land and Water Company, as sales agents, paid the cost of a major publicity campaign and placed two large signs on the property — one overlooking Santa Monica Canyon and one at the mouth of Potrero Canyon. Newspaper articles were sent to such "Hot Belt" communities as San Bernardino, El Centro, and Phoenix, as well as to Los Angeles newspapers.

Promotional brochure of the 1920s. *Clearwater Collection*

Jack Sauer's first gas station, at the southwest corner of Beverly (Sunset) Boulevard and La Cruz Drive. *Courtesy Jack Sauer*

Competition for lot buyers was keen. Each Sunday the *Los Angeles Times* was full of lavish ads: "The Magic Story of Chevy Chase" . . . "Popularity is absorbing the hills of Hollywoodland" . . . "Capitalists, Writers, and Artists are coming to Del Mar." Nearer home, Frank Meline pushed sales of Alphonzo Bell's properties; the city of Santa Monica publicized its array of glamorous beach clubs; and several new tracts — including Canyon Mesa — were opened for sale in Santa Monica Canyon.

Huntington Palisades countered with artistic drawings and photographs of its scenic coastline and giant eucalyptus trees. Buyers were collectively offered a three hundred-foot stretch of private beach and were promised decorative stairways leading to a park at the base of the bluff. All Palisadians had access to the new Association bathhouse, which was completed in January, 1927, and opened the following summer. "The Lighthouse," as it was called, stood on the shoreline at the site of the Long Wharf and provided dressing rooms and dining facilities, all under the management of J.D. Abraham.

The first home in Huntington Palisades was completed before the end of 1926 — a twelve-room Colonial house built at 601 Ocampo Drive by Phillip A. Lee at a cost of $15,000. Also under way were the Albert M. Jarvis home on Ocampo and the handsome adobe hacienda of Captain Overton Walsh on Frontera.

At the same time, the Association expanded its saleable holdings by laying out new developments on Temescal Heights and Western Heights, even though sales on their other properties were lagging. The resident leaseholders became equally grandiose and demanded a large, modern hotel, a sightseeing railway down the side of Temescal Canyon, a golf course, croquet courts, sewers, a weekly newspaper, a radio station, and a viaduct over Santa Monica Canyon — few of which have even yet come to pass.

Hopes hinged on the completion of Beverly (Sunset) Boulevard, which would bring an increased flow of traffic through the community and, if all went well, a flood of new customers. Dr. Scott presided over the opening ceremonies on January 20, 1926, and within a short time, commuters were able to ride on comfortable new motor coaches from Castellammare to Pershing Square. The line was established by Francis Brunner, a native Santa Monican who had operated the Santa Monica-Topanga bus line since 1922, using buses labeled "Southern California's Prettiest Drive." With the backing of Alphonzo Bell, Brunner obtained the Beverly Boulevard franchise; subsequently he sold his rights to the Pacific Electric, who operated the service for many years.

At this strategic time, Ray Corr's gas station in Temescal Canyon closed, and Florian "Jack" Sauer, who had been purchasing agent at the Sawtelle Veterans' Home, opened an up-to-date service station on Beverly Boulevard to accommodate the expected influx of motorists. In no time Jack's flair for merchandising and his zeal for public service attracted nationwide attention. Heeding the "growing flocks of aviators" that skirted the Santa Monica Mountains in search of the airport, he painted the name "Pacific Palisades" and a directional arrow in bold black and orange on the station's roof to point the way to Clover Field. For this gesture, Sauer received an official commendation from the Guggenheim Foundation.

Publicity now focussed on the new highway and the advantages of living along this scenic and convenient route. Press releases pointed out that UCLA, the projected Occidental College campus, the Mandeville Canyon Botanic Gardens, the new Los Angeles Athletic Club golf course (Riviera), and the Uplifters Club were all located within minutes of Pacific Palisades.

Local businessmen jumped on the bandwagon and backed several controversial expansionist schemes, including the extension of Reseda Boulevard over the mountains from the San Fernando Valley to Pacific Palisades, a three-mile breakwater running parallel with the coast from downtown Santa Monica to Santa Ynez Canyon, and a viaduct over Santa Monica Canyon. The concept of a viaduct to provide a convenient connection between Pacific Palisades and Santa Monica had been proposed first by Abbot Kinney and was revived at this time by business people in both communities. Leslie Storrs of the Santa Monica Planning Com-

Plan for the proposed breakwater that appeared in *The Palisadian*.

Will Rogers, Jr., Jim, Betty Rogers, Mary, and Will Rogers with Sarah, the pet calf, in the old weekend cabin, about 1927. *Courtesy, Will Rogers State Historic Park*

mission remarked:

It requires very little imagination to vision a series of viaducts from Inspiration Point and the Huntington Palisades to Twenty-sixth Street at the California Riviera. . . . The economic factor is, after all, the determining one, and it is obvious that the construction of the viaducts will make for a desirable movement of money within the Bay District.

Several private developments were also linked with the completion of Beverly Boulevard. Perhaps the earliest was the Will Rogers ranch on the western slopes of Rustic Canyon. Rogers had purchased his first acreage in 1923 from Alphonzo Bell, but the family continued to make their home in Beverly Hills and used a small cabin on the property for weekends. Gradually Rogers acquired a total of 224 acres; he built a barn and polo field and began enlarging and improving the house.

In 1926 Will announced that he and his family would make the ranch their permanent home and that he would move his world-wide base of operations to Pacific Palisades. His crews accordingly went to work on a six-mile system of roads, five miles of bridle paths, and a nine-hole golf course.

The family became a part of the community.

Rogers and his sons, Bill (Will, Jr.) and Jim, played polo regularly at the Uplifters and at Riviera and participated in the equestrian events at the Methodist playing field. Occasionally Mrs. Rogers and their daughter, Mary, would join them, all staying on for dinner and sociability. Will was also a favorite patron at Ballantyne's Restaurant in Santa Monica Canyon, where he ordered crisp-fried ham, and from time to time stopped off at Doc Law's drug store for a soft drink and conversation.

The Rogers' Rustic Canyon neighbors to the south were Ralph Dallugge and his wife, Margarita, whose family, the Guirados, owned ranches in the Montebello area and oil-producing land at Santa Fe Springs. The Dallugges purchased eighty-five acres adjacent to the Uplifters in 1924 and built a sprawling log-faced "hunting lodge," which provided ample room for their seven children. It was decorated with Indian rugs and handsome rustic furniture, hand-crafted on the premises, using the native woods, sycamore and redwood. The fence surrounding the property was built of beer barrel staves imported from Mexico.

Originally this was intended to be a weekend and vacation retreat, but their permanent home, planned

Above, Will Rogers' original home in Rustic Canyon. Later it was enlarged and enhanced. The grounds were landscaped; roads and pathways were built in the surrounding hills. Will had his own polo field and constructed a small golf course for the pleasure of his friends. *Young Collection*

Below right, Will Rogers practicing one of his favorite sports—roping. *Swarzwald/Patterson Collection.*

Below left, Will reviewing his daily newspaper column, written at the ranch. *Young Collection*

115

Above, Mrs. Margarita Dallugge's bedroom was furnished with a handmade sycamore bed and chest, Indian rugs and baskets, following the rustic theme of the entire house. *Below,* the home as it appeared in the 1920s, the branches of the tree festooned with bird cages. *Courtesy the Dallugge family* and *Diane Phillips*

for the mesa to the west, was never built. Ralph Dallugge took great pride in his ranch and entertained hosts of celebrities, including William Jennings Bryan and members of the movie colony. He planted a large orchard of avocados, cherimoyas, and sapotes in the canyon, and an even wider variety of fruits on the western mesa. The area around the house was landscaped with conifers, shrubs, and ferns, and a concrete replica of Yosemite Falls was built on the steep western wall of the canyon. At night, hidden music and colored lights provided a dramatic *son et lumiere* display for his guests.

Plans for another lavish estate were announced in August, 1925, by millionaire art collector Adolph Bernheimer, who had made his fortune in the Pacific silk trade. He had purchased eight acres of land at the far western end of Pacific Palisades from the Methodists for $100,000, a parcel that included the highest point along the immediate coastline and six hundred feet of Beverly Boulevard frontage. Previously this site had been used as a mule camp for highway construction crews. Now, in a leap from rags to riches, it was to be transformed into a $3,500,000 Japanese showplace, exceeding in size and concept the Bernheimer brothers' famous Oriental gardens in Hollywood.

Adolph Bernheimer had studied sites here and in San Francisco before choosing Pacific Palisades —attracted by the natural beauty of the setting and by the religious and educational ideals of the community. He engaged a New York architect to draw the plans and built a summer house to use as headquarters until the estate was finished.

Opposite the Bernheimer property, the new Beverly Pacific subdivision was also opened in 1925 and attracted some attention during the building and heyday of the gardens. Sales, however, were slow; only one or two homes were actually constructed during the first year. By then it was becoming apparent that the succession of new subdivisions from Westwood to the sea was rendering choice lots in and around Pacific Palisades a glut on the market.

For a time the boom seemed only to be slackening. In reality the beautiful dream was coming to an end for the Pacific Palisades Association and for Dr. Scott. An article in the January, 1927, issue of the *Progress* announced simply that an election had been held and a new administration was taking charge. Scott resigned as president of the Association, ostensibly to devote himself to the land sale effort, and was replaced by wholesale nurseryman Walter Armacost. To accomplish the reorganization, a finance committee was formed, with R.C. Gillis, Dr. Lewis T. Guild, and Armacost as members, and A.M. Chaffey as chairman. Dr. Oren B. Waite was appointed vice-president and business manager.

The financial pinch dated back to mid-1924, when property sales began to slump, even as carrying

The Bernheimer residence and gardens, ca. 1926. *P.P.H.S. Collection*

Bernheimer Residence
Pacific Palisades Calif.   Santa Monica Bay

BERNHEIMER GARDEN

Japanese Garden
eimer Residence

Sacred Ox and Minister

Bernheimer Residence
Pacific Palisades

118

Beautiful Waterfall
at Bernheimer Japanese Gardens

Temple of Heaven
and Shrines of Nikko

Bernheimer
Japanese Garden

costs and development expenses continued. Records show that land sales totalled $1,088,000 during the first half of 1924, fell to $580,000 during the last half, and to a total of $250,000 in 1925 and 1926. The coup de grace was administered by the purchase of Huntington Palisades in 1926, which increased the bonded indebtedness from $808,000 at the end of 1925 to $3,500,000 on April 1, 1928, and jeopardized the million-dollar improvement program.

During this time, Dr. Scott frequently sought advice and help from his friend, Robert Gillis. When liquidation of the Association's assets seemed inevitable, Gillis agreed to take over the property, pay the bills, continue the development program, and make cash payments of $25,000 a year to the Association as a replacement for lost fees from the leaseholders. The Pacific Land Corporation, an independent entity, was set up for this purpose.

The Association was permitted to retain the institutional land and all structures in Temescal Canyon, fifteen acres on the western mesa for permanent educational buildings, five hundred feet of beach at the mouth of Temescal Canyon, an adjacent site for a clubhouse or bathhouse, and a few miscellaneous lots. Gillis also offered to contribute property on Via de la Paz to be used for a new church.

Meanwhile, the Methodist Church had responded to the crisis by transferring Dr. Scott to a church in Hawaii — a move the family was reluctant to make,

with six children to educate and the eldest ready for college. Scott decided instead to go into real estate as a broker, encouraged by the warm personal relationships he had established with Gillis, Alphonzo Bell, and the Janss brothers. In Westwood, a Janss development, lots were selling in one new tract after another, while other subdivisions languished.

Dr. Scott was successful in his new profession, putting together the sale of a large piece of beach frontage to Will Rogers and negotiating the sale of a site for the Bel-Air Bay Club to Bell. As the Depression deepened, Scott's friendships with Will Rogers and R.C. Gillis grew in significance. He relied increasingly on Gillis for advice on business matters and often visited Will Rogers at his ranch, valuing his philosophy and his homespun brand of humor. In later years, Scott became a close friend and admirer of Dr. Ernest Holmes, founder of the Church of Religious Science, and contributed articles to the *Science of Mind* magazine.

The Scotts moved closer to the city in the early thirties and for a time had a large home on Westmoreland Avenue. When their children were grown, the Scotts continued to live by their Christian ideals and shared their house with young people in need. Ironically, before Dr. Scott died in 1952, his life completed its circle. He spent his last days in the same Methodist hospital where several of his children had been born, and felt he had come home again.

View looking east on Beverly (Sunset) Boulevard in the late 1920s, with the new Castellammare Mesa subdivision on the left and Bernheimer Gardens on the right. *Courtesy Huntington Library*

10

ALPHONZO E. BELL

A remarkable chain of developments along the fringe of the Santa Monica Mountains — Bel-Air, California Riviera, Bel-Air Bay Club, and Castellammare — all grew from the vision of one man, Alphonzo Bell. Today each retains its distinctive character and bears the unmistakable hallmark of prestige.

Bell's dream began to take shape in 1922 when he acquired title to 1,760 acres in Bel-Air and began to develop it in his own fashion. A few months later, on February 5, 1923, he and several other men formed the Los Angeles Mountain Park Company and purchased 22,000 acres from the Santa Monica Mountain Park Company (owned by Robert C. Gillis and Arthur H. Fleming) and the Santa Monica Land and Water Company (owned by Gillis) at a price of $5,400,000, or $250 an acre — giving Bell a princely expanse of scenically beautiful mountain property that extended from Bel-Air to the sea.

Bell had much in common with the founding fathers of Pacific Palisades, who combined a strict moral and religious background with a worldly appreciation of land and money. Born in Los Angeles in 1875 of Scottish, Irish, and English ancestry, Bell was a staunch Presbyterian; he believed in a literal observance of the Sabbath and abhorred both liquor and gambling. He was one of the first graduates of Occidental College and spent two years at San Anselmo Theological Seminary, a Presbyterian school.

According to Bell's biographer, John Pohlmann, Bell was essentially too shy for the amount of public speaking required by the ministry. However, he may also have been lured away from the pulpit by his zeal for tennis and his interest in real estate. He rapidly reached local championship ranks in tennis and met his future wife, Minnewa Shoemaker, on the tennis courts. In 1902 they were married and six years later moved to Santa Fe Springs, where Bell had purchased land.

The first traces of oil were found on the property by

Bell himself in 1904, but it was not until after World War I, when he was on the brink of bankruptcy, that the oil companies began to drill. After the first well began production in 1921, he was financially secure, receiving royalty checks of from $20,000 to $300,000 a month.

The family moved abruptly in 1922 when a fire in a nearby oil well briefly threatened their home, and they stayed temporarily with their three children at the Beverly Hills Hotel. Bell negotiated the purchase of the Bel-Air property the same year, organized the Los Angeles Mountain Park Company in 1923, and

Alphonzo E. Bell, *Courtesy UCLA Special Collections*

the following year took his wife and children on their first trip to Europe. Names which appealed to Mrs. Bell as they toured the Mediterranean coastline in their chauffeur-driven Rolls Royce soon graced the street signs in Bel-Air and in Bell's other developments.

Bel-Air was designed with meticulous care and set an example for future subdivisions. Handsome rock walls and choice foliage lined the roads, which wound over the hillsides in graceful curves. A championship golf course and Spanish-style clubhouse were finished in 1924, as were stables and riding trails. Bell built his own home, Capo di Monte, atop the highest hill and surrounded it with elaborately terraced gardens.

Along the way Bell assembled a tightly knit team, with Wilkie Woodard as engineer, Mark Daniels as landscape architect, and Frank Meline as sales agent. Lot sales tended to lag, however, as Bell at first forbade his agents to transact business on Sundays or to sell to motion picture people — a move that incurred the wrath of William Randolph Hearst and his newspapers, in the light of Hearst's relationship with Marion Davies.

Bell viewed himself as an idealist. When he acquired his mountainous domain, he let it be known that he considered his millions a public trust. His goal was to turn the hills, covered with native growth and rich with game, into the finest residential district in the world. Every tree was studied, every road laid out with care, and a review board was set up to govern the choice of architecture. He thereby conveyed the impression that selling property at a profit was a side issue.

While work was progressing on Bel-Air, chance played a role in the development of the Riviera. For years the Los Angeles Athletic Club had been searching for a country home for its members, similar to the Uplifters Ranch, but with sufficient space for a golf course and other sports. In 1923 they discovered the perfect spot, just over the hill from the Uplifters, in neighboring Santa Monica Canyon. Three plots totaling 640 acres were available — 200 acres in the canyon and 440 acres on the mesa to the west, all part of Alphonzo Bell's recent purchase.

Bell was enthusiastic. Not only would such a facility meet his high standards, but it would promote sales of the adjoining property. He approached Frank Garbutt, the guiding light of the LAAC, with an offer of free land in exchange for developing the course. The two saw eye-to-eye. Garbutt, William May Garland, and E.P. Giffin of the LAAC worked with Bell and Gillis to arrange the $2,200,000 deal.

Real estate agent John A. Vaughan agreed to assemble a syndicate, pay off the bonds, subdivide and sell the residential property, and donate the canyon site plus ten acres on the mesa to the LAAC for a golf course. The Riviera tract would be an exclusive community with European charm, its Mediterranean-style estates insulated against the ugliness of the commercial world.

Formation of the syndicate was completed in 1925, with financial aid from Bell and the LAAC, and by December tractors began clearing the dense foliage. Garbutt chose George C. Thomas Jr., who had recently completed the Bel-Air course, to design the best possible layout on the rough terrain. The

Frank Meline's California Riviera subdivision, ca. 1927. The panorama, *below,* faces north from a vantage point near Beverly (Sunset) Boulevard and Napoli Drive, with the tract office and Robert Gillis's lemon grove on the right. *Above,* a close-up of the tract office. *Both, courtesy Huntington Library*

Above, an aerial panorama of the Riviera Country Club and the California Riviera subdivision, showing large Mediterranean-style homes being built among the lemon trees. *Courtesy Spence Collection/UCLA*

Left, a similar view facing southeast from the hillside, in the vicinity of Casale Drive. *Courtesy Huntington Library*

picturesque oaks and sycamores were preserved wherever possible and more trees were planted; soil was brought in from the San Fernando Valley to contour the fairways; and the famous barranca (stream bed) was preserved to form a natural hazard. When play began in 1927, the proudly named Riviera Country Club boasted the costliest eighteen-hole course in the world.

A massive, Spanish-style clubhouse, designed by J. Bernard Richards of Santa Monica, was placed atop the mesa where it offered magnificent views of the course, canyon, and ocean. By this time the LAAC had acquired 243 acres in the canyon and 47 acres on the mesa at a cost of $264,000, plus an outlay of $651,157.91 for construction of the golf course, service structures, and partially completed clubhouse. Visiting dignitaries were lavish with their praise, calling the course "The Pine Valley of the West Coast" and the clubhouse "The Grand Hotel of Golf."

Extensive equestrian facilities were added, beginning in 1928, and eventually included four polo fields, training tracks, a steeplechase course, stables for 350 horses, grandstands capable of seating five thousand spectators, and fifty miles of riding trails reaching up into the hills.

From its beginning, the Riviera Country Club attracted both motion picture personalities and socialites. Mary Pickford and Douglas Fairbanks donated the first trophies and played golf as well. When the polo fields were opened, supplementing those already in use at the Uplifters Ranch and at Will Rogers', Pacific Palisades became a mecca for golfing buffs, the international polo set, and aspiring equestrians of every age.

Reflecting the wide array of luxury properties on the market and the real estate slump which began in the mid-twenties, lot sales moved slowly. Frank Meline, Bell's first sales agent at Bel-Air, brought his company in to promote business and built a tract office on the property. His firm assumed responsibility for the LAAC property and for the California Riviera, while Vaughan promoted an adjacent tract to the southwest named the Vaughan Riviera.

The next venture which was at least influenced by Bell was Castellammare, located on the steep coastal slopes west of Santa Ynez Canyon. The announcement was made in mid-1925 by the actual developer, the Frank Meline Company, who held title to the property and formed a syndicate to attract investors. The offer was oversubscribed in less than thirty days, and by August the project was ready to go. On October 4, the *Times* advertised the opening of the tract and instructed the untraveled reader to pronounce the word correctly — "Cás/tel/la/máh/rey," meaning "Castle by the Sea."

Today, the original Castellammare (di Stabia) is a small Italian port and unpretentious thermal resort

A portion of the Castellammare business block, the highway pedestrian overpass, and the bus that provided transportation for the handful of residents. *Courtesy Huntington Library*

a few miles south of Naples. In Roman times, however, it was quite grand and rivaled Pompeii, with Greek and Roman villas scattered over the hillsides, facing out over the blue waters of the bay. The town was destroyed in the eruption of Vesuvius in 79 A.D., but it was rebuilt and regained its popularity as a watering place.

Meline's look-alike community proved expensive, as development of the steep terrain cost $10,000 a lot. Roadways, staircases, and a highway overpass to the 700-foot private beach — all were built of heavy cement to withstand erosion. Sales were sporadic, but by May, 1926, a second unit (on the mesas to the north and northeast) had been added, and by the end of 1927 foundations had been laid for twelve homes.

Although lots sold for as little as $3,500, most purchasers were affluent and planned large estates. Conditions set by Meline required homes to be built in the Italian Renaissance tradition, "patterned after the old Castellammare style of architecture in vogue along the Mediterranean." As part of the tract, a Mediterranean-style commercial building was constructed at the base of the hill, near the overpass; at various times it housed a drug store, a cleaning establishment, and a succession of restaurants. The dining room in the tower had an ocean view and was popular with banquet groups. The business block was also the terminus for the bus line, which had so few passengers that it was virtually a taxi service.

The first home to be built was the Villa Leon, truly a "castle by the sea." Even today it remains the most visible landmark along the Palisades-Malibu coastline, and is often mistaken for its tucked-away

neighbor, the Getty Museum. The builder, Leon Kauffman, was of Austrian descent. He migrated to the United States in the late 1890s, arriving in Washington state, and traveled around the West before settling in Los Angeles with his wife, Clemence, a native Californian of French descent. He began buying sheepskins to use in manufacturing wool and set up a processing plant in Vernon.

The Kauffmans traveled widely and accumulated a valuable collection of art and furniture. When Castellammare was platted, they purchased the entire Castle Rock plot of six lots and began planning a home that would serve as a showcase for their treasures and provide a weekend retreat near the sea. In the process, their concept grew in scope, and resulted in the thirty-five room Villa Leon which became their permanent home.

Kenneth McDonald, architect of the Flood mansion in San Francisco, and contractor H.W. Baum collaborated on the project from 1926 to 1928, employing the finest artisans and materials. The exterior was of reinforced concrete, faced with plaster and artificial stone; the art work and statuary were created by E. Merril Owens; and the ornamental iron work, which used the ram's head motif as a symbol of the wool business, was by James C. Kubic. *Architectural Digest* featured the home in 1928, showing such interior details as the Italian marble entrance hall with its circular staircase and the living room with its frescoed ceilings, carved paneling, and "echo" pipe organ.

The landscaping plan included formal gardens around the Villa itself and an elaborate Chinese garden on the slope between the home and the coast highway. There were bonsai trees, walks, pavilions,

Above, a dramatic view of the coastline, facing southeast from Castellammare, with the letters of the promotional sign silhouetted against the waters of the bay. *Courtesy Huntington Library*

Below, the portals of the Villa Leon, as seen from the curve of Porto Marina Drive. *Swarzwald/Patterson Collection*

waterways with miniature boats, and a collection of rare birds in round lacquer cages. Today, due to landslides, this is only a memory.

The Kauffman family occupied the Villa from 1928 to 1935. During this time, their daughter, Lorraine, was married, and their son, Lazare, was in the East, attending Harvard Law School. Clemence lived only five years after they moved to Castellammare, and Leon himself died two years later, in 1935. Thereafter, the premises were maintained by caretakers until the estate was settled in 1952.

The completion of Beverly Boulevard from Los Angeles to the sea in 1926 made Castellammare more accessible and triggered work on several other new developments. By August of that year, Bell's hydraulic machinery was at work in Santa Ynez Canyon, moving 122,000 cubic yards of earth to make way for a 100-foot-wide highway and storm drain and creating buildable lots along the right-of-way. The earth-moving also left a depression at the bottom of the canyon which filled with water and became a man-made lake.

Two months later, the Los Angeles Mountain Park Company sold 847 acres in Santa Ynez Canyon to Judge Arthur A. Weber and George W. Ley for a price in excess of $4 million. They immediately subdivided the western ridge and

The use of hydraulic equipment in Santa Ynez Canyon to prepare the way for Beverly (Sunset) Boulevard and future development. *Courtesy Huntington Library*

created the prestigious Miramar Estates on a series of natural terraces. George Stiles, manager of the tract, announced construction of several large homes, one of which was to be Weber's own. Mark Daniels, landscape architect for both Bell and the Pacific Palisades Association, was engaged by the Meline Company, agents for the subdivision, to direct the landscaping.

The promotional activities at Miramar Estates garnered widespread publicity on the real estate pages of the Sunday newspapers. A storybook version of the romance of the original ranchos was accompanied by a description of the Miramar's superb location at the ocean terminus of Beverly Boulevard: "Where the Declining Sun Gilds the Foothills with Glowing Topaz Hues."

As part of the development, a fine restaurant, the Casa Miramar, was built on several descending levels, each offering a spectacular view. It was readily accessible to the city via the new busline and offered lunch, tea, and dinner at modest prices. More than one prospective buyer was converted by the developers' hospitality and the scenic outlook.

The real publicity coup, however, was the construction of the *Los Angeles Times* Demonstration Home on a challenging hillside lot. Each week, pictures and text delineated the process in detail for prospective home-builders, using the project as a model of design, quality of construction, and up-to-date planning.

Readers were urged to visit Miramar Estates and consult with the experts, architect Mark Daniels and builder George Ley. Daniels was described as a man of many talents — an engineer who had designed railroad bridges in the northwest, one of the developers of Atascadero and Pebble Beach, and landscape engineer for the National Park Service under Franklin K. Lane.

Grading for the house began in September, 1926. By November, framing and plumbing were well under way, and by Christmas time, plaster was being applied. A good-natured race between house-builders and road-builders was an incentive to both crews. The palatial structure was opened to the public on April 29, 1928, complete in every detail. The furniture was copied from Spanish museum pieces and made locally by Spanish craftsmen. Bertha Coler of Pacific Palisades, who supplied the drapes, lamps, and antiques, was singled out for special praise; her fabrics — mainly tapestries and brocades — were imported and of unique design.

Marion Rouzie, the Uplifters' organist, played the great pipe organ as visitors explored the mansion. They were most impressed with the cloistered patios and the billiard room, which had a panoramic view of the coastline through floor-length windows. This mode of architecture, according to Daniels, was

Above, a gathering of Uplifters and other equestrians at the opening of Miramar Estates. The Casa Miramar, housing a restaurant, display room, and tract office, follows the contour of the hill beyond. *Below left,* the sign at the entrance. Adelbert Bartlett, photographer. *Courtesy Carolyn Bartlett Farnham*

Below right, the interior of the restaurant. *Courtesy Esther Malcolmson*

Above, Mary Pickford presided at the ceremonial ground-breaking for new facilities at the California Botanic Garden. *Clearwater Collection*

Below, an aerial view looking north up Mandeville Canyon, showing the plantings of the botanical gardens at the mouth of the canyon and the development of Westridge Road, *on the left. Courtesy UCLA|Spence|Collection*

ideally suited to the California coast, its climate and surroundings. In this land of little wind and balmy weather, the out-of-doors should be seen and enjoyed.

At the same time as Castellammare and Miramar Estates were being developed, Frank Meline chose Los Liones Canyon, situated in between, as a site for his own estate. The plan did not survive the depression of the thirties, but the shrubs and trees he planted enhance the beauty of the winding canyon approach to Castellammare even today.

Bell's next project was a botanical garden and a related subdivision in lower Mandeville Canyon. The announcement was made in February, 1927, with Bell, R.C. Gillis, and Henry O'Melveny listed among the organizers. The resulting Garden Foundation, sponsor of the California Botanic Garden, acquired 3,500 acres from the Los Angeles Mountain Park Company and announced the issuance of $2,500,000 in bonds. Out of the total acreage, 2,200 would be sold for residences, the profits to be held in trust for the gardens.

Dr. E.D. Merrill, dean of the College of Agriculture of the University of California was named director general of the project, and an expedition was financed to bring home specimens from the wilds of French Indo-China. This and other such

The Times Demonstration Home, later the residence of Marta and Lion Feuchtwanger.
Courtesy Marta Feuchtwanger

ventures were expected to supply materials to an experimental laboratory on the premises. The gardens thus were planned both as a tourist attraction and as a world-renowned educational center, where the public could obtain advice on seeds and plants and be given rare species judged suitable for local gardens.

By late summer 115,000 specimens had been obtained, mostly in the form of donations, from major collections here and in Europe, and the work of identifying them and preparing them for display began. Eventually 200,000 specimens were acquired. Research was also conducted on fire-retardant plants, using the hilltop acreage devoted to fire-breaks.

There were several newsworthy problems. During fire season the botanical gardens and the Los Angeles Mountain Park Company posted their own guards to patrol the hills and worked out their own plans for fire protection. Deer were so numerous that deer repellent was necessary to protect the new trees, and bird muzzles were suggested when a marauding kingfisher gobbled up all of the goldfish from the ponds.

Progress was slow, since funds from the sale of residential property were necessary to support the gardens. In July, 1928, President Remsen Bird of Occidental College spoke at the dedication and announced that 140 acres had now been deeded to the gardens. He urged the accelerated sale of homesites and solicited private contributions for the required buildings.

Thousands of visitors came to see the wild-flower exhibits and lingered to explore the miles of paths. They crossed the stream on a rustic bridge and found their way to the Forest of Fame and to the Devil's Garden with its collection of "oddities." A grove of sacred trees was planned, including bo trees from India and frankincense-yielding balsams. Thriving eucalyptus trees were given to UCLA to form a grove on the new campus.

Interest in the botanical gardens was fortified by the prospect of bringing Occidental College to nearby Brentwood. As a member of the Occidental College Board of Trustees and chairman of its Grounds and Building Committee, Bell offered to give the college 1,000 acres of land. Departing from precedent, he proposed that 150 acres would be used

Promotional ad for Castellammare, printed in the *Los Angeles Times* on Sunday, October 4, 1925.

for a new men's college, to be called the "Chapel Hill" campus, while the women's college would remain in Eagle Rock. The remaining 850 acres would be sold by the Los Angeles Mountain Park Company, the profits to accrue to both campuses. The chosen site was located between Kenter and Boheme Canyons — the buildings on the heights and the athletic field below. The residential area was to be called "Tiger Tail Estates."

The idea of separating the sexes had been suggested when the Eagle Rock campus was new, but at this point it was strongly opposed by both students and faculty. Ultimately, the trustees decided that $250,000 worth of land must be sold before any definite commitments could be made. The move was still being considered in 1929, when the whole scheme collapsed, and the dissension created by Bell's good intentions served to retard progress at the parent campus itself.

Another elaborate plan surfaced in 1927-28, when Bell purchased land from the Methodists and established the Bel-Air Bay Club on thirty-one acres of oak-covered hillside and adjoining beachfront east of Santa Ynez Canyon. The new complex was intended to complement the facilities offered by the

Bel-Air Country Club, its Spanish-style architecture and gracious atmosphere similarly harking back to the days of the *rancheros,* a favorite theme for sub-division ballyhoo.

The story of this favored bit of coastline was presented to prospective members in an embossed, leather-bound promotional volume, *Bel-Air Bay: A Country Place by the Sea* by Edward F. O'Day, with illustrations in pastel-toned water colors. O'Day's version of history led back in time "over hills as sweetly curved as the meanderings of Spanish romance, down purple canyons heavy with the haze of legendry, past springs of fancy, over streams of enchantment, to the white strand of the crescent beach where the breezes of Old Pacific carry from mysterious horizons the salty memories of Cabrillo and Vizcaino."

O'Day either unearthed or concocted tales of "love and hate, gaiety and sudden death, lutes and litanies, ghosts and hidden treasure — aye, and the gallows tree." Not forgetting the ladies, he added, some were "fair and chaste, others fair but frail. In the story of Bel-Air theirs is a charming, tender, sad participation" — a tantalizing observation.

In a more practical vein, members were offered

the advantages of "a city home, a country club, a mountain cottage, and a bathing lodge." Grading began in 1927, but actual construction was delayed until 1929 due to legal disputes over ownership of the beach, which had been artificially widened by state-installed groins.

Surrounding the club, sixty-seven "cottage" sites were available for purchase by members of the club; they varied in size, but all were situated to provide ocean or mountain views. Mediterranean architecture was recommended and tile roofs were required. The first home in the tract was built by A.F. Price in 1929-30, and was designed by the famous black architect, Paul Williams. By the time it was completed the Depression had struck and the single large structure stood on the hillside in bleak and isolated glory for many years. Later the house was sold to Noel Marshall Seeburg, the juke-box king, who added an indoor swimming pool and other embellishments.

O'Day's fanciful panegyric to the charms of the Bel-Air Bay Club failed to mention the legends associated with Burning Canyon, between Bernheimer Gardens and the clubhouse. This natural phenomenon had been known to the early settlers and was a favorite landmark in the 1920s. Mysteriously, it not only emitted sulfurous odors, it also gave off a slender cloud of steam by day and an ominous reddish glow at night.

Bell's engineer, Wilkie Woodard, wrote in *The Palisadian* in 1929 that Burning Canyon had been avoided by the Indians and Spanish alike as one of the abodes of the Evil Spirit. Offering his own explanation, unconfirmed by geologists, he observed that Bernheimer's hilltop to the west was "thoroughly calcined" and theorized that in ages gone by, the mountain had burned "until the fire had eaten its way through the hill and was burning in the canyon."

Be that as it may, the Bel-Air Bay Club held its informal opening on March 24, 1930, and formal ceremonies that summer. The clubhouse and grounds, designed by architect Elmer Grey and landscape architect Mark Daniels, occupied seven acres, the Mediterranean-style building standing ninety feet above the sea and utilizing elevators and a tunnel under the highway to give access to the private beach. Planned but never built were a "second beach" halfway up the hill, a large salt-water swimming pool, stables, and tennis courts.

Membership in the Bel-Air Bay Club was limited to six hundred, each member to be part-owner of the club and the club grounds. Bell, however, held the mortgage, set the tone, and dominated the board meetings. In deference to his wishes, members were forbidden to bring flasks of liquor to club parties during Prohibition, as was customary elsewhere, and those who broke the rule were subject to suspension.

Bell's optimism with regard to the future of his land reached its zenith in 1927. Even as he was laying the foundation for the Bel-Air Bay Club, Bell was outlining new ventures — a Spanish village at the mouth of Santa Ynez Canyon, a complex of connecting roads in the hills, even a hilltop observatory at the head of Santa Ynez Canyon — plans given impetus in 1924 by the completion of the first portion of Mulholland Drive along the crest of the Santa Monica Mountains.

With a wave of his hand, Bell told reporters that everything they could see from the shoreline at Santa Monica would one day be developed — from Mulholland and the Topanga divide to the sea —and that no expense would be spared. He seemed little aware that the precarious state of the economy and the community's reaction to some of his tactics would make his plans increasingly vulnerable.

The "Tiderock," a small shop on the beach selling shells and other tourist items in the early 1920s. Later this was the site of the Bel-Air Bay Club. *Courtesy Angelina Marquez Olivera*

Above, the Bel-Air Bay Club, shortly after its completion in 1930, showing the main clubhouse and the facilities on the beach. *Courtesy Huntington Library*

Lower left, the Bel-Air Bay Club tract plan from the promotional brochure. The street names and the design of the club were subsequently changed. *PPHS Collection*

Lower right, Sunday afternoon at the cabanas, with a front view of the main clubhouse. *Courtesy Huntington Library*

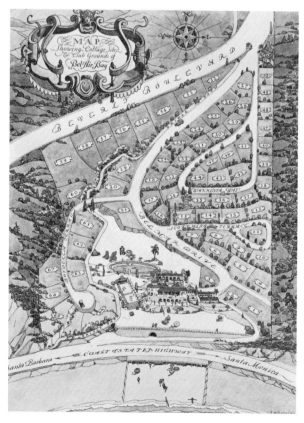

11

THE CEMENT CONTROVERSY

The first act in the "tragedy of Alphonzo Bell" was, for the most part, played out in the mountainous terrain behind Pacific Palisades. As John Pohlmann tells the story, the scenario began in 1925, when Joe Gilliland, Bell's engineering and mining consultant, discovered a rich limestone deposit on Bell's land and saw the potential for the manufacture of cement. No word of this discovery, however, reached the public until 1928. At that time Bell petitioned the Los Angeles Planning Commission to grant a variance in zoning and the battle began.

The first business deal was made on March 3, 1928, when the Los Angeles Mountain Park Company contracted with Chapin A. Day, operator of a large limestone quarry in Utah, and Samuel W. Traylor, an industrialist from Allentown, Pennsylvania, to mine and process various rock deposits on its landholdings in the Santa Monica Mountains. On this, as well as all future matters, Bell was represented legally by Eugene Overton of the firm of Overton, Lyman, and Plumb.

The news reached Pacific Palisades just as the first issue of the new weekly *Palisadian* appeared on subscribers' doorsteps, and the recently arrived editor, Telford Work, found himself in a hornets' nest of controversy. The lines between opposing forces were rapidly drawn and changed but little over the years. For a time Work's fledgling newspaper gave Bell his only journalistic support in the Los Angeles area.

To start the ball rolling, Bell petitioned the Los Angeles City Council Planning Committee for special permits for two separate operations — a quarry and a cement plant — and asked for rezoning of 497 of his remaining 11,000 acres of land. The projected quarry site itself, occupying 25 acres, was located in remote Traylor Canyon, three airline miles inland from the ocean, between Santa Ynez and Temescal canyons. There, a jagged outcropping of rock was said by Bell's experts to contain one of the "purest and largest" limestone deposits in the country. Alumina shale and silica shale, both necessary

to the production of cement, were also present nearby in large quantities.

It should be noted that the Methodists had operated their own do-it-yourself quarry in Temescal Canyon when Pacific Palisades was founded, and that Bell, at the time of his application, was operating two quarries and a primitive rock crusher in Santa Ynez Canyon. Sandstone, shale, and gravel from the latter sites — 1½ and 3½ miles from the coast — provided material for roads and walls in Bel-Air, Castellammare, and Miramar Estates. Despite regular blasting and the use of heavy trucks, no protests had heretofore been launched, and the residential zoning of Bell's land had been imposed after his existing quarries were already in operation.

The new plan was part of Bell's vision for development of the mountains. He projected building 300 miles of roads over the rough terrain — two transverse routes parallel with Beverly Boulevard and several laterals connecting Beverly Boulevard with Mulholland Drive. He estimated these would cost $30 to 34 million and that by using his own rock and cement, the work could be done more efficiently and economically. Later, the precipitous quarry site itself would be recontoured and integrated into the overall development scheme. Already, Bell's engineers were out in the field, surveying and staking.

The whole concept was presented as a vision of beauty. There were to be small neighborhood commercial centers, equestrian stables, two country clubs, a golf course, and an old-world village at the mouth of Santa Ynez Canyon, with its own beach club and yacht harbor. Over 200 miles of landscaped drives and 180 miles of equestrian trails were planned, utilizing medieval arches where trails and roads intersected. All was to be as handsome as Bell's existing showplace, Bel-Air.

The site chosen for the cement mill was the former goat farm in Las Pulgas Canyon, ominously near Pacific Palisades. Bell promised to house the machinery in an architecturally attractive structure with a landscaped 3/4-mile access road from Beverly

Boulevard, and guaranteed to keep truck traffic to a minimum. Rock would be brought from the quarry by tram and the finished product taken by truck along the coast highway, or by tram to the summit and by truck to the San Fernando Valley beyond. He also suggested that sandstone from the existing quarries could be used in building the breakwater which was being planned by the state to run parallel with the Pacific Palisades coastline.

The loudest opposition came from the Hearst press, growing more and more blatant and emotional as the controversy raged, while a similarly impassioned campaign was waged at a lower pitch by the *Los Angeles Times.* Hearst apparently still rankled over the restrictive nature of the Bel-Air subdivision, while the *Times* was believed to have firm ties to the powerful "cement trust." This group of prominent Angelenos had managed to control cement prices to their advantage and had even contrived to restrict competition from imports.

Locally, where the issues were immediate and personal, both sides offered sound reasons. Sylvia Morrison, representing the Women's Forum and other groups, voiced the concern of many Palisadians over the preservation of the area's natural beauty and of the community's founding values. She noted that the original property had been sold under lease for just such restrictive protection, and that the Huntington property had been purchased at great

cost to prevent the sort of encroachment that Bell's plan represented.

A second group of protestors were major landowners from the affected area, including Harry Sexton who owned property in Las Pulgas Canyon. The most vocal and persistent were the developers and residents of Castellammare and Miramar Estates, particularly Judge Arthur A. Weber and Joseph Schenck. They formed an alliance with Dr. Frank Barham, publisher of Hearst's *Los Angeles Evening Herald,* who owned a magnificent hilltop estate on the eastern rim of Santa Ynez Canyon.

It was ironic that the *Times* Demonstration Home opened that spring, with much advance publicity. The location, they announced, was "chosen from all others because of its faultless view of rolling hills and sweeping prospect of mountains, bay, and coastline." The notion of a quarry and commercial development within view when such expensive lots were up for sale was something less than appealing.

The businessmen of Pacific Palisades were generally sympathetic with Bell's rights and were favorable to the plan, seeing 350 prospective jobs in the offing and hope of more homes at a moderate price. However, they voiced fears that the area would become available only to the wealthy, and asked for assurance that local Caucasians would be employed whenever possible, rather than imported Mexican labor. Offered the opportunity to make a

Hilltop estate of Dr. Frank Barham, publisher of the *Los Angeles Herald* and one of Bell's adversaries in the cement controversy. The home, built on the eastern rim of Santa Ynez Canyon, was destroyed by fire in 1964. Adelbert Bartlett, photographer. *Courtesy Carolyn Bartlett Farnham*

The TRUTH About Bell's Proposed Quarry Location

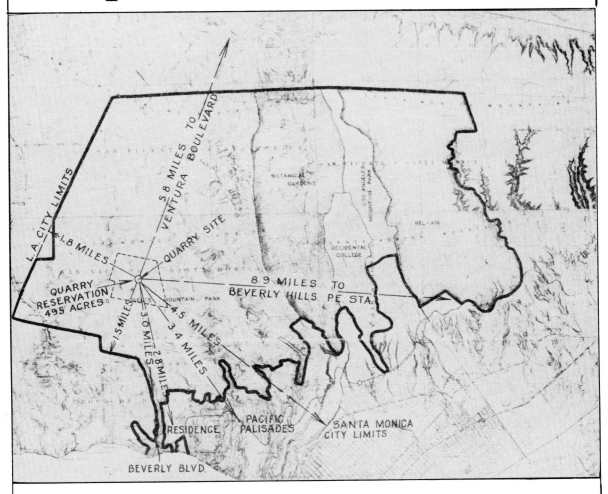

Secluded by Miles of Mountains

Distance of the existing quarry site from nearest property owned by other interests—1.5 miles.

Distance from nearest residence towards ocean—2.8 miles.

Distance from Mr. Bell's projected Italian village at the ocean front and Beverly Boulevard, where "slurry" pipe will emerge—3.5 miles.

Distance from Santa Monica city limits—4.5 miles

Distance from Pacific Palisades business center—3.4 miles. Distance from Pacific Electric Station, Beverly Hills, 8.9 miles.

Distance from Ventura Boulevard in San Fernando Valley, 5.8 miles.

All of these measurements represent air line distances, have been determined scientifically by engineers, and are a matter of record.

It should be added in this connection that the quarry will be TOTALLY HIDDEN for all time in the floor of the canyon 350 feet below the crests of the Santa Ynez-Temescal divide on the east and the Santa Ynez-Topanga divide on the west.

Only One Site Asked

No additional site is required and none will be asked for.

There will be no application for a permit to build a cement plant, as no cement plant is to be built in this district.

The rock quarry and crusher will be located centrally in the 495-acre tract so that they will be entirely surrounded by undeveloped land and the operations will forever be protected from encroaching on or becoming a menace to adjoining lands.

The 495-acre parcel does NOT extend to the crests of the Santa Ynez-Temescal divide and contains no peaks whatsoever.

No portion of the property is visible from any point in the Pacific Palisades.

Property owners of the district who desire to go over the ground in person are invited to phone Santa Monica 31141 or OXford 1175 and horses and guides will be provided without obligation.

LOS ANGELES MOUNTAIN PARK CO.

A typical Bell ad, reprinted from *The Palisadian,* January 18, 1929, in which Bell promises that there will be but a single quarry site and that it will be hidden by "miles of mountains."

What Scares the Little People So?

Why are the little people so scared when brave Capt. Alphonzo Bell leads his forces forward in the battle to make the Santa Monica mountains resemble the No Man's Land of France? Is it the fearsome Captain Alphonzo and his three musketeers that frighten them? Is it the cement tanks, the rock crushers or the dynamite explosions that scare them?

No, gentle reader, 'tis not big Captain Alphonzo and his three musketeers that bring terror to the little people—the homeowners and the humble taxpayers. What terrifies them is an army invisible in this picture but which follows this noble leader. It is an army of golden armored millions, of serried ranks of "grands," of battalions of "centuries," of cohorts of "ducats," of winding lines of "long green." The little people have a right to be scared—but the battle has just begun and the little people are great folks to rally when their homes are in danger.

Cartoon from the December 6, 1929, issue of the *Los Angeles Herald,* showing planning commission chairman Perry Thomas and two other members of the commission in action. *Courtesy California State Library*

personal inspection of the site, William H. Day, president of the Pacific Palisades Improvement League; Telford Work, secretary of the Pacific Palisades Business Council; realtor Tom Gettys; and businessman Jack Sauer made the trip on horseback and gave their approval.

Writing in *The Palisadian*, Work urged citizens to keep cool and evaluate the situation sensibly. This led to a note from an irate reader, "Stop your crawfishing and get off the fence." Promptly, Work came out in support of Bell's plan, but continued to print opposing points of view.

The watchdog civic group, the Pacific Palisades Improvement League, was similarly torn. Adding other community issues to their concerns, those opposed to Bell split off and founded the Pacific Palisades Protective Association. Among their energetic supporters were such community leaders as Sylvia Morrison; real estate agents Gus Martin, W.S. Rothery, and Louis Evans; and an outspoken attorney, Thorwald Siegfried.

Heeding the opposition, Bell withdrew his application shortly before the May 28 hearing. *The Palisadian* took advantage of the lull to interject a few humorous notes. Work wrote a tongue-in-cheek editorial marveling at the amount of free advertising given Pacific Palisades and pointing out that even the hoity-toity *Los Angeles Times* called this the "finest residential area in California." As publicity, he said, the controversy "eclipsed the historic success of Anna Held's milk baths and Godiva's bareback horse rides, or bare Godiva's horseback ride, or whatever it was." Work also noted with amusement that Judge Weber now referred to "our" Pacific Palisades, whereas those same "high hat" Miramar Estates residents prior to the cement conflict had insisted on receiving mail from the Santa Monica Star Route instead of using the Pacific Palisades name and postal delivery service.

Vacationing Jack Sauer sent home a postcard of the Three Brothers, a granite outcropping at Yosemite, and wrote: "The other side of this card shows a wonderful deposit of pure limestone. I intend to start a cement plant at once, but don't tell anyone."

The mood darkened when the plan was revamped and introduced in person by Bell at a Santa Monica Chamber of Commerce meeting in late November. He urged residents to study the new concept and to take company-sponsored trips, on foot or on horseback, to the quarry site to see for themselves, instead of relying on accounts in the *Times* and the *Examiner,* both of which continued to misrepresent the facts as he saw them.

According to Pohlmann, Manchester Boddy of the *Illustrated Daily News* was undecided about the project but after receiving several thousand dollars from Bell, he presented Bell's version in a series of articles and full-page ads. Similar ads were placed by Bell in the Beverly Hills *Citizen News, The Palisadian,* and other community publications to answer specific questions and give his point of view. These three papers and a majority of the suburban weeklies also gave Bell their editorial support. The debate continued for months on the pages of *The Palisadian,* as Work offered his studied opinion that the new industry would provide jobs for local workers and income for the merchants and that adequate safeguards would be provided.

Bell's next move was a request to the city planning commission for a zoning exemption under Section Four of the code. The Pacific Palisades Improvement League voted to look into both sides of the plan and eventually supported it, while the Protective Association stepped into the foreground of the organized opposition.

The new proposal provided that blasting would occur only once or twice a year at the remote quarry and the rock would be processed at the site. A noiseproof, dustproof concrete building, designed in Spanish style and attractively landscaped, would be built in Traylor Canyon by Traylor and Day at a cost of $3 million.

Using a new process, the rock would be pulverized and mixed with water to form a slurry, which would be conveyed by a buried eight-inch pipeline to the mouth of Santa Ynez Canyon, and out along the ocean floor to a single buoy. There, a specially designed tanker, built by Bell, would take on the slurry and carry it to San Pedro Harbor, where a cement mill would be constructed on a suitable industrial site.

Critics warned against setting a precedent that might bring other industries to this jealously guarded scenic and residential area. They feared that the quarry site might be visible from their homes and that the sound of blasting and the pall of dust would be damaging to property values. Bell's good intentions and high business principles were not publicly questioned. Instead, his opponents were apprehensive that Bell might be overruled or superseded in his ownership by others who might install the processing mill or in other ways spoil the land.

The Pacific Land Corporation, the Santa Monica Land and Water Company, and the Pacific Palisades Association — who had millions of dollars in obligations outstanding, and hundreds of lots remaining unsold — lodged a formal protest with the Los Angeles City Council, accompanied by a letter from Robert C. Gillis. With regret, he challenged his friend and former business associate,

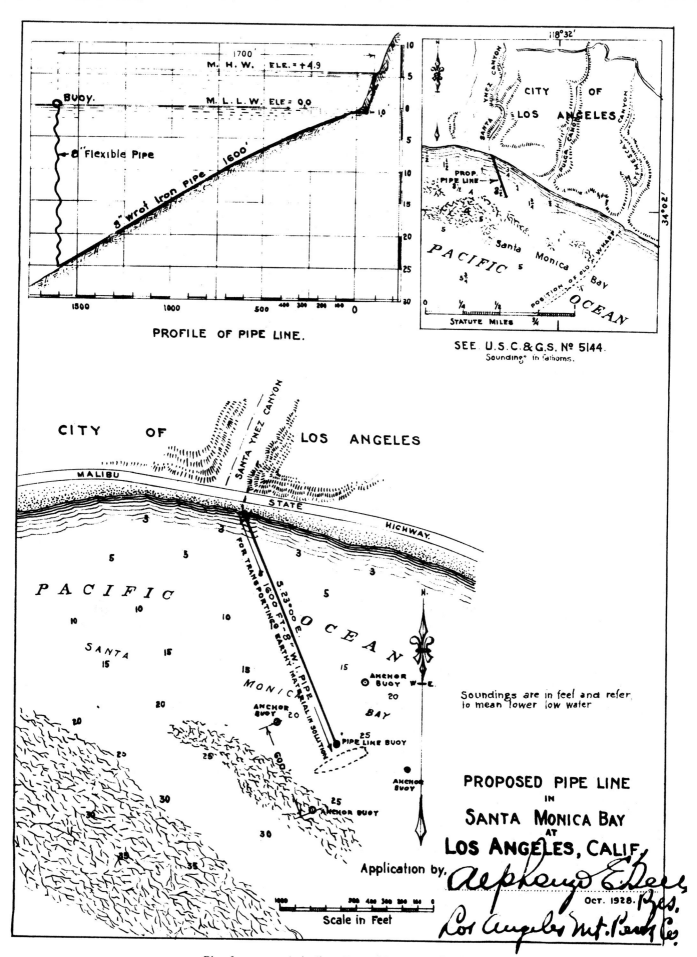

PROFILE OF PIPE LINE.

SEE U.S.C.&G.S. N⁰ 5144.
Soundings in fathoms.

Soundings are in feet and refer
to mean lower low water

PROPOSED PIPE LINE
IN
SANTA MONICA BAY
AT
LOS ANGELES, CALIF.

Application by,

OCT. 1928.

Scale in Feet

Plan for proposed pipeline. *Ernest Marquez Collection*

140

Cartoon by Ewing. Copyright, 1929, *Los Angeles Times.* Reprinted by permission.

stating that "such development would prove a cloud of distrust over residential and educational activities, and in consequence, I am opposed to the opening of this great area to anything suggestive of industrial development."

Raging citywide, the struggle became vituperous and unreasonable. Such notable public figures as the Reverend Bob Shuler and engineer William Mulholland came to Bell's defense, even as new charges appeared in the press and were carried before the commission in a well-financed campaign. Bell tried to counter each overblown charge in his ads. He printed diagrams and photographs of the terrain to exhibit the privacy of the site; he offered severe deed restrictions and even bought out a new stockholder, David Howells of Utah, to assure for himself a controlling interest in the cement operation. Meeting accusations of "slag and slime" on the golden strand, he argued credibly that he would not be apt to pollute his own beaches.

Bell doubtless contributed to his own woes by a poor sense of timing and showmanship, as in December, 1928, when his men surreptitiously laid the pipeline under the coast highway at night. They had obtained last-minute permission from the state, but the stealth of the action, as well as the deed itself, drew fire. Then, on May 22, 1929, Bell hoped to

allay his neighbors' fears by detonating a test blast at the quarry site. Instead, he ordered a truck bearing seismographic monitoring equipment off his property and virtually incited a riot. The *Herald* pictured Bell as a hardened boss:

> Aided by a gang of Mexican quarry workers who went into the fray at the order of Alphonzo Bell himself, henchmen of the Los Angeles Mountain Park Company today forcibly ejected seismologists and blasting experts. . . . F.H. Judson, an elderly scientist . . . was cut severely about the hands as he was thrown from the seat of his automobile and landed on the rock floor of the canyon. Bell, Gilliland, and attorney Eugene Overton directed the attack . . . .

The *News* and *The Palisadian* gave their own low-key version of the incident, stating that the blast of 9,500 pounds of powder sent 70,000 tons of rock sliding down into Santa Ynez Canyon with "a low grunt." The opposition belittled the size of the blast and commented instead on the dust and the noise.

Will Rogers even entered the fray with a cutting parody of the whole succession of events, printed on the front page of the *Los Angeles Times* on January 28, 1929. Rogers, who had a Section Four permit for his stables, led off with a bogus application to construct a garbage-sorting plant at his ranch for the manufacture of fertilizer and to retrieve a product called "slipus." Anticipating the familiar objections, he wrote:

Instead of using trucks, "we have a way to overcome that. We will bring in the garbage by airplane, sort it out on the premises, render it up into fertilizer and then send it out by radio."

As to the class of labor, "instead of having all university or college men . . . the work will be done by the better grade of tourists, who want to exercise but are not notorious enough to get into the golf clubs."

And the odor "has been taken care of. We will use the 'damp' method of treatment. We use cologne. The entire hills and valleys will be saturated with jockey club and lily of the valley."

As for the appearance of the plant, "I guarantee that it will be no attempt at 'early Spanish' or 'late Hollywood,' there will be no architect, so there will be no possible chance for it to be unsightly."

Finally, "I have gone over every phase of the plan with my accomplices and they say (knowing politics as they do) that we can't lose a thing but the friendship of everyone living west of Figueroa street."

The hearings before the planning commission lasted from March until September, with *Examiner* attorney A.T. Sokolow, *Herald* publisher Frank Barham's attorney Arthur Smiley, and the Protective Association's advocate Thorwald Siegfried waging a desperate battle. At the conclusion the commission, by a vote of three to two, gave Bell permission to operate three quarries — for limestone, alumina shale, and silica shale. The opposition promptly took the case to the full city council, where hearings began in January, 1930.

The three members of the planning commission who favored Bell were singled out for attack by the Hearst press. They charged, with inferences of collusion, that commission chairman Perry Thomas and Joe Gilliland were golf partners at the Bel-Air Country Club and that Gilliland had been seen cavorting on the beach at the Bel-Air Bay Club with Thomas, who was scandalously dressed in the bottom half of a pair of women's pajamas. Cartoons appeared showing such antics in the most lurid and damaging light, including a parody of the Bay Club incident in the *Los Angeles Herald* on December 13, 1929. Bell was shown in the full regalia of a nineteenth century French officer, flanked by Thomas in "pajametts," and the other members of the commission dressed in garb indicating various forms of illicit payoff.

The case dragged on and on. In February, 1930, the city council granted the permit, but it was never put in force. The opposition immediately started referendum proceedings and filed an appeal with the state supreme court, where it was scheduled for June.

By this time the Depression had caused the real estate market to collapse and had seriously depleted Bell's finances. He needed cash to pay off his debts. On May 19, 1930, he announced that he had sold all of his holdings except Bel-Air to Eastern interests for $10 million, the largest real estate transaction in Los Angeles history.

The option to buy the property was never exercised, and the controversy faded from view. Then, without warning, early in the morning on February 16, 1931, Bell's men laid an additional segment of pipeline, this time from the highway to a buoy some 150 feet offshore, giving the press another field day. In June a newly elected city council reversed the zoning permit and put an end to Bell's hopes. Two years later Traylor sued the Los Angeles Mountain Park Company for breach of contract and agreed to a settlement in 1934, finally ending the matter six years after negotiations began.

According to Pohlmann, it was regrettable that Bell listened for advice to men whose standards were different from his own. There was no doubt that the cement operation was a profit-making one, for all the advertising puffery, and should be seen in that light. As it was, Bell became embroiled in a dispute which sullied his name, squandered his fortune, and wasted years of his life. Bell was less a businessman than a visionary and promoter, whose talents were best expressed in the rarified atmosphere of Bel-Air and the Riviera. Only his oil interests actually made a profit, and the projected development of the mountains might have shackled him with the greatest white elephant of them all.

After the stock market crash of October, 1929, Bell's debts continued to mount. Fortunately, the discovery of new oil deposits in Santa Fe Springs and in Santa Barbara County made it possible for him to continue his comfortable life style and to devote his energies to the enhancement of Occidental College.

Some degree of retrenchment was also necessary, since high real estate taxes, payments on principal, and interest on $6 million in bonds were too much even for Bell. Thus, in 1938, Webb and Knapp absorbed most of the debt and under the ownership title of Mountain Park Associates took over twelve thousand acres of land. The remaining unbonded land, including almost a mile of beach frontage, was retained by Bell under the name Residential Land Corporation. Plans for the Brentwood campus of Occidental College were abandoned in 1929, and the property was subdivided by the Residential Land Corporation in the late thirties.

Bell's rock deposits paid off handsomely. In October, 1935, the federal Works Progress Administration began quarrying both the sandstone and the high-quality limestone for use on various flood

The Gentle Art of Covering Up

Cartoon from the December 13, 1929, issue of the *Los Angeles Herald. Courtesy California State Library*

View of the quarry in Traylor Canyon today, a short distance from homes in Palisades Highlands. Photograph by Thomas R. Young.

control projects. Ultimately millions of tons were used in reinforcing the banks of the Los Angeles River, San Gabriel River, Ballona Creek, and other watercourses.

The hermetically sealed operation took place behind locked gates, under the supervision of the United States Corps of Engineers for the government and Joe Gilliland for Bell. At its height, three thousand men were employed at wages of $60 to $90 a month. The government also invested more than a million dollars in equipment and provided scores of buses to transport the workmen, most of whom came from other areas. Privately owned cars were parked outside the gates on Sunset Boulevard.

Jedd Fuller, writing in *The Palisadian*, described the middle quarry as a beehive of activity, with cranes, derricks, mammoth shovels, and powerful electric lights for night work. Huge blasting operations, employing more than twenty tons of explosives placed deep in tunnels, from time-to-time caused a "deep roar and a rumbling of the earth," while two hundred trucks carrying five thousand tons of rock a day passed in a steady procession out onto Sunset Boulevard and the coast highway at the rate of forty trucks an hour. Surprisingly, no protests were registered, either over the increased

traffic or over the thumps and thuds from the blasting, and the community was scarcely aware when work was completed and the project closed down, sometime after World War II.

Although the ill-starred cement venture left behind some bitter antagonisms in Pacific Palisades, it did lay the foundation for community pride and advocacy. Future environmental concerns were best voiced by Sylvia Morrison, who took the Bell-sponsored tours of the limestone quarry site — visitors scrambling up sheer slopes on ladders and hiking or riding horseback through the chapparal — and came away thrilled with the natural beauty of the canyons. Taking a cue from Yellowstone National Park, she urged the establishment of a Whitestone National Park in the Santa Monica Mountains, named after the by-now-infamous cliffs.

Currently, Topanga State Park, established in the 1960s, incorporates portions of Santa Ynez and Quarry canyons, but does not include Traylor Canyon itself. It is interesting to note that one of the supporters of a major park in the Santa Monica Mountains was Alphonzo Bell, Jr., who from 1960 to 1977 represented Pacific Palisades and Santa Monica in Washington, D.C., as congressman for the 16th District.

12

THE GREAT DEPRESSION

A vigorous editorial voice was provided for Pacific Palisades by Telford Work and his new weekly newspaper, *The Palisadian,* which made its debut on May 4, 1928. Work was born in Colorado, came to California in 1911, and attended Venice High School, where his father was the first principal. He earned the first journalism degree ever awarded by USC, while his wife, Ada, a native Californian, took her teachers' training on the Vermont campus of UCLA.

After serving in the army in World War I, Work moved with his family to the San Joaquin Valley — first to Parlier, then to Selma — purchasing five local newspapers and founding a small chain. In March, 1926, he was invited by Dr. Charles H. Scott to come to Pacific Palisades as director of public relations for the Pacific Palisades Asssociation, and when the new Huntington Palisades subdivision was put on the market, he became advertising manager for the Santa Monica Land and Water Company as well. In July he took over as editor of

the *Progress,* the Association's monthly house organ. *The Palisadian* was launched two years later with the cooperation of the land company and area advertisers and maintained its solvency through the sterling efforts of the Ladies' Aid of the local Methodist Church, whose members earned bonus money for their organization by selling subscriptions.

By 1928 the community had begun to feel the effects of a lagging economy and tensions were rising. The feud over Alphonzo Bell's cement plant was followed by an equally emotional controversy over management of the landholdings by the real estate interests and the Pacific Palisades Association. Confronting these and other civic issues, Work stated his point of view with characteristic candor.

The era began on a positive note when R.C. Gillis and the Pacific Land Corporation were given a vote of thanks for donating four and a half lots on Via de la Paz for the new Methodist church and for contributing $10,000 to initiate the church building fund. Cost of the structure, to be designed by the

Pacific Palisades Community Methodist Church. *Clearwater Collection*

145

architectural firm of Thomas P. Baker, was set at $45,000. The cornerstone was laid on August 18, 1929, and the first service in the new building was held the following February, with Dr. Alfred Inwood, pastor of the church, and Dr. Oren B. Waite, its first pastor, officiating. Although the church was designated Methodist Episcopal, sixteen different denominations were represented in the membership, and it served as a community church.

Another new addition to the central area was a clubhouse and vacation home for the "We Boys" and the "J.O.C." — the only such structure ever to occupy the "Church Vacation Homes" site. The "Boys" were a group of men who had attended Sunday School together forty years earlier at the First Methodist Church in Los Angeles. Inspired by their teacher, Eva Todd Burch, their friendship and religious dedication lasted a lifetime. Many of them married young ladies from another of her classes, who formed their own group, the "J.O.C." ("Jesus Our Companion").

The spacious Spanish Revival-style structure was purchased at auction in 1927 for $3,000 and moved from Los Angeles to a spot on Haverford Avenue near Founders' Oaks — a laborious process that lasted for three successive nights. An additional $5,600 was spent on remodeling and decorating to provide dining, recreational, and sleeping facilities. Renamed "Aldersgate Lodge," the building still functions as a popular place for groups meeting under religious auspices.

The old ranch buildings in Temescal Canyon, which had served as the Association's warehouse and lumberyard, were demolished in 1928 and the wood transported to Topanga Canyon to build a Boy Scout cabin at Camp Slauson. Several old tent houses on the Assembly Grounds were replaced by a new building the following year; the camp office was moved to Mr. Warrell's former meat market; and the renovated cafeteria was opened to the public as the Temescal Cafe.

A pleasant addition to the commercial center appeared around 1930 when two up-and-coming women, Ethel Wilson and Alice Tinsley, established the White Gate Tea Room in the old "Bishop's Cottage" on the rim of Temescal Canyon, serving luncheon and afternoon tea. It is said that their most famous patron was Douglas Fairbanks, who regularly stopped by for a piece of tasty lemon pie.

The concept of planned community growth so dear to the founders of Pacific Palisades received the blessing of city officials in 1928 when the first official zoning took place — quite informally — in the office of *The Palisadian*. Using a fistful of colored pencils purchased at the neighborhood drugstore, Huber Smutz of the Los Angeles City Planning Department in one afternoon zoned all 2,800 lots in Tract 9300. Within a week the city council gave its approval. There were no notices to property owners and no hearings; yet, with the exception of an enlarged business district, that zoning remains in force today.

The "We Boys" Lodge, now Aldersgate, located at 925 Haverford, near Founders' Oak Island. Drawing by Helen Luitjens, from the *Pacific Palisades Sketch Book*. Used by permission of the publishers.

The first annual Ex-Servicemen's Dinner, in the spring of 1928, hosted by Florian "Jack" Sauer in the Dining Hall in Temescal Canyon. This event led to the founding of the Pacific Palisades American Legion, Post 283. *Seated, left to right:* Norman Winston, R.L. Stadler, John E. Stadler, G.H. Eaton, Dave P. Thomas, Lew Thomas, Edwin Michel, C.D. Clearwater, F.J. Sauer, C.D. Wooldridge, Telford Work, Harry Keller, W.W. Culp, Jerry Dunbar, William Kendall Robinson, Ray Corr, Leon Faubion, W.L. Blanchard, and Bill Johnson. *Standing:* _____, German ex-soldier, Fred Sedding, Nancy Kendall Robinson, and Harry Du Rocher. *Courtesy Jack Sauer*

Community services in Pacific Palisades were gradually improved, largely through the efforts of the American Legion Pacific Palisades Post 283, which was founded in 1928. Jack Sauer, who had been active in the Brentwood unit of the organization, contacted the local veterans, hosted the first dinner meeting, and successfully organized the new post —Clifford Clearwater serving as the post's first commander and Jack its second. Since then the original group of 19 charter members has grown steadily and today numbers 328.

Protection from brush fires was one of the Legion's earliest concerns; this task had generally been left to Bell's mountain patrols with help from local volunteers based in Temescal Canyon. The residents suddenly recognized their vulnerability in September, 1928, when fire broke out north of Peace Hill, and the fire trucks, coming from Sawtelle, chugged up Rustic and Mandeville canyons before locating Temescal, on to the west. By then the fire had been contained by Association and land company employees. Recognizing the need to acquaint citizens with the terrain, the Legion organized automobile tours of the mountains and began lobbying for a fire station. At the suggestion of Legion commander Jack Sauer, the Santa Monica

Land and Water Company donated property on Beverly (Sunset) Boulevard for the new facility, which was inaugurated in 1929 with Captain J.A. Tanzola in charge.

Similarly, police protection was non-existent until 1928, when the city police department was badgered by the Legion into renting temporary office space in the Business Block for $10 a month. A year later a motorcycle officer was assigned to make nightly visits. According to *The Palisadian*, it was a predictable event: "riding a saddle-seat made out of horse hide [the officer] sputters through here over Beverly Boulevard about 11:30 each evening.... Remember then the hour of Paul Revere's ride! He comes and goes at 11:30. Schedule your misfortune, tragedy, hard luck, or whatever it may be, accordingly."

In response to continued complaints, a patrolman set up headquarters at Sauer's gas station. He was the object of instant admiration when he captured a desperado who had shot and killed his wife in Las Pulgas Canyon and was trying to escape. The agile officer reportedly jumped on top of the fleeing auto at the foot of Santa Monica Canyon and took the culprit into custody.

The community also began considering provisions

for air traffic when Will Rogers buzzed across town in his plane one July day in 1928 and landed on his polo field. At the same time, other large landowners were planning fields, including William Randolph Hearst who was said to be building an airport near the site of his proposed Tuna Canyon estate, leading to speculation that there would soon be scores of private and semi-private fields in the Santa Monica Mountains.

An article in *The Palisadian* predicted that the Temescal athletic grounds, Uplifter polo field, and both of Will Rogers' playing fields would soon be in constant use as landing fields, and that a local committee should begin securing and preparing other suitable sites. Jack Sauer, who already had a sign on the roof of his gas station for the guidance of pilots, also offered to put in a supply of aviation gasoline.

Early risers who were abroad at 4:30 A.M. on August 26, 1929, peered skyward through the fog to watch the Graf Zeppelin as it passed over the town twice at an altitude of 500 feet, almost scraping the rooftops, before it landed at Mines Field (today's Los Angeles International Airport) in its flight around the world. Its silvery form loomed overhead, motors whirring and lights shining eerily from the windows of the gondola.

Futuristic dreams of air travel and the prospect of multiple airports in the vicinity were diverting ideas, but the day-by-day needs of the community were financed by land sales. In 1928, only twenty-eight new homes were built, although $37,000 was spent on advertising and the Santa Monica Land and Water Company opened a handsome new tract office on the southwest corner of Chautauqua and Pampas Ricas. Subsequently the building was converted into an attractive home — one of six hundred which today occupy the Huntington Palisades tract.

As revenues fell, progress lagged on the promised improvements, and maintenance suffered. Vacant lots and parkways often went uncleared, and many of the original plantings died from lack of care. Paving of streets in Huntington Palisades did continue, however, and Beverly Boulevard was improved with gutters, curbs, and sidewalks.

Public criticism of both the Pacific Land Corporation and the Pacific Palisades Association and their management role reached the surface in 1929. Thirteen bondholders formed the Pacific Palisades Property Owners' Association and, with editorial support from *The Palisadian,* sued for a financial accounting. The newspaper, in fact, ran a weekly series of articles containing a detailed list of

Lindsay Gillis and his plane, a plywood Aero-Marine-Klemm, after landing on Will Rogers' polo field, ca. 1930. The unusual craft was adapted from a German glider, with a two-cylinder French-type motor built to cruise at low speeds and land at thirty miles an hour. *Courtesy Colleen Gillis*

grievances. The Association and the land company responded by printing a booklet in which they defended their position point by point, citing the ongoing expenses that had to be met, the costs of promotion, and the progress made in reducing the debt.

The basic facts, on which all finally agreed, were that the bonds outstanding in 1932 totaled $1,295,000 (reduced from $2,209,500 in 1926), with $2,000,000 receivable and an estimated $5-6,000,000 in saleable real estate carried on the books at 1925 prices. At this point the picture was so bleak from the practical point of view that scavenging agents from outside the community were offering a paltry $50 for a $1,000 bond.

The bondholders and representatives of the underwriters formed a committee and in June, 1933, announced a foreclosure plan. The California Trust Company (a subsidiary of the California Bank) was named depository for the bonds and was placed in charge of all the properties — listed as the Pacific Palisades and Huntington tracts, Temescal Canyon, the Huntington Beach Assembly Grounds, Bundy Bathhouse, and a sizeable stretch of beach property. The Santa Monica Land and Water Company was designated the exclusive sales agency for all lots not already sold or under contract of sale in both the Huntington and original Pacific Palisades tracts. The Business Block was not included in the listing and in 1936 was sold to the Santa Monica Land and Water Company.

By the time of the foreclosure sale on May 4, 1934, most of the ninety-nine-year leases had been exchanged by the leaseholders for ownerships. The remaining bonded lots and acreage were sold for $200,000 to the bondholders, who formed the Palisades (Land) Corporation and in short order began to sell off the various holdings.

The Pacific Palisades Association held its last Summer Assembly in Temescal Canyon in 1933 with the aid of two other church groups. The featured speaker was the eminent author, India-based missionary, and future Palisadian, Dr. E. Stanley Jones, lecturing on "The Gospel in the Age of Uncertainty." There were additional speakers from USC and UCLA, a drama school, and a series of motion pictures in the outdoor theater in Rustic Glen. The largest crowds in history responded and contributed generously to the free-will offering. In subsequent years, the facilities were rented by a variety of groups who continued to present worthwhile, if less ambitious, religious and cultural programs.

Several major problems remained unsolved, including the ultimate fate of Temescal Canyon, the beachfront, and the parkland along the bluff — all considered essential to the quality of the community. The Palisades Corporation in 1931 offered a mile-long strip of land along the bluffs between Potrero, Temescal, and Las Pulgas canyons as a gift to the city for park purposes, but for economic reasons the offer was rejected. The park department, which had once sought to expand its properties and services, stated that it could no longer afford the upkeep.

Lower Temescal Canyon was similarly caught in the economic squeeze. In 1929 the city had offered to pay $20,000 to develop this scenic area as a park, but the church-sponsored Pacific Palisades Association demurred, fearing relaxation of its Sunday-use restrictions and interference with its institutional programs. Again in 1934 the city offered to spend $15,000 on a recreational center and swimming pool there if given the land; this time the Association and the Palisades Corporation refused even to negotiate, alleging the uncertainty of their liquidation plans and the status of properties then being sold.

Community leaders also hoped to save enough space in Temescal Canyon for a future high school campus and recommended a site on the western mesa which could be connected to the athletic field in the canyon below by means of a tunnel under Sunset Boulevard. Both plans came to an abrupt end in August, 1935, when lower Temescal Canyon was sold to motion picture director Roy del Ruth —eighty acres for $100,000. The new owner fenced the property, demolished unwanted structures, built new roads and a polo field, and planted a grove of trees at the entrance. The Lodge became the del Ruth home. *The Palisadian* deplored the loss of desperately needed recreational facilities for the young people and questioned the future of the Assembly Camp and the beach. Clearly the Pacific Palisades Association and the Palisades Corporation gave top priority to paying off the debt and redeeming the value of the bonds.

Indeed, the battle to secure the Pacific Palisades beachfront for public use lasted for many years. In 1926 Dr. Scott and R.C. Gillis initiated a complex series of individual transactions that resulted in the sale of approximately two thousand feet of Association and Pacific Land Corporation beach property to Will and Betty Rogers for a total price of $977,372. By 1928 the Rogers holdings extended from a point west of the Lighthouse to the state-owned beach at the mouth of Santa Monica Canyon, excluding the privately owned Huntington Palisades beach. Will subsequently acquired the Bundy Bathhouse at the foot of Chautauqua and entered into negotiations to purchase five acres of land on the small mesa halfway up the hill (opposite Vance Place).

His intentions were clear. In his biography, Will is quoted as saying that he made such a handsome

profit buying beach property in Santa Monica and later selling it to Hearst that he bought a much larger parcel at the base of the Palisades as an investment for his family's future, implying plans either for resale or development.

In 1931 he tried to have his land rezoned for commercial use and failed. A few weeks later he withdrew his request when the state purchased 3,333 feet of adjacent beach frontage from the Pacific Land Corporation for $1,000,000 ($600,000 of which went toward payment on the mortgage indebtedness and much of the remainder for expenses), and the county leased 2,700 additional feet west of Temescal Canyon from Bell. Significantly, it was a county-wide study by the Olmsted Brothers in 1928 that convinced public agencies to acquire as much unimproved beach land as possible while it was still available, and thereby put the quietus on plans such as Will Rogers'.

In June, 1931, Will refused to pay his obligation in full to the Pacific Land Corporation and the Pacific Palisades Association because, he argued, commercial prospects for the beach property had been misrepresented to him. As a result of this action, he lost his title to the bathhouse, but retained his other properties.

Attention focussed on another beachfront property in November, 1932, when the Pacific Electric Railroad discontinued service to Santa Monica Canyon and relinquished possession of its narrow strip of trackland. Several ownerships were involved, but the state completed the purchase in 1934 for $450,000 and secured the strip for public use.

Even as these negotiations were under way, the Pacific Land Corporation, the Southern Pacific, and the Santa Monica Swimming Club all sought rezoning on several hundred feet of state-owned beach at the mouth of Santa Monica Canyon to permit them to build restaurants or refreshment stands there, leading canyon merchants and local citizens to mount a protest campaign. The "hot-dog controversy" continued until 1935, when rezoning was denied and two tunnels were built under the coast highway to make existing facilities in Santa Monica Canyon available to beachgoers.

Nothing came easily for Palisadians. Civic groups banded together to obtain an $85,000 appropriation

Views of the Lighthouse were regularly used in promotional literature, such as to the left, in a 1927 issue of *Pictorial California.* The landmark structure, which was purchased by Will Rogers in the late 1920s and used by the U.S.O. during World War II, later became a snack stand and lifeguard station. In 1972 the structure was scheduled for demolition and the tower was to be transported to Pepperdine College in Malibu. However, it was so severely damaged in the process that it had to be abandoned.

for a new school building to replace the four temporary frame structures on Via de la Paz, and assembled with pride when the Pacific Palisades Elementary School was dedicated on June 12, 1931. Even then, the community was considered so isolated that the principal, Theresa Sletten, was named an ex officio police officer and was also expected to function as a pound master. This involved picking up stray dogs from the school grounds and transporting them across town to the Boyle Heights animal shelter.

Bus service to Castellammare and Pacific Palisades, which had been heavily subsidized by Bell and the Pacific Land Corporation, was drastically curtailed in 1931, when revenues dwindled and support for the service was withdrawn. Francis Brunner came to the rescue and maintained a regular schedule until 1935, at which time public demands to reduce the fare to five cents led him to sell the franchise to the Santa Monica bus lines.

As the purse strings tightened, work on major highways continued, while less urgent public works projects were shelved. The new Roosevelt Highway was dedicated on June 29, 1929, by Governor James Rolph of California who performed the ribbon-cutting ceremonies, thereby opening the route along the Malibu coast to north-south travel and laying "fifty miles of virgin seaside beauty . . . before the eyes of thousands of appreciative motorists."

The highway's narrow, two-lane pavement was

Pacific Palisades Elementary School, which was dedicated on June 12, 1931. *Clearwater Collection*

Heavy equipment straightening and regrading the old "Marquez Road" access route to Pacific Palisades. The new road was named "Chautauqua Boulevard." *Clearwater Collection*

soon outdated. The state began the work of widening the roadbed almost at once — a complicated process that lasted for years. Groins were installed to extend the beach; deep cuts were made into the base of the unstable bluffs; and a large portion of Castle Rock was blasted away before protests could be heard and heeded. The state abandoned its plans for an ambitious three-mile-long breakwater, leaving it to the city of Santa Monica to build a shorter version. This created a small-craft harbor near the Santa Monica pier and had little effect on the beach below Pacific Palisades.

Instead of constructing a viaduct from Seventh Street in Santa Monica to the edge of Huntington Palisades, the city of Los Angeles widened and improved existing roads on the floor of Santa Monica Canyon. The bona fide ties with the old Rancho Boca de Santa Monica lost another round when Marquez Road was widened and straightened and renamed "Chautauqua Boulevard" from the coast to Pampas Ricas, leaving the historically significant Marquez name on only a small stub of road in the Beverly Pacific tract. Several routes for the proposed Reseda-to-the-Sea highway were also considered and mapped by state and city engineers, but no action was taken.

Another significant change occurred in 1933, when the West Los Angeles Chamber of Commerce decided to switch the name of Beverly Boulevard to "Sunset" and to capitalize on the romantic image of "Sunset to the Sea." The new name became official in July, 1934, and the route itself became one of the

world's most famous and glamorous thoroughfares.

Sepulveda Boulevard was opened to through traffic on October 20, 1935, providing a much-needed link between the San Fernando Valley and the coast. A ceremonial auto caravan drove along the historic route from Seal Beach to Ventura Boulevard and returned to the Sunset Boulevard intersection for the customary speeches.

Interest in parks continued as the Palisades Corporation offered three canyon properties to the city for this purpose — Las Pulgas, Potrero, and the Temescal picnic grounds. Alphonzo Bell also urged a park on a major portion of his mountain land, extending from Rustic Canyon to Santa Ynez. Unfortunately, there were no takers.

The effects of the Depression were felt in every home during the early thirties, and the community responded with sympathy. Cliff Clearwater and the American Legion sponsored a welfare relief board to centralize the local emergency effort. Families in need were asked to call Mrs. L.A. Warrell, wife of the local butcher, who sent women volunteers out to investigate and arrange help.

English-born actress Beryl Mercer, who had contributed generously to various welfare causes, staged a benefit variety show on February 17, 1933, to raise money for local unemployed men and sold most of the one thousand tickets priced at fifty cents to better-heeled donors outside the community. Following her example, local groups sponsored similar events. Will Rogers appeared in a benefit for the Santa Monica Community Chest and observed,

"Then we got to frame up something to do for our little neighbor, the Pacific Palisades." The proceeds from such efforts were used to pay unemployed workmen to clear lots, trim trees, and improve the parkways — all of which had been neglected due to the financial pinch.

The Palisadian sponsored free cooking classes in cooperation with the gas company and the PTA each year, beginning in 1930. These sessions provided the ladies with several days of sociability and fun, as well as useful new recipes, prizes, and even a bit of free food to take home. Attendance often approached seven hundred, truly remarkable when the number of households in Pacific Palisades was less than three hundred.

Ideas for padding slim household budgets were shared. Some women raised vegetables; others sold homemade preserves; and the Edison Company suggested that going without toast for breakfast would save five cents a week. The authorities deplored the fact that hunters were hauling truckloads of deer carcasses out of the Malibu hills and selling the meat for food; instead, the unemployed were urged to hunt for wild mustard greens and sunflower bulbs.

The community was resourceful in providing its own pleasures. In addition to summer programs and activities for every age group, young people could join a Boy Scout troop under Robert Norris's leadership, Alice Kinsley's Girls Scouts, Ivy Hodder Bailey's Campfire Girls, or Beatrice Clark's Bluebirds. Later, Beryl Mercer organized a dance at the Miramar Hotel for the older teen-agers; it was so successful that the Woman's Club thereafter sponsored family dancing at the formerly sacrosanct Assembly Grounds.

The local Methodist Church lost its beloved Nancy Kendall Robinson to the more affluent Westwood Methodist Church in December, 1932, but she continued to teach piano classes at her Sunset Boulevard home and remained an inspiration to her many pupils. Years later, after William Robinson had died and Cap Wooldridge was widowed, Nancy Kendall Robinson and Cap were married. When Mrs. Robinson herself died in 1967, a scholarship was established in her honor at UCLA and is supported by a yearly benefit concert. Captain Wooldridge remained a resident of Pacific Palisades and sang at special events until shortly before his death in 1982 at the age of ninety.

Taking Mrs. Robinson's place as musical director at the church was eighteen-year-old Winifred Andrews, an exceptionally capable pianist who assumed her responsibilities with verve and skill. Herbert and Alice Andrews and their four children (Winifred, Ina, Howard, and James), who had

moved to Pacific Palisades in 1926, were all talented musicians, playing and singing together for their own pleasure and for the benefit of their friends and neighbors. Dr. Andrews not only commuted to his medical practice in Hollywood, but composed music, organized nature study activities for the community, and brought a major natural history conference to the Assembly Grounds two years in a row.

As had been hoped, the proximity to UCLA contributed to the cause of culture and learning. After the campus opened on September 20, 1929, many faculty members either moved to Pacific Palisades or came to the Assembly Grounds to teach classes. Some — such as geography professor George McBride, who was president of the Civic League for many years, and historian Brainerd Dyer — were active in community affairs, while others, such as Arthur Steiner and Constantine Panunzio, were popular summer speakers.

One of the giants of Methodism, Reverend Toyohiko Kagawa of Japan, visited the Assembly Grounds in 1931, saw the street that bore his name, and admired the glories of the natural setting. Revered as the "Gandhi of Japan" and "Kagawa of the Slums," he was a world figure in the peace movement. He and other Japanese ministers held an

Hundreds of women enjoyed the cooking classes sponsored by *The Palisadian* during the Depression years. *Clearwater Collection*

153

Children picnicking in "the glen," a wooded area between the elementary school and the Business Block, which is visible in the distance. *Clearwater Collection*

hour-long prayer meeting on the lawn adjoining The Lodge each morning at sunrise, bowing toward the east, and each evening went to the canyon rim and sat quietly on benches, facing the setting sun.

A variety of new social and economic measures were introduced when the Roosevelt Administration came into power in 1933. One of its first actions, the bank closure, had little local effect since merchants and customers were generally friends and were able to deal on a credit basis. The threat that Prohibition would be repealed was far more menacing and partially came to pass on April 6, 1933, when 3.2% beer was legalized. A few optimistic souls, including Will Rogers, hoped that the milder brew might satisfy beer lovers and prevent the return of hard liquor and saloons. Palisadians, however, stood resolute and frowned on the restaurants and taverns in Santa Monica Canyon, where the 3.2% brew could be served legally.

The community had already suffered one embarassing brush with vice in 1932, when a raid on a Chautauqua Boulevard residence uncovered a supply depot for liquor and resulted in the arrest of two men, one of whom lived on the Assembly Grounds. The proprietors had installed a bar with a sawdust floor, free lunch counter, and tables with celery centerpieces — a replica of a tavern they had operated at the Pioneer Days celebration in Santa Monica the previous year. It was a short-lived venture, opening on Friday and closing on Sunday with the unexpected arrival of the police.

When the Eighteenth Amendment came to a vote in June, 1933, Palisadians stood six to one against repeal, the most lopsided ratio in the state. The sale of liquor was legalized in December, but Telford Work and others successfully fought the granting of off-sale and on-sale licenses in Pacific Palisades for many years — arguing that it violated both the deed restrictions and the commitments of the founders and the community, as cited in the advertising and sale of leaseholds and lots. Despite strong opposition, the Palisades Drug Store was granted a package liquor permit in 1935, since the Business Block in which it was located did not fall under the aegis of the new Civic League and the deed restrictions.

The new federally funded alphabetical agencies — the SERA, PWA, and WPA — augmented the community's self-help programs and made possible such major public works projects as brush clearance, street maintenance, construction of fire roads and firebreaks, and installation of sewers. These basic improvements were much appreciated in Pacific Palisades where the continued sale of lots was critical to financial recovery.

The first of several Depression-era disasters to plague the area was the Long Beach earthquake, which struck at 5:55 P.M. on March 10, 1933, and claimed 113 lives. Although damage in Pacific Palisades was limited to fallen cans and bottles and a few cases of jangled nerves, the elementary school remained closed all week. The American Legion organized relief efforts, sending food and cash to those in need, while Clifford Clearwater, Jack Sauer, and other volunteers served as guards in the stricken areas.

Mathematics teacher Paul Spring, son of Founder Louis D. Spring and a resident of Pacific Palisades, was one of the lucky ones. Thanks to the late hour, he was not in his customary place at Edison Junior High School in Long Beach when the smokestack of the incinerator fell through the roof, carrying his desk and the whole front of the room to the floor below.

On New Year's Eve in 1934, a destructive flood washed out the bridge on Sunset Boulevard over Rustic Canyon creek, endangering passing motorists. Emil Sandmeier, Will Roger's major domo, discovered the hazard around midnight when he was driving several staff members, who had been his guests for the evening, back to the ranch. Finding the roads impassable, the group went up the hill on foot and passed word of the washout on to the Rogers family.

Will left the house at once, taking his new Christmas poncho and a lantern, and rode on horseback down to the devastated area. He stood watch all night in the drenching rain, warning travelers, until at daybreak work crews came to put

154

Above, the Minnie A. Caine washed ashore during a storm on September 26, 1939, near the Bel-Air Bay Club. *Clearwater Collection*

Beach development was viewed as a threat by Palisadians, who campaigned long and hard for public ownership. These signs appeared in 1938. *The Palisadian*

up barricades. Then he set out to assess the damage to his own property, and at two o'clock in the afternoon, still wearing the poncho, he rode his horse up to the living room door and greeted his visitors. The bridge remained a shambles for over a year, while the new government agencies took turns attempting repairs.

Pressing for action on this and other issues was the Civic League, formed in 1935 to fill the gap left by the demise of the Pacific Palisades Association. The Civic League acted as a watchdog over deed restrictions and spoke for the community on such matters as street paving, schools, bus service, parks, zoning, and the everpresent need for sewers. The installation of a trunk line for the sewer system and connections to the various parts of town was a *cause celebre* for many years.

Ownership of *The Palisadian* passed from Telford Work to Clifford Clearwater on September 7, 1934, another benchmark in the history of the community. Work officially left the paper at this time to become manager of the Los Angeles Newspaper Service Bureau, a cooperative association of twenty suburban daily and sixty weekly newspapers which published legal notices on a local basis. However, he continued to take an interest in *The Palisadian* and contributed occasional editorials.

When asked recently which was the most significant of all the battles fought by *The Palisadian* during his editorship, Work cited persistent efforts to preserve the distinctive character of the community, including its "Pacific Palisades" post office designation. It required constant vigilance not to give in to the great megalopolis of Los Angeles and to become mere numbers in the postal zip code, a fate that has obscured the community identities of Brentwood, Westwood, and Sawtelle.

Work also paid tribute to Beatrice Clark, society editor of the paper since 1928. She played an active role in every phase of community life, helped to extend the newspaper's coverage to outlying areas, and took over as manager when Work was out of town. A favorite with the young people, she was affectionately known as "Ma" Clark.

Cliff Clearwater's commitment to the future of Pacific Palisades was well known. He had worked to obtain needed physical improvements for the community and had been deeply involved in humanitarian causes. The new editor began his regime in 1934 with a special edition honoring the local American Legion post and thereafter ran a timely series of articles on patriotism.

Gathering of prominent citizens of Pacific Palisades in 1957. *Left to right, standing:* Ruth Millard, Mr. and Mrs. Telford Work, Beatrice Clark, Ella Lorin, Mr. and Mrs. E.J. Kennedy, William K. Robinson, Mrs. Phillip A. Lee, Rube Stadler, Robert E. Norris, Leonard A. Warrell. *Seated:* Ella French, Mrs. Norris, Helen Little, Nancy Kendall Robinson, Mrs. Warrell, Alice Kinsley. *Courtesy Beatrice Clark Kottinger*

13

FRINGE BENEFITS

In spite of the Depression, excitement and glamor hovered on the fringes of Pacific Palisades all during the 1930s and gave the residents cause for pride. The positive side of the ledger received a hearty assist from the presence of the Olympic Games in Los Angeles in 1932, an event that attracted worldwide attention. Palisadians supported the effort by selling fifty-cent Olympic pins and welcomed participants with warm-hearted hospitality. The Riviera Country Club agreed to house the equestrian events, which were held from August 10 through 13, and built elaborate new facilities to accommodate them.

Among the first contestants to arrive were the equestrian teams, who were given generous space on the sports pages. The Japanese riding contingent was especially popular and had a full schedule of social events, including a Fourth of July party at the Bel-Air Bay Club as guests of Winifred Napier of Castellammare. Later in the summer the Uplifters entertained a thousand Olympic participants and guests with a barbecue and polo match at their Ranch.

The Dutch equestrians and their wives took up residence in a house on Iliff Street, and the Americans stabled their mounts at Will Rogers' ranch. Prior to the games, the Riviera Country Club hosted the International Equestrian Review and staged a polo match between Riviera and the University of Arizona to entertain the visitors and inaugurate the new field. The Los Angeles Athletic Club's *Mercury* magazine waxed jubilant: "All of the screen colony was present. Malibu must have looked deserted. William McAdoo was there. So was Sonny Whitney. Titled nobility from many lands. Uniforms. Monicles [*sic*]." The newspapers took note and soon put Riviera on the map.

When the games began, twenty thousand spectators filled the stands and found vantage points on the adjacent hillsides. The first event was the dressage, won by the favorite, Francois LeSage of France and his horse Taine. Thereafter, the American team forged into the lead. Will Rogers, who attended every day, commented in his column that the

Americans were doing so well he didn't believe the judges would notice them. To everyone's surprise, they won the three-day event and placed well all down the line.

The most gripping moment of the meet came on the third day, when the gruelling cross-country run was held on a course which began at Riviera and finished at Fox Hills. Colonel Kido of Japan, who was leading in the event, turned his mount aside at the final jump when he realized that the horse was too exhausted to make the attempt. Sacrificing twelve years of preparation, Kido not only won the affection of the Americans, but was singled out for honors by the emperor of Japan.

The dashing and popular Baron Nishi, a member of the Japanese equestrian team, clearing a jump at Riviera Country Club. *Courtesy Los Angeles Athletic Club*

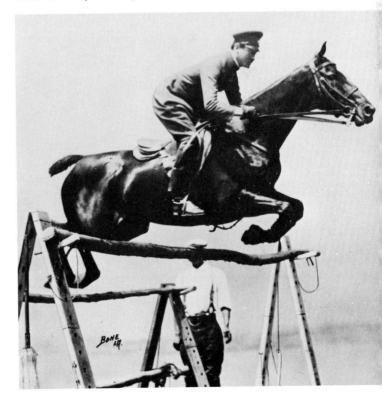

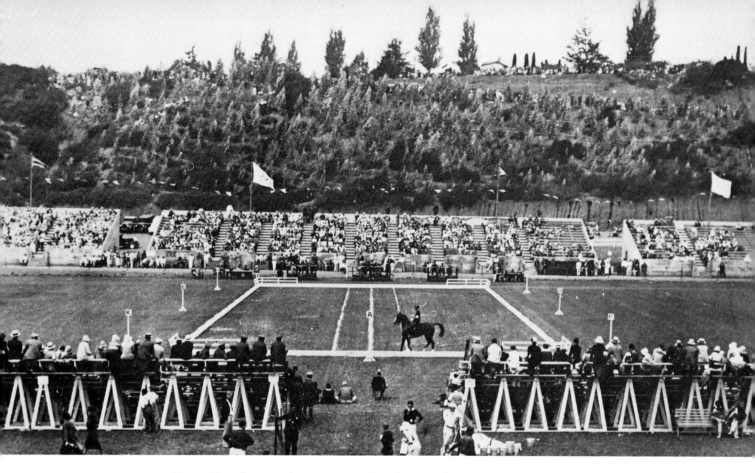

Above, Olympic equestrian event staged on the polo field at the Riviera Country Club. *Courtesy Los Angeles Athletic Club*

Below, finish of the Olympic cycling race, photographed from the pedestrian bridge over the coast highway at Castellammare. *Courtesy Elliott Welsh*

On the same day, cyclists in the 100-kilometer road race started off at Moorpark, proceeded to Oxnard, and crossed the finish line at Castellammare. The individual event was won by an Italian, Attilio Pavesi, in 2 hours, 28 minutes, 5.6 seconds, and the team event by the Italians.

Pacific Palisades, meanwhile, still suffered an identity crisis in the reporters' datelines. *The Palisadian* observed wistfully: "Why is it that sportswriters on the metropolitan papers persist in alluding to the Riviera Club as being in Santa Monica when . . . the club is not in Santa Monica and gets its mail at the Pacific Palisades post office? . . . And why do they keep saying that the Netherlanders have taken a house in Santa Monica . . .?"

Nevertheless, the Riviera Country Club cast a welcome aura of fame over Pacific Palisades and the surrounding area. Snowy Baker's "Riviera Riders" included such well-known folk as Greta Garbo, Elissa Landi, Jack Holt, and Lady Chaytor, who enjoyed relaxed excursions into the nearby mountains, while his junior group, the "Geebungs,"* found equal delight in Snowy's paper chases and bandit hunts. Benefit horse shows and top-flight polo matches captured the attention of sportsmen throughout the country, and the golf course achieved national recognition when it was chosen to host the Los Angeles Open Golf Tournament in 1929 and 1930.

Alphonzo Bell's California Botanic Gardens in Mandeville Canyon, a favorite destination for Snowy's riders, fared less well. It closed in 1929, and although financial support was sought from UCLA, USC, and the county, the effort was in vain. In 1932 Bell forfeited his $2,200,000 second mortgage, having previously lost substantial sums paid in interest on the bonds and spent on maintenance of the gardens. In April, 1933, the entire parcel, including the 140 acres actually developed as a garden, passed into the hands of the newly organized Garden Land Company for subdivision and sale.

Even when property sales lagged, the more exclusive sections of Pacific Palisades attracted wealthy residents whose very presence gave zest to the community. The McCormick estate in Huntington Palisades was one of the most imposing of these properties. Located on a point of land overlooking the ocean and Potrero Canyon, it occupied fourteen lots (13.77 acres) which cost $365,000 in 1928, supposedly the highest price ever paid for a residential lot in the entire United States.

The owner of this "summer home" was Virginia

*A whimsical name suggested by Snowy Baker. It was taken from "The Geebung Polo Club," a ballad written by Australian poet A.B. "Banjo" Patterson, who also wrote "The Man from Snowy River."

McCormick, a member of the International Harvester family of Chicago, whose year-round residence was in Pasadena. The main house was spacious, with large bedrooms upstairs and a suite downstairs for a woman companion who also served as Miss McCormick's secretary and manager. Connected to the house by gardens and walkways were a full-scale guest house, gardener's cottage, theater, laundry, swimming pool, and a garage with servants' quarters. According to *The Palisadian,* the entire complex contained one hundred rooms and was maintained by a staff of thirty servants.

Miss McCormick decided to move to Pacific Palisades from Montecito following the Santa Barbara earthquake and arranged the purchase through Arthur Fleming, whose wife was related to the McCormicks. Palisadians seldom saw their mysterious neighbor, aside from her arrivals and departures in her limousine, but she had many visitors — family, friends, and a variety of entertainers — some invited for dinner, others for a prolonged stay.

She loved music and engaged local musicians, visiting European artists, and even whole orchestras to appear at private concerts in her theater. As part of the daily routine, a young lady from Santa Monica also arrived each evening and was instructed to play a specific piece on the piano at the exact moment Miss McCormick came down the stairs for dinner.

From the outset the site of the estate proved vulnerable. In 1932 a steam shovel operator on the coast highway below was killed in a small slide; later in the year the highway was closed for over a week

Aerial view of the McCormick estate, overlooking the mouth of Potrero Canyon, taken shortly after the buildings were completed in 1929. *Spence Collection/UCLA*

when a retaining wall and a section of the garden came tumbling down. Moisture from irrigation was blamed for causing the rock to become slippery and slide-prone. Under the direction of Stanford University oil geologist Harry Johnson, engineers drilled four tunnels into the bluffs, hoping that the water might be sealed off and the forward movement of the hill halted. Their solution was to run pipes into the cliff and dry out the soil by means of hot steam. The tunnels were abandoned during World War II, but the access doors still may be seen along the coast highway today.

A different sort of excitement attended the completion of the Hugo Ballin home on Almoloya Drive in Huntington Palisades in December, 1928. Ballin, who had recently returned from Europe, was a successful novelist and a veteran of twelve years in the motion picture business. He had directed ninety-one movies and now planned to devote himself to writing and painting. As a muralist, he required a large working space and incorporated a two-story north-light studio into his home.

His wife, Mabel, was a stage and screen actress with many friends in Hollywood. The first callers at the home in the sparsely settled neighborhood included Rupert Hughes, Marion Davies, Harold Lloyd, Gloria Swanson, and Cedric Gibbons. All during the Depression, Ballin was kept busy with commissions to paint decorative friezes and panels for the dome of B'nai B'rith Temple, the Griffith Park planetarium, Los Angeles County Hospital, and the *Los Angeles Times* building at First and Spring streets in downtown Los Angeles.

Palisadians were both scandalized and titillated when Ballin's ninth novel appeared — *Dolce far Niente,* a satire on Santa Barbara social life. A review in *The Palisadian* called it "raffish and sybaritic . . . illustrated with ironical drawings," and dubbed Ballin a "Jekyll and Hyde," as they contrasted the theme of his novel with the inspirational tone of his murals.

Ballin's sense of humor led him to perpetrate a hoax on the National Academy of Design in New York and on Edward A. Jewell, art editor of the *New York Times,* who often criticized Ballin's work. He entered a competition in New York with his own signed painting of Dolores del Rio and a hastily produced likeness of a Mrs. Katz from Venice which he signed "A. Gamio." The result was high praise from Jewell for "Gamio" and brickbats for Ballin: " . . . such vulgarities had best be forgotten as soon as possible." When Ballin's double identity was revealed, Santa Monica Canyonite Arthur Millier, art editor of the *Los Angeles Times,* shared Ballin's amusement at Jewell's discomfiture.

A few blocks from the Ballins, artists George and Olive Barker had their home and a pair of studios,

scenically located on the rim of Potrero Canyon. George had spent a year in Paris and was known for his portraiture, while Olive had trained in music and art at Oberlin and specialized in water colors, particularly scenes of New Mexico.

Artists of various sorts were discovering the area. Author David Malcolmson came to Pacific Palisades from Illinois in 1928 and began giving classes in creative writing under UCLA auspices to a loyal group of aspiring literati. David and his wife, Esther, later moved to Santa Monica Canyon, where they joined a community of talented neighbors: sculptor Merrell Gage, art critic Arthur Millier, architect Thornton Abell, sculptors Holgar and Helen Jensen, photographers Peter Stackpole and Edward Weston, and artist Nicolai Fechin. Canyonites were a gregarious lot, fond of badminton games at Al and Nora Edmundson's court and Sunday night gatherings at the Malcolmsons'. All pooled their talents each spring to make the Canyon School art show a resounding success.

Somewhat later, in 1937, Harry and Frances Usher built the "House of Usher," a large Mediterranean home on Chautauqua Boulevard. Rumors were circulated that it was planned for seances, since the Ushers were intrigued with the occult and had studied astrology. They distributed their own system of astrological charts to dime stores across the country and were popular stage and parlor entertainers. Harry started his career in New York as a vaudeville actor and was joined by his wife, who was a mind reader. In their act, Frances was blindfolded and read Harry's mind as he went out into the audience. After coming to Pacific Palisades they appeared frequently on community programs.

Perhaps the most intriguing of all the Depression-era estates were those built by Anatol Josepho and the mysterious Jessie Murphy in the upper reaches of Rustic Canyon. Anatol was a White Russian who had fled to New York during the Revolution and made a fortune through his invention of the photomaton, a coin-operated instant photo portrait booth which he sold to a group of businessmen for a sizeable sum shortly before the market crash. He and his wife, Ganna, came to California in 1928 and lived with their two sons in a home on Rockingham Drive, overlooking Mandeville Canyon, where they often hosted Snowy Baker and his Riviera Riders for picnics and barbecues.

While riding through the hills, Anatol found a site for his own version of Shangri La — an eighty-five-acre parcel of land in Rustic Canyon, rich with springs and shaded by oaks and sycamores. He purchased the land in 1932 and set to work building the mile-long road into the canyon from the top of the Riviera, operating the steam shovel himself.

Architect George Anderson, with a background

Views of the Josepho Ranch as taken by Anatol himself. *Above,* the house as seen from the swimming pool across the creek; *below,* the caretaker's house, "inventor's cottage," and barn, as seen from the terrace of the home; and, *lower right,* bridges built across a tributary stream which flowed down a small canyon past the house. *Josepho Collection*

Above, Architect's rendering of a lavish four-story home proposed for the Murphy Ranch. *Courtesy Eric Wright*

Below, the double-generator power station on the Murphy Ranch. Photograph by Thomas R. Young.

of motion picture set design, and builder Paul Levine cooperated with Anatol in achieving a plan — the house, outbuildings, swimming pool, and pastures, all placed in harmony with the watercourses and the contours of the land. Many Indian artifacts, which were unearthed when the excavation was made for the pool, were carefully retrieved and preserved by Anatol. Unfortunately, all have been lost.

The family lived in the canyon for fifteen years, entertaining Snowy and his fun-loving troop and their many friends. Will Rogers and Leo Carrillo, whose home was in Santa Monica Canyon, were especially close; the three men would sit on the corral fence for hours, talking about politics and world events. According to Ganna, Will taught Anatol to chew gum, while Leo taught Anatol a few spicy swear words, and Anatol introduced them both to 100-proof vodka.

Theirs was a life of comfort in a wilderness setting. The boys captured and killed rattlesnakes, cured the skins, and displayed the rattles as trophies. Anatol collected honey from the swarms of bees to package as gifts for the holidays. Deer families grazed in the meadows near the main house, while red foxes, coyotes, skunks, and bobcats were less frequent visitors. The family kept a stable of eight fine horses, a couple of donkeys, and a few cows.

Under construction at the same time as the Josepho home was the Murphy Ranch, located immediately downstream, but concealed by a flank of the canyon wall. There, behind a barbed wire fence, fifty men were at work, constructing elaborate terraces, a 375,000 gallon water tank, a 25,000 gallon fuel tank, and a double-generator power station large enough to supply a small town. The architect was Welton Becket, newly arrived from Washington state; this remarkable installation was his first local commission.

The true story was made public many years later. The land was purchased in 1933 from Mountain Park Associates by "Jessie M. Murphy, a widow," but the Josephos learned that no such Mrs. Murphy ever existed. The actual owners were Norman and Winona Stephens, who spent four million dollars laying the groundwork for a Nazi stronghold in this isolated spot. They had fallen under the spell of a German named Schmidt who convinced them that he had supernatural powers and that a war would soon come in which the United States would be defeated by Germany. The ranch was to be a self-sufficient community where their chosen band would survive the bombings and remain isolated until they could emerge and form a nucleus to implement the new order.

The Josephos, who were Jewish and might well have been concerned, knew only that there were locked gates, armed guards, and patrol dogs. Farther afield, workmen began telling tales of Silver Shirt maneuvers, and a terrified resident of the Uplifters who was interested in spiritualism blamed Schmidt for a mysterious fire that burned her cottage to the ground.

Behind the barriers, terraces were built on the hillsides, fitted with water pipes and planted with three-to-five thousand orchard trees — including an olive grove with its own press. Paved roads and cement staircases led from the ridge down to the canyon floor, where the stream was diverted into a concrete flume. The only residential structures ever completed were a couple of cottages and a two-story steel garage with a tile roof. Left on the drawing board were plans for a hotel-sized mansion, with indoor swimming pool, gymnasium, and workshops, and for a three-story barn. Becket, in fact, was superseded on the project by Paul Williams, who specialized in large-scale residences.

A stone's throw away, at the Rogers Ranch, Will was busy enlarging his own home and added to his domain by purchasing an additional sixty acres of land in upper Rustic Canyon. In 1934 his career was at its height, with movies, lectures, plays, radio programs, columns, articles, and benefit appearances making demands on his time. Here on the ranch he could be at ease: ride horseback, rope calves, and enjoy his friends. Each morning he wrote his daily column in front of a large window which looked out over the hills. Ironically, the dateline read "Santa Monica."

Pioneer businessman Jack Sauer recalls that

163

during these years Will Rogers was his service station's best customer, since each member of the Rogers family had a car and they had many guests. One day Will's car hit a rock while he was driving across the Riviera on a dirt road; a tire blew out and he was stranded. Jack responded to the emergency call with one of his employees and found Will, sitting on the running board with his portable typewriter, pounding out his syndicated article for the next day's newspaper.

Although Will's friends included the rich and famous, his home life centered on his family, and he liked nothing better than an old-fashioned barbecue out in the patio. By 1935, however, Will was showing signs of fatigue from his busy schedule. He built a small hideaway log cabin in Rustic Canyon, a mile or so upstream, and planned to relax there with Betty when time permitted. Fate intervened. In his travels Will had been intrigued with Siberia, which reminded him of his home in the old Indian Territory of Oklahoma. He and Anatol talked of returning to Siberia together, with Anatol acting as interpreter, but Anatol was in the East early in August when Will arranged his ill-starred flight around the world with Wiley Post.

On the Sunday morning before Will's departure, he and Betty took a long ride around the ranch and visited the Rustic Canyon cabin. In the afternoon they watched the end of a polo game at the Uplifters Ranch. Will roped calves until supper time, went with Betty and his son Bill to a nighttime rodeo at Gilmore Stadium, and left for San Francisco that evening. A few days later, on August 16, 1935, the world was stunned to hear that Will Rogers and Wiley Post had died in a plane crash in Alaska. Betty and her sister were visiting in Maine when they received the message and made the long, sad journey back to their home by train.

A tribute in *The Palisadian* expressed his neighbors' sorrow. Will had been a friend of the milkman, the iceman, the gardener, and the caretaker; he patronized the local merchants, subscribed to the local newspaper, and contributed to local aid programs. They remembered him best, "sitting astride the topmost fence rail at his corral," talking about his horses and telling anecdotes. His very presence and his humorous outlook on everyday problems were welcomed by all. The Uplifters held their own ceremonies on Sunday, September 29, with Fred Niblo giving the official eulogy, and

The Will Rogers hideaway cabin in Rustic Canyon, completed a short time before Will's death in 1935 and subsequently destroyed by fire. The only significant portion of the original structure remaining is the indoor-outdoor fireplace. *Courtesy Will Rogers State Historic Park*

The George E. Barrett home in Las Pulgas Canyon, designed in the Norman-French style by John Byers, architect, and Edla Muir, associate. *Swarzwald-Patterson Collection*

dedicated the polo field to Will.

By the mid-thirties there were many new faces at the Uplifters Club. The brotherhood was deeply involved in polo, and the old-time spirit had changed. Harry Haldeman and several of his friends had resigned in protest in 1928 over the increased burden of debt required to build the new polo facilities and had left the Ranch. Two years later, the Uplifters' popular riding instructor, Snowy Baker, left to take over the equestrian activities at the Riviera Country Club.

The Depression also took its toll. As many of the original householders fell behind on their payments, they were forced to confer with the Uplifters' lawyer, Joseph Musgrove, and to agree to his hard-headed terms. In the process, Musgrove ended up owning several of the most desirable properties, including Marco Hellman's magnificent log cabin.

The newcomers who were associated with the motion picture industry brought both money and glamor. Their homes tended to be larger and more sophisticated in style than the rustic originals. Charles Rosher, Mary Pickford's cameraman, built a two-story, half-timbered home; Sol Lesser, a Spanish ranch-style dwelling; and author Lewis Browne, an adaptation of a Moroccan mosque. The clubhouse and grounds were run for profit by a professional manager, and now, with Prohibition a thing of the past, liquor could be served openly in the new Polo Lounge.

Social life still focussed on the Annual Outing, as Dr. Kress presided over the Saturday circus each year, and motion picture producer Sol Lesser staged one of the more imaginative High Jinks. A few courageous women stayed on the Ranch during the week-long stag follies, but lurked out of sight behind discreetly drawn blinds.

In 1935 the Uplifters had an unscheduled preview of World War II, when 750 pounds of lead bars were accidentally released from the bomb rack of a Northrup plane and fell over a wide area of the club grounds. One of the slugs landed with a mighty crash on Dr. Fred Nichols' driveway and shattered into a thousand pieces, terrifying Mrs. Nichols, while other fragments fell near the Lewis Browne home. The pilot had no idea of the consternation below, believing he was flying over a wilderness area.

Not to be outdone, the estates to the west of Pacific Palisades had a flair of their own. Equipment went to work in Las Pulgas Canyon in April, 1935, removing the old ranch house, the movie set, and remnants of the goat farm — each with a store of precious memories. The new owner was George Barrett, who had retained architect John Byers and his associate, Edla Muir, to design a rambling Norman-French home in a picturesque natural bowl in the hills.

Barrett had purchased seventy acres north of Sunset Boulevard and added forty more acres to the south. He planted a grove of avocado trees on the site of the former family garden plot and replaced the old horse corrals with a modern stable for his Kentucky-bred saddle horses. The home was situated where five hundred goats had once been corralled; the old apiary formed the front yard; and the trees which had sheltered the hives now shaded a sweeping expanse of lawn. Barrett acquired the remains of Jesse Vore's nursery stock which provided many varieties of trees and shrubs for the landscaping. In the lower canyon he built homes for his children, his mother, and his aunt, as well as a guest house and a scenic bridle trail to the beach.

Barrett had the Midas touch. He had made his first million in the stock market before he was twenty-one and was many times a millionaire by the time he reached Pacific Palisades. Subsequently he parlayed his fortune through the timely purchase of property in the Malibu Colony business district, acreage at Trancas, and oil-producing ranch land around Santa Barbara. According to Jack Sauer, it was Barrett's ambition to own a chain of ranches in the Santa Barbara area, so he could travel on horseback for a week and spend each night in a different one of his haciendas.

Thelma Todd, in the kitchen of her restaurant at Castellammare. *Wide World*

In the late thirties Barrett sold the property to Hamilton and Jean Garland, whose comfortable income was derived from an eastern stove-manufacturing enterprise and from cranberry bogs. Jean Garland was a handsome woman who had been a dancer and on a trip to England had caught the eye of the bachelor Prince of Wales. She dressed in the latest fashion, in glorious colors, but surrounded herself with white. Not only was the terrace tastefully decorated with white wicker furniture, but there were white cockateels in cages, and outside on the grounds all of the animals — horses, dogs, lambs, and peacocks — were pure white. Later the Garlands moved to Arizona where their ranch was similarly outfitted — this time in black.

On to the west, the Bernheimer Gardens flourished and became a major tourist attraction. Although its owner, Adolph Bernheimer, was quiet and seclusive, wore thick glasses, and seldom mixed socially, he nevertheless liked to sit in the sunshine, chatting with visitors or listening to their comments, and occasionally shared a Gibson cocktail with a friend. His life was more-or-less managed by a Mrs. Halstead, who came in 1929 as his nurse. She graduated to gardening and from 1931 on, was head gardener and generalissimo of the estate.

At first Bernheimer refused to charge an entrance fee, and the Gardens' only income was from a small shop that sold pictures, plants, bulbs and seeds. Later, he opened an Oriental tearoom and began charging admission. Through it all, he kept the grounds in immaculate order, with beds of roses, tuberous begonias, primroses, fuchsias, and annuals to provide a background of seasonal color.

It was nearby Castellammare, however, that captured front-page tabloid-style newspaper coverage when motion picture actress Thelma Todd's lifeless body was found in movie producer Roland West's garage on December 16, 1935. As the story unfolded, it involved the restaurant, the Joya Inn, which West had opened in the Castellammare business block and named after his first wife, Jewel. When the popular comedienne became associated with the venture, the name was changed to "Thelma Todd's Sidewalk Cafe" to capitalize on her fame, and both partners often stayed in a second-floor apartment over the dining area.

On that fateful Sunday, Todd came home from a Hollywood party by cab. It was 3:45 A.M., and West had already locked the door to the cafe and had gone up to his home on the hill. Finding the door locked, Todd had apparently climbed the long flight of stairs to West's garage, where her own car was kept. On Monday morning her maid found her body half-in and half-out of her car, the garage door closed and the ignition key on.

Above, the Castellammare area after the 1938 fire. Note the business block and the highway pedestrian overpass in the right lower corner. The West home is off the picture on the upper right. A network of roads and walkways interlaces the seaward slope of the mesa, with the Villa Leon on the left, near Castle Rock, and the Claude I. Parker estate (now the J. Paul Getty Museum) at the head of the adjacent Cañon de Sentimiento. *Spence Collection / UCLA*

Below, the Castellammare business block, with the sign "Thelma Todd's Sidewalk Cafe" prominently displayed. Roland West's home is atop the hill to the right. *Swarzwald-Patterson Collection*

Jack Sauer, responding to a call from West, picked up Dr. Phil Sampson and arrived on the scene shortly after relatives and the homicide team had gathered. The *Times* described the grisly sight — her blood-stained mauve and silver evening gown, her tousled blonde hair, and a fortune in jewels around her neck.

The investigation involved many Hollywood names, but the mystery was never solved. Testimony revealed that she had received extortion notes and a phone call from the "Ace of Spades," threatening to blow up the cafe, and rumors persisted that the underworld wanted to move in with gambling, which the actress had refused to condone. Suicide was ruled out, since her career was going well; she was excited over her Christmas plans and prospects for the future. The prevailing theory was that she had stumbled on the stairs, cutting her face, and that she had crawled into the car to sleep, turned on the engine to keep warm, and died of carbon monoxide poisoning.

For years an aura of tragedy and fear surrounded the cafe. In *Farewell, My Lovely,* Raymond Chandler used the Castellammare setting to create suspense:

He opened the front door cautiously and peered out into the foggy air. We went out and down the salt-tarnished spiral stairway to the street level and the garage.... For two minutes we figure-eighted back and forth across the face of the mountain and then popped out right beside the sidewalk cafe. I could understand now why Marriott had told me to walk up the steps. I could have driven about in those curving, twisting streets for hours without making any more yardage than an angleworm in a bait can.

Most of the developments on the fringe of Pacific

Roland West's elaborate hillside villa, Castello del Mar. Thelma Todd's body was discovered in one of the garages which were located several tiers below the main house. *Courtesy Katherine LaHue*

Palisades were hauntingly bleak during the mid-thirties — a sprinkling of Mediterranean mansions on the hillsides. Chandler caught the mood:

...I swung the car to the right past a big corner house with a square white turret topped with round tiles.... We slid down a broad avenue lined with unfinished electroliers and weed-grown sidewalks. Some realtor's dream had turned into a hangover there. Crickets chirped and bullfrogs whooped in the darkness behind the overgrown sidewalks....

There was a house to a block, then a house to two blocks, then no houses at all.

Chandler's vivid descriptions were obtained first-hand. For several years he lived on Hartzell Street in Pacific Palisades — a prosaic location where, in contrast with the hard-boiled style of his plots, he and his wife led a quiet life. He even fretted over his neighbor's daughter when, in his opinion, she lingered too long in her boy friend's Ford roadster after coming home from the Saturday night movie. The daughter, incidentally, was Martha French, and the boy friend was her husband-to-be, Charles Patterson.

Real estate sales throughout Pacific Palisades rallied in the late 1930s, as the Palisades Corporation began selling off its last remaining properties, and the Douglas aircraft plant in Santa Monica expanded its facilities. Notices on the bulletin board at Douglas listed homes for rent in Pacific Palisades for as little as $15 a month, offering the first month free as an inducement. More than one hundred new homes were started in 1938, while many existing homes, long vacant, also found buyers.

The Civic League, headed by UCLA professor George McBride, continued its battles for sewers, street maintenance, police protection, a local library, and other perennial causes, with parks and playgrounds generally heading the list. In an arrangement with the county in November, 1936, the city acquired "Bell Beach," extending from the Bel-Air Bay Club to Castle Rock, leaving the acquisition of Will Rogers Beach, between Santa Monica Canyon and the Lighthouse, as the most pressing local concern.

The Beverly Hills National Bank, trustees for the Rogers property, accented the urgency when they sought permission from the city to subdivide the beach and installed fences to prevent the area from reverting to public use. The city gave its approval in 1938, and workmen began staking out the foundation of a house. The community quickly launched a vigorous protest, which led members of the Rogers family to cancel the plan.

In a related action, the Civic League successfully fought back a proposal to turn the Jones Bowl Auto Camp into a residential area and trailer park by conjuring up "lurid visions of cats, children, dogs, and parrots" and pointing out that the new owner had applied for a liquor license. Here it should be said that Dr. Scott had originally envisioned the Jones Bowl highway frontage as a site for a hotel and other recreational facilities, with a church-sponsored "pleasure park" on the beach itself, similar to the layout at Ocean Grove, New Jersey.

Plans for a blufftop park received a temporary setback in 1937-38, when the land along Via de las Olas was sold to Theodore Earl, and a heavy wire fence went up. Jack Sauer and his Civic League committee on parks acted at once and brought the appropriate officials out to inspect the property. As a result, the city acquired 4½ acres from two ownerships — Earl and the Palisades Corporation — and created a park along Via de las Olas and Asilomar which was officially dedicated on Memorial Day in 1940.

The del Ruth property came on the market again a few months later, and the Civic League once more attempted to obtain all of Temescal Canyon for a park and recreation center. The city park commission refused to purchase the land, but agreed to equip and maintain the facilities. Within weeks, movie director Jack Conway bought the 80 acres for $100,000, called his new spread "All Hollows Farm" and again the community went empty-handed.

Seeing the need for recreational opportunities for youth and wishing his gift to serve as a token of appreciation to his adopted country, Anatol Josepho purchased 110 acres of land adjacent to his own ranch in Rustic Canyon and donated it to the Crescent Bay Council of the Boy Scouts for a camp

Above, dedication ceremonies at Camp Josepho on June 7, 1941. *Left to right,* Anatol, Roy, and Ganna Josepho, with Leo Carrillo. *Below,* general view of the opening day's Camporal which attracted a thousand Boy Scouts and Scout leaders. *Clearwater Collection*

— paying $19,000 for the site and adding $31,000 more for improvements. Parents and interested citizens donated time and money and built a dining hall, handcraft building, caretaker's lodge, and several campsites with fireplaces.

The dedication of Camp Josepho was held on June 7, 1941, with Leo Carrillo, Sheriff Eugene Biscailuz, and one thousand Scouts and Scout leaders present. At noon, seventy-six patrols marched in parade, and flocks of carrier pigeons were released in honor of the occasion. To make the new facility more widely available, Anatol also set up a fund to provide camperships for needy Scouts.

Extremes of weather and a potpourri of bizarre events marked the decade of the thirties. Measurable snowfalls in December, 1931, and January, 1932, delighted the children and provided an excuse for an unscheduled school holiday. On the latter occasion, two inches fell, enough to catch on the inhospitable surfaces of palms and prickly pears and to be made into satisfactory snowmen.

Oft-expressed fears of Santa Monica Canyonites over the inadequate state of their storm drain, which ran under Channel Road, were realized in March, 1938, when rain fell steadily for several days and left devastation all along the base of the mountains. Water and debris pouring down from Mandeville

Snowman in front of the Smith home at 1000 Galloway in December, 1931. *Courtesy Frances Smith Stewart*

and Rustic canyons met at Channel Road and formed a huge wave which swept over the clogged-up entrance to the culvert, deposited a deep layer of sand and gravel around the business structures at the mouth of Santa Monica Canyon, and washed out the coast highway.

Rustic Canyon was a tangle of fallen branches and uprooted shrubbery, and the Uplifters lost their amphitheater. At the Assembly Camp in upper Temescal Canyon, one casita and several tent bases washed away; the Jones Bowl road through the auto camp was cut; and the Via de la Paz road to the beach was strewn with boulders.

Many residents of Santa Monica Canyon hoped that the business district might now be abandoned and the mouth of the canyon turned into a park. However, the county moved the storm drain and made it into an open trench that ran behind the business structures — a change which permanently frustrated park plans, but successfully reduced future danger from floods.

Even more devastating were the fires. The first to pose a serious threat to the Palisades started in Temescal Canyon in October, 1938. It was started by children playing with matches at the upper picnic ground and burned thirty acres before being controlled. No homes were lost, but the Assembly Camp was evacuated, and one family took advantage of the situation by leaving without paying rent on their cottage.

Then, on Wednesday, November 23, the most destructive fire in the county's history started when the caretaker on the Trippet Ranch in Topanga Canyon threw out a pan of hot ashes. Driven by a forty-mile wind the flames roared through Topanga, Las Tunas, and Las Flores canyons and destroyed more than seventy-five homes before reaching the sea.

W. W. Culp, head ranger for the Bell interests, was in the hospital when the fire broke out; his cabin and that of Joseph Gilliland, both in Santa Ynez Canyon,* were burned, as was the Hottentot Riding Academy on Sunset Boulevard. Aided by high-pressure mains and better roadways, firemen were able to save all of the homes in Miramar Estates and Castellammare, Dr. Barham's estate on the rim of Santa Ynez Canyon, George Barrett's in Las Pulgas Canyon, and J. Walter Rubin's on Las Lomas Drive, even though flames raced through the oat fields and turned the eucalyptus trees into torches.

The firemen made a stand at the Assembly Camp, watching as the blaze reached Sunset and threatened

*Jack Sauer recalls Gilliland's comfortable cabin near the junction of Santa Ynez and Quarry canyons, where the ruins may be seen today, but does not remember Culp's. *The Palisadian* mentioned both.

the lower canyon with showers of sparks. Shortly after dawn on Thanksgiving Day, the fire swept over Peace Hill, sparing the cross, and raged on to destroy C.B. Brunson's cabin in Rivas Canyon. Caretaker Leo Urban returned to find all of his possessions gone — including cash kept under the bed.

Will Rogers' home and stables were saved, and in upper Rustic Canyon, firemen pumped water from the Josepho swimming pool to protect the ranch and thereby prevented the fire from moving into Mandeville Canyon. Unable to gain access to the Murphy Ranch, fireman had to notify the residents of the impending danger by commercial radio.

By the time the fire was brought under control Sunday evening, it had consumed 22,000 acres. Constance Cockrell recalled a similar fire in November, 1911: "It is a picture no artist could ever paint — the gentle stillness of the night, the placid calm of the ocean, and the raging, leaping, unconquerable flames. Yet always, in the midst of the flames, the unmoveable, unhurt, and indestructible mountains."

Throughout the thirties, the social and religious center of Pacific Palisades continued to be the Community Methodist Church. The Association moved to Pasadena and was liquidated in 1937, but the church itself and many of its educational functions thrived. Dr. Alfred J. Inwood served as minister from 1926 to 1929 and Dr. James F. Dunning from 1929 to 1933. Reverend John Gabriel-

Above, view looking northwest toward Topanga from the corner of Sunset Boulevard and Via de la Paz as the 1938 fire approached. On the right is the Van de Kamp's Bakery windmill, a short-lived addition to the business district. *The Palisadian*

Below, Leo Urban, caretaker of the C.B. Brunson estate in Rivas Canyon, dolefully surveys the remains of his cabin. *Clearwater Collection*

THE FLOOD
OF '38

Malcolmson Collection

Clearwater Collection

Storm damage from the 1938 flood was most severe at the mouth of Santa Monica Canyon and at the foot of Sunset Boulevard in Santa Ynez Canyon. (Pictures are individually credited)

son, 1933 to 1939, had the honor of presiding over the burning of the mortgage on November 22, 1935. Many pioneers had remained active members of the congregation, and the children who had been raised in the extended family environment of Temescal Canyon by this time were in high school and college, dating and being married.

Margaret Jane Work Pollock remembers from her own childhood the very special atmosphere of Pacific Palisades: the inspiration of daily contact with great men who came to lecture and to teach; the fun of collecting and assembling specimens for the neat-as-a-pin museum under Dr. Clark's aegis; the weekly movies at Rustic Glen in the summertime; and the Merry Melody Makers, a group of young people who put on variety shows under Esther Day's guidance. Everyone could rattle a chime or play an instrument and feel included. Not all were as talented as Fern Buckner, who went on to New York as the featured violinist on Fred Waring's popular radio program, or as the Williams brothers, who played in the Los Angeles Philharmonic Orchestra.

For teenagers the meeting place was church. They sang in the choir on Sunday mornings, hiked in the hills in the afternoon, met at Epworth League in the evening, and walked home together at night, "talking their heads off." Even the marginally pious came to church for the sociability. The young people had picnics and parties; they tooted around town in Model A Fords with rumble seats and spent idle summers at the beach.

Each age group included familiar surnames — Andrews, Work, Hoch, Anglemyer, Clearwater, Mercer, French, Christianson, Westenhaver, Norris,

Koenig, and Curtis — all of them neighbors, schoolmates, and friends. New families were a welcome addition. It was a red-letter day when the Weeks, missionaries from India, arrived with their five children. Don wowed the audience by appearing at a benefit talent show in exotic costume and won second prize with a rendition of Indian songs. Carlisle Manaugh took the place of Major Bowes and vigorously banged on the gong when performances faltered.

Binding it all together — the town and the people, their hopes and their dreams — was the physical setting of mountains, canyon, stream, and ocean. It was an integral part of the lives of the young. Nancy June Robinson Evans expressed the depth of this influence in a tribute to her mother, Nancy Kendall-Robinson Wooldridge:

The pastoral pioneer lands of the early days were accessible to the dreamer. They were places where the real and the ideal came together — places where there did not have to be a pot of gold at the end of the rainbow, for the rainbow was sufficient. Here, people were seen whole, not in fractions. An identity was established for a child growing up in such a place, nurtured and secure in such peaceful and beautiful surroundings — in the way the walls of Temescal Canyon rose gently upward and enclosed that paradise home — in the way the stream flowed down through the middle of the canyon . . .on its way to the sea.

For us small children "Fairyland" was at the 'top' or headwaters of that stream. We knew this beyond any question of doubt. We never got there, but we never lost the certainty that if we went just a little farther we would find it. And what is this but hope? Jumping from one stepping stone island to another along the way was a great adventure. It is in the sights and sounds and smells of nature that one truly learns. She is the most excellent teacher of all.

A group of young people in the late 1930s, lingering in front of the Methodist Church after Sunday School. *First row, left to right:* Margaret Jane Work Pollock, Ina Andrews Bitting, Martha French Patterson Wynegar, Loren Wilson. *Second row:* Jim Gabrielson, Carlisle Manaugh, Donald Weeks, Jack Gabrielson, and Joan Mercer Bitting. *Courtesy Ina Bitting*

14

WORLD WAR TWO

Radio sets carried news of the Japanese attack on Pearl Harbor on Sunday morning, December 7, 1941. As luck would have it, Jack Sauer had already scheduled a test run to an aircraft spotting station in the detached garage of a home at the top of Bristol Avenue for two o'clock that afternoon. Undaunted, his crew of thirty potential watchers, which included Zola Clearwater, Harry Usher, Mary Sauer, and movie star Pat O'Brien, assembled on Sunset Boulevard and drove up the hill in a caravan. Zola and Mrs. Nathaniel Charnley took the first watch and scanned the skies with a pair of binoculars borrowed from Pat O'Brien, while Jack reported by phone to the downtown control center and learned that his Palisades unit was the first such group in the city — by far — to be organized and to report for duty.

Jack, who had acted as the American Legion's civil defense chairman, promptly became chairman of the Pacific Palisades Civilian Defense Council. Knowing from experience that the community was so isolated it would have to be responsible for its own emergency measures in the event of sabotage or attack, Jack promised a useful spot to every man, woman, and youth who offered to help. Four hundred volunteers responded, as residents forgot past controversies and acted together with the dedication and zeal of pioneer days.

The American Legion Auxiliary opened a recreation center for servicemen at the Legion clubhouse in Harmony Hall, and Gladys Peabody took charge of the Motor Transport Mobil Kitchen. Teams of volunteers picked up coffee and sandwiches at the Riviera Country Club and made deliveries to 250 servicemen at various guard posts along the coast, from Malibu to Palos Verdes. Since no official provision had been made to feed the local unit, curbstone wits dubbed it "the lost battalion."

Fears of invasion were intensified as barbed wire was strung up along the bluffs and signs were posted alerting residents to the possibility of enemy landings on the beaches. To bolster the coastal defense system, three 3-inch guns, mounted on tractors, rumbled down Via de la Paz one day and were placed along the bluff in cement mountings, facing at different angles out over Santa Monica Bay. The whole community rattled during target practice, and after the rains, when the men had to stand on "duckboards" in the mud, there was widespread anxiety that the earth would be loosened and the whole bluff would collapse — as it did, years later.

Dr. Clarence F. Ott, an independently wealthy doctor who lived in a large pillared house on Chautauqua Boulevard and was in semi-retirement, immediately obtained a hard-to-get station wagon from a friend in Oakland and at his own expense had it converted to an ambulance. The Red Cross, however, noted a greater need at the North American aircraft plant and purchased the ambulance for the company's use.

Dr. Ott then set up an emergency casualty station at 15314 Antioch Street and made an adjacent room into a fifteen-bed ward. He donated some equipment and arranged for the rest — an operating table, electric generator, instruments, and supplies — and had a nurse on duty six days a week. Dr. Uhl, head of medical civil defense for Los Angeles, inspected facility, pronounced it the best in the city, and used it as a pattern for other areas.

Fears of enemy attack were confirmed on December 10, when radio stations announced the approach of enemy aircraft and an immediate blackout was ordered. A second alert was sounded the following night, and on February 23, 1942, a Japanese submarine reportedly lobbed shells into an oil installation near Santa Barbara.

Two days later Los Angeles experienced its one and only "air raid." Secret radar screens picked up an unidentified object approaching the coastline at 2:00 A.M., and at 3:06 A.M., some sort of flying object — said by some observers to resemble a balloon — appeared over Santa Monica. Residents rushed out into their yards to watch as searchlights

Above, standing in front of the fully equipped casualty station on Antioch Street are the hard-working members of the Civilian Defense Council. *Left to right:* Major Jirah Downs, David C. Stadler, Mrs. Hamilton Garland, Mrs. H.J. Keller, Mrs. L.J. Chambard, Miss Ruth Millard, Mrs. Coragern Reppy, Mrs. R.J. Morrison, Florian J. Sauer, Mrs. R.E. Westenhaver, Harry Usher, Mrs. Ida B. Kibler, Anatol Josepho, Willard Auch, Robert J. Foster, C.D. Clearwater, and Dr. C.J. Ott. *Clearwater Collection*

Below, the AWVS Motor Transport car loaned by Winifred Knowlton (shown standing, with a basket) delivered coffee and sandwiches nightly from the Riviera Country Club to more than 250 soldiers on outpost duty. *Clearwater Collection*

converged on the target, and anti-aircraft batteries burst into action, shooting off more than 1,400 rounds of 3-inch shells and lighting up the sky with tracer bullets. While the public-at-large accused the Army of being trigger-happy, some qualified observers and the top brass stoutly maintained that planes had been sighted. Three years later, Lieutenant General John DeWitt of the Western Defense Command stated officially that the planes in question might have been launched from a Japanese submarine or that they might have been unauthorized civilian craft. To this day the true cause of the alert remains a mystery.

All in all, the scare gave meaning to local defense measures. Blackout restrictions were vigorously enforced to minimize the danger of enemy action against such targets as the Douglas aircraft plant nearby. Each home had its blackout curtains, and block wardens patrolled the streets to warn residents if cracks of light appeared. No street traffic was permitted during blackouts; at other times automobiles ran with their parking lights, the upper half masked with black tape, and advertising lights were dimmed. The intersection of Chautauqua and Sunset was deemed a hazard when five autos in a month ran over the curb and suffered one to four blowouts apiece. Thereafter, the curbs were painted with black and white zebra stripes, and protective posts were installed.

The air raid wardens' corps under Dave Stadler's leadership went into action with each alert. Before the sirens were installed, a "telephone tree" was used to contact 160 volunteers for medical, firefighting, and police duties. The necessary supplies — armbands, steel helmets, and gas masks — were all provided by the community. Santa Monica Canyon had an independent defense council, and each geographical area had its own roster of wardens and fire watchers, the list including such notables as actors Jack Holt and Tom Moore, conductor Richard Lert, sculptor Merrell Gage, screen writer Frank Dazey, and producer-director Joseph Mankiewicz.

In Huntington Palisades, chief warden Denis Lee requisitioned an old wagon from the Pacific Land Corporation and equipped it for firefighting, with

Young men's Sunday School class on November 9, 1941, at the Methodist Church. A short time later most of them had gone into the service. *Front row, left to right:* Clint Creed, Don Van Olinda, Jack Stephenson, Rodney Powell, Mourley Wheeler, Bob Titus, and Doc Crane. *Second row:* Reverend Taber, _____, Dick Stead, Dave Oswalt, _____, Chuck Norris, Bob Lindstadt, George Richards, Dick Shaver, Robert Stephan. *Back row:* Bob Thomas, Nat Charnley, Dave Huycke, Al Jenewein, Jackie Sauer, Louis Clearwater, and Roger Cotton. "Doc" Crane was a friend and mentor to the boys and a founder of the "We Boys" Lodge. *Courtesy Bee Clark Kottinger*

squirt cans, buckets of sand, and fire hoses. It took a dozen men to push it across the mesa to Corona del Mar — downhill there and uphill back.

A big "Junk Rally" was held in September, 1942, to support civil defense efforts. Prime donations included old road-building equipment no longer needed by the Uplifters and a new rubber mat from Anatol Josepho's horse trailer. Permanent salvage bins were set up as collecting stations for fats and metals.

Gasoline was the first scarce item to fall under nationwide rationing, followed by sugar. Later, ration books were issued with red coupons for meat and fats, blue coupons for shoes, coffee, and processed (canned and frozen) foods. Much attention was given to the point values assigned to each scarce item. Housewives were asked to declare their supply of sugar and canned goods to discourage hoarding. Shortages inspired a rash of Victory Gardens and an exchange of new recipes, now that meat was scarce and such popular party foods as marshmallows, bananas, and whipping cream had disappeared from grocers' shelves.

Nature unexpectedly provided Palisadians with a gourmet feast on June 26, 1945, when hundreds of thousands of lobsters were washed up onto the shore by the waves and were gathered into gunnysacks by gleeful beachcombers. University of California scientists speculated that microorganisms in the water had so depleted the oxygen supply in the water that the crustaceans took flight.

The Palisadian offered a helping hand to cooks and gardeners alike by running weekly columns of timely hints and suggestions. Residents wrote in, reporting on the size of their squashes and bemoaning the loss of their produce to gophers and deer. The Bernheimer Gardens offered plants and seeds to local patrons and set up a demonstration Victory Garden under a federal program, adding ornamental vegetable beds to the usual floral displays.

During the war the Gardens suffered a series of misfortunes: Bernheimer's own residence, Hilltop House, was seriously damaged by slides; patronage fell off due to gas rationing; and the Oriental Gardens themselves became suspect in the wave of hostility toward anything Japanese. Bernheimer had to explain repeatedly that he and all of his employees, including the gardeners, were loyal Americans, and that the concept of the Gardens was Chinese, even though some of the art works had come from Japan.

As Pacific Palisades mobilized for war, some residents found new careers at the aircraft plants; others worked long hours as volunteers. Mrs. Robert E. Westenhaver and Mrs. Galitzen organized the American Women's Voluntary Services which

Zola Clearwater admiring the tall corn in her Victory Garden. *Clearwater Collection*

coordinated a variety of activities for the benefit of servicemen. The joint Pacific Palisades-Brentwood AWVS unit had a membership of one thousand and included such prominent local women as Virginia Bruce, Jean Garland, Vilma Ebsen, Mmes. Jack Conroy, Buster Crabbe, and Grover Jones. In addition, more than two thousand persons were enrolled in physical fitness, motor mechanics, and home nursing courses under AWVS auspices. To support their programs, the group organized a series of benefits and maintained an antique shop in the Lee Building.

The Mobil Canteen alone was a major volunteer effort. Local women continued the emergency program and prepared hundreds of sandwiches daily for delivery to the guard posts. Transportation was provided by two station wagons — one belonging to the AWVS and the other loaned by Winifred Knowlton. Groups of three or four teenage girls made the rounds with an adult driver, the most dedicated being Vilma Ebsen, who had succeeded

Mrs. Peabody as supervisor of the canteen service. It was a banner day when the girls riding with her discovered that one guard contingent was composed entirely of handsome Ivy League college men; return visits to that post were in popular demand.

Another project was instigated by the army, who gave secret orders to the unit to hold parties for departing servicemen. Every effort was made to give them a good time. The movie colony turned out en masse — Dixie Crosby, Bob Hope, Joan and Constance Bennett, Kay Francis, Dale Evans, and many more providing homes, entertainment, and hospitality, with Westside teenage girls serving as hostesses. For larger groups, the Riviera Country Club and the Uplifters Club made an even wider variety of recreational facilities available.

Rustic Canyon provided its own excitement when FBI men raided the Murphy Ranch — immediately after Pearl Harbor — and conducted Herr Schmidt off to the pokey. They discovered that he had hidden a short-wave radio on the property and had been transmitting messages to the Germans. Nothing more is known, except that he died in prison during the war. The swastika-clad marchers and the spiritualism cultists who had frequented the property became less visible, and the Stephenses thereafter managed the ranch as a self-sufficient farm.

The Josephos, who had previously been unaware of the true situation at the Murphy Ranch, whole-heartedly joined the community defense effort. Anatol became a fire marshal and purchased an old truck which the city equipped with pumpers and tanks and had available for use on narrow mountain roads where conventional equipment would be useless. It was manned by volunteers and kept at the fire station. Anatol and Ganna also entertained hundreds of servicemen at the ranch over the years under the sponsorship of the AWVS, providing a day of relaxation with food, entertainment, and swimming in the pool.

The Uplifters, as usual, performed their civil defense tasks in style, particularly Chief Warden Robert Bowman who made his rounds in handsome tailored outfits, color-coordinated from head to toe, often matching the shades of his Cord and Lincoln automobiles. Nora Edmundson taught first-aid classes in Dr. Kress's garage, where a cache of medical supplies and other equipment was stored, and Latimer Road residents planted Victory Gardens on the meadowland along the creek.

Able-bodied men being scarce, women were added to the list of wardens. The Uplifters liberalized their rules and admitted their first lady member — Olive May, a widow with two grown daughters, who became eligible for a membership quite unwittingly by purchasing three wooded acres by the stream for a homesite and patriotically signed on as an air raid warden. One night when an alert was sounded, a party was in progress at the home of writer Coningsby Dawson across the creek and lights continued to blaze. Failing to reach him by phone, "Ollie May" put her own safety aside and scrambled across the swollen stream in the darkness to deliver the warning.

To test their preparedness the Uplifters staged practice drills in front of the clubhouse, the warden handing out sealed envelopes with assignments. The hardest job was manning the heavy fire hose, which was mounted on four-foot wheels, and running with it down the street to the simulated fire site. The Spanish class therefore decided to hold a big benefit spaghetti supper to finance new fire equipment for the canyon's use. The event happened to fall on invasion day, so the volunteers gathered in Onis Rice's tiny kitchen, cooking batch after batch of pasta and sauce while the radio brought them the latest war news.

The Uplifters Ranch gained prominent new summertime residents from 1944 to 1948 when Governor Earl Warren and his family visited the

Actor Tom Moore served as a member of the mounted home guard, based at the Uplifters' polo field. *Courtesy Eleanor Moore*

Above, serving hot dogs to the soldiers at the Josepho Ranch. The party was held in the enclosed barbecue area, which was behind the main house. *Left to right:* Phyllis Westenhaver Tebbe, Barbara Kirk Raker, Ganna Josepho, Nina Wilson, and Mrs. Koenig. *Courtesy Phyllis Westenhaver Tebbe*

Below, Phyllis Westenhaver Tebbe with some of the soldiers who attended an AWVS party at the Josepho Ranch. The view is from the terrace of the Josepho home, looking across the bridge toward the swimming pool. *Courtesy Phyllis Westenhaver Tebbe*

Marco Hellman cabin as guests of Joseph Musgrove. The governor came down from Sacramento for weekends, while Mrs. Warren and five of their six children remained at the Ranch. *The Palisadian* noted with pleasure and pride that the family's favorite pastimes included swimming at Will Rogers State Beach, grunion hunts at Malibu, and sailboat excursions out to Santa Cruz Island.

Farther down Rustic Canyon, World War I veteran David Malcolmson put his writing and his classes aside and returned to Illinois to operate the family farm for the war effort. His newest novel, *The Man Who Killed Hitler,* recently had caused a major uproar, especially among the Germans, who sent out spies to track down the author.

The book was actually the product of a collaboration between David, who provided the idea and wrote the story, and Ruth, Countess Yorck, a German-Jewish refugee who supplied the background material. The publisher, George Palmer Putnam, gave the manuscript to one of his staff writers who rewrote and sensationalized it, and proceeded to publish the book anonymously. It became an instant success, was published in several languages, and made into a movie. Putnam heightened the drama of the book's release when he disappeared — supposedly the victim of a kidnapping — and resurfaced miraculously in Bakersfield with a copy of the book in his hand for reporters and photographers to see. Subsequently David received a share of the royalties but was never given due credit for the authorship.

Over the hill in Sullivan Canyon, Dorothy and Arthur Loomis had their own pastoral retreat on 140 acres of land retained by Dorothy's father, Robert Gillis, after he sold the major portion of his holdings to Alphonzo Bell. There Gillis had a hideaway cabin for himself and houses for the Japanese and Mexican farmhands who tended the orchards and livestock and raised chives commercially.

When war was declared the Japanese were interned, and the Loomises, with various members of their family, moved onto the property and operated the ranch with the help of Pablo, the remaining workman. With two sons serving in the combat zone, the Loomises were grateful for the busy life on the ranch. They transformed the chive patch into a pasture, where they kept cows and raised calves for meat. Arthur practiced up on his technique and did the milking before he went into his brokerage office in Beverly Hills each day. They made their own cheese and butter, using a hand-operated churn, and each season harvested a bumper

American Women's Voluntary Services' ambulances and nattily uniformed personnel. From left to right; Betty Dyons, Kay Tomson, Barbara Orr, Virginia Orr and Cynthia Sammons. *Clearwater Collection*

crop of fruit and vegetables.

There was no lack of adventure. An attempt to raise turkeys failed when the young ones proved too inept to roost and had to be lifted bodily and placed on their perches, and the old male turkey was so cantankerous that he chased the Loomises around the orchard. Chickens were easier. The first batch of pedigreed fowl, purchased from an Uplifter, failed to produce eggs, but a second mongrel batch of hens yielded a steady supply. Snakes were the greatest hazard. Both rattlers and king snakes invaded the chicken coop and coiled up in the nests. They were a constant worry until, following Pablo's advice, the Loomises brought in an army of cats.

The first Palisadian to become a war hero was Santa Monica Canyonite Jimmy Edmundson, who became an army pilot and was stationed at Hickam Field in Honolulu at the time of Pearl Harbor. Wounded by shrapnel, he nevertheless requested transfer to a combat unit and was sent to a bomber squadron. He was credited with sinking a Japanese submarine in Hawaiian waters on January 16, 1942; thereafter he participated in over a hundred combat missions and was awarded the D.F.C. Following his discharge with the rank of major general, Edmundson returned to Pacific Palisades, and in 1961 headed the first full-fledged American Legion Fourth of July parade.

The atmosphere of tension and fear of imminent invasion began winding down in 1943-44, and dimout restrictions were eased. Once again shop windows were illuminated, and the street lights, although kept shielded from the sea, were turned back on. The attention of residents focussed on the annual war chest campaigns and war bond drives, which were regularly over-subscribed by an ample margin, and on ways of assisting returning servicemen.

The McCormick property on Corona del Mar played a role in meeting just such a need. It had been vacant since 1941, when Virginia McCormick died without leaving a will. To settle the estate, administrators held an auction of her furnishings, and for the first time the public could troop through the buildings, admiring her museum pieces and the five grand pianos that had satisfied her craving for music. Community plans to turn the estate into a park and art gallery failed to make any progress due to objections from neighborhood residents.

The United States Shipping Board stepped in and took over the property on a one-year lease in 1944, over fresh protests by Huntington Palisades homeowners, and turned it into a rest home for sixty-nine merchant seamen. Furnishings were obtained from luxury ocean liners which had been converted into transport vessels.

The formal opening, attended by representatives of the armed services, the community, and various Scout groups, was held on April 23, 1944. Speakers included Isadore Dockweiler, Charles Bickford, and neighbor Charles Laughton, who thrilled the crowd with a reading of Lincoln's Gettysburg Address. In short order, the ladies of Pacific Palisades formed an auxiliary and showered the men with homemade gifts and food items.

News from the camps and the fighting front appeared in *The Palisadian,* as many young men who had grown up in the community went off to war. One of the youngest was Jackie Sauer, who left Santa Monica Junior College to enlist in 1943 and was commissioned a Lieutenant in the Army Air Corps in March, 1944. He was trained as a bombardier-navigator and was sent with a liberator crew to England for bombing runs over Germany.

A few weeks later, Jack and Mary Sauer received the dread news that their son had been killed on the crew's thirteenth mission on September 8, the first Palisadian known to have perished in combat. The plane had been struck over Munich by heavy anti-aircraft fire which severely damaged the nose section. All of the crew members returned safely to their base except Jackie, who died while helping an injured crewman. Cliff Clearwater wrote a personal tribute in *The Palisadian* to his son's close friend, and the community held a memorial service at Legion Hall.

The end of the war in Europe was announced on Monday, May 7, 1945, at 11:00 P.M. and was celebrated quietly with "thanksgiving, hope, and prayer." A few weeks later, on Memorial Day, ceremonies at the Community Church honored those who had died in the service of their country: Lieutenant O. Carman Richardson, Major Albert H. Bohne, Ensign Wayne A. Seath, Private John Alden Speers, Lieutenant John D. Sauer, Lieutenant Joseph Bowman, Donovan W. Jacobs, William E. Lyons, Richard C. O'Reilly, and Clyde Freeman.

The local casualty station closed in June and the contents were donated to worthy organizations. The long-awaited announcement of V-J Day became official at one minute after four o'clock in the afternoon of August 14, 1945. It was a time for rejoicing. There were smiles and tears and an embrace for friends and strangers alike. In Santa Monica auto horns sounded and everyone poured out into the streets. Downtown Los Angeles and Hollywood were jammed. Radio reporters conducted random man-on-the-street interviews, while listeners at home remained close to their sets, hungry for news. Gas rationing and restrictions on canned goods ended the next day, and by the end of November virtually all rationing was discontinued. For most Palisadians the world returned to normal.

15

WEIMAR-BY-THE-SEA

For one group the anxieties of wartime were not over. The average Palisadian was little aware that the influx of refugees from Europe before and during World War II turned the immediate area into one of the great intellectual centers of all time — an "American Weimar." This epic migration began in the 1920s when Hollywood and the film industry attracted scores of European actors, directors, and writers, several of whom found in Hollywood a flamboyant and lucrative niche.

The artistic hub of Europe in the twenties was Berlin. Its theaters and concert halls attracted an outpouring of talent and provided an opportunity for exchange of ideas that fanned the creative spark. The modernist mode in music and the expressionist theme in art, film, and literature spread to other cultural centers from the experience of Berlin.

The chilling events of the thirties, set in motion by Hitler's rise to power in January, 1933, led to a dampening of this spirit and a gradual migration of European artists of many nationalities — both Jewish and Gentile — to safer countries, and eventually to the United States. When German forces entered Austria in March, 1938, and began the conquest of Europe, an increasing number of artists came to America and joined one or another of the refugee colonies.

Hollywood offered opportunities for employment in the arts and provided a place to meet old friends. The warm climate and the mountainous coastline also attracted Europeans from the north who had traditionally sought refuge from the cold at resorts along the Mediterranean and now found homes on the West Side in Beverly Hills, Brentwood, Pacific Palisades, and Santa Monica. Here the more successful writers and composers were able to collect royalties from their European and American publishers and to reconstruct their lives in a comfortable, even luxurious fashion, while the less fortunate among them struggled to earn enough to pay their bills.

Los Angeles thus provided a safe harbor for an unprecedented array of artistic talent; at the same time this land of palm trees and gentle breezes was traditionally indifferent to newcomers and inhospitable to new forms of art. The refugees themselves tended to lead isolated lives, even Germans apart from Austrians. Yet, their appearance in the predominantly Anglo-Saxon, Protestant community of Pacific Palisades presaged the later arrival of others with different ethnic and religious backgrounds. This small nucleus of world-renowned artists, mostly Jewish and Central European in origin, also brought a heady infusion of talent and a worldly sophistication to the local scene that was beyond the scope of the familiar Chautauquas.

The first such refugees to live in Pacific Palisades were the Viertels, both from Austria, who came to Santa Monica Canyon in 1929. Berthold Viertel, an established writer and theatrical director, had come to Hollywood under a three-year contract to Fox Studios; his wife, Salka, discovered Santa Monica while house-hunting and thought the beach town would be an ideal home for their three sons. Extending her search to Santa Monica Canyon, she rented — and later bought — a house near the ocean at 165 Mabery Road, which became a world-renowned haven for artists and visiting dignitaries.

In Salka's book, *Kindness of Strangers,* she describes her first visit to the canyon:

> On my left was a road winding uphill and on my right shacks and adobe huts and lots overgrown with weeds and geraniums. I faced a clapboard schoolhouse, small and rural, on which the roads seemed to converge. Children, mostly Mexicans, played on the slides and swings of the recreation ground. All this was peaceful and quiet: old sycamores and gnarled oaks, a swollen brook which rushed toward the Ocean highway.

Through the real estate agent, Mr. Guercio, she found the house — English-style with a magnolia tree in bloom and a fence overgrown with honeysuckle and "pink Portugal" roses. The rooms were sunny and spacious. "From the windows one could see the ocean and the sharp profile of the hills on the other

A portion of a 1930 panorama, focussing on Salka Viertel's home at 165 Mabery Road in Santa Monica Canyon which became a favorite gathering place for émigré artists. *Young Collection*

side of the canyon, and I could hear the waves pounding on the shore." Little matter that the house was in receivership and that the sofa and armchairs were covered with black velvet and the rest of the living room was filled with "shabby rattan garden chairs."

Salka, herself an actress, had the good fortune to meet Greta Garbo, a neighbor with whom she enjoyed early morning walks along the beach. This friendship led to an acting role for Salka in a German version of *Anna Christie* and to a career with MGM as Garbo's screen writer, her credits including such films as *Queen Christina, Anna Karenina,* and *Marie Curie.*

In their personal lives, the Viertels drifted apart, as Berthold's work took him to Europe and New York, and Salka's kept her in Hollywood. Sunday gatherings on Mabery Road, however, reflected Salka's warmth and good nature and attracted such varied guests as Charlie Chaplin, Johnny Weissmuller, Oscar Levant, Dmitri Tiomkin, Miriam Hopkins, Max Reinhardt, Arnold Schoenberg, Thomas and Heinrich Mann, the Lion Feuchtwangers, Franz Werfel and his wife, Alma Mahler Werfel.

Salka became a citizen in 1939, and her sons attended Canyon School. Peter, who later became an author and playwright, wrote his first book, *The*

Canyon, in 1940, at the age of nineteen, telling the fictionalized story of his own boyhood. At the end, the beauty of the canyon is destroyed by fire and flood, and the innocence of his youth perishes as well: "All through the canyon you could see the tops of cars sticking up out of the muddy current. Down to the sea . . . down to the sea it took everything. Telegraph poles, toys, furniture, garbage cans, and always mud, heavy and brown, that was the water's brother."

The first émigrés to live in the heart of Pacific Palisades were the Tochs, who arrived in 1936 — Ernst, Lilly, and their daughter, Franzi. Toch was riding the crest of his fame as a "modernist" composer and was given an enthusiastic welcome in *The Palisadian.* He had recently written the music for the movie *Peter Ibbetson,* and his new work "Pinocchio" was scheduled for performance by the Los Angeles Philharmonic Orchestra. Critics praised him as a "tone painter and a poet" and commented that he wrote with delicacy and wit.

The Palisadian urged Toch to use the "irresistible charm of Pacific Palisades" as a theme for a new tone poem, "weaving the heartthrobs of this place . . . into a musical fabric . . . formed of the natural beauties of its setting, the hopes, joys, heartaches and noble dreams of its founders and pioneers, and the echoes of the exquisite music and inspirational addresses heard on the great Assembly programs."

This encyclopedic request was never gratified. However, the Tochs did rent a Spanish-style house on De Pauw Street, facing Potrero Canyon, that had a view of the mountains and a glimpse of the ocean. The setting was an inspiration to Toch, as were his daily walks in the hills. A few years later, after the Tochs had moved, a geologist friend's warnings were confirmed: the house, whose site was unstable, tumbled into the canyon.

Toch, who was Viennese by birth, developed his musical career in Germany and moved to Berlin in 1928. He returned from a United States tour in 1932 to find the Nazis in power; his publisher had deserted him; his music was being burned and his concerts cancelled. The family fled to New York where Toch's acquaintance with George Gershwin led to a commission by Warner Brothers Studios and the move to California. Here to greet them were German-born Vicki Baum and her husband, Viennese conductor Richard Lert, who had built a home on Amalfi Drive. According to Marta Feuchtwanger, Vicki Baum became a "pathfinder and counselor" for the refugees, whether they had a large income or none at all.

The Tochs moved to Toyopa Drive in 1937. There were happy moments as well as sad. When their furniture arrived from Germany, the Tochs took the huge packing crates, rented a small parcel of land on the beachfront at Malibu, and put together a shack where Ernst could be alone and work on his music. In the grand European manner, they called it the "Villa Majestic."

Sadness entered their lives in December, 1937, when Toch's mother died in Vienna. While attending the ritual prayers for the dead at the local synagogue, Toch decided to base a new composition on the *Haggada,* a scripture read to the family at the Passover table. A few months later, Hitler's armies invaded Austria and occupied Vienna, adding new meaning to Toch's *Cantata of the Bitter Herbs* — a universal message of liberation from oppression.

The danger in Europe intensified with the Nazi takeover of Austria in 1938, and from then on, the émigrés who were established in the United States spent their lives trying to save those who had been left behind. It was not an easy process. To bring refugees to America sponsors had to provide affidavits and assume financial responsibility for five years. In addition, the quotas were painfully small, considering the backlog of desperate applicants waiting in Europe, and there were visas to be obtained. Citizenship was another hurdle, requiring character witnesses to appear in court, a time-consuming imposition on any but close friends.

The Tochs, who became citizens in 1940, were successful in saving several of their relatives, but the effort took its toll, physically and emotionally, as Ernst accepted any kind of work — films, private students, and lecturing — to obtain the necessary funds. Their daughter, Franzi Toch Weschler, remembers this period as a difficult and lonely one for the family, much as they loved Pacific Palisades. Their immediate neighborhood was sparsely settled, and their house on Toyopa had few neighbors. Franzi was the only Jewish girl in the grammar school, and while she was welcomed, she had no close ties to the community. The family's friendships were with the other refugees, who provided solace and old-country comforts. One enterprising lady named Lotte Spitz ran a catering service from a refrigerator installed in the trunk of her passenger Chevrolet and made the rounds, delivering European-style sausages, Viennese chocolates, and other

Conductor Otto Klemperer, Prinz Hubertus von Lowenstein, Arnold Schoenberg, and Ernst Toch, strolling in upper Rustic Canyon. *Courtesy Ernst Toch Archive/ UCLA Music Library*

delicacies to refugee households — an important concession since few of the refugees had cars.

Toch's musical career suffered a personally devastating decline as the need to earn a livelihood forced him to write movie scores to order — often horror or chase scenes which capitalized on the eerie effect of his unique tonal patterns — and to take on a heavy teaching schedule at USC. Although he received three Academy Award nominations for Paramount Studio mystery films, it was not until after the war that he could resume the track of his artistic career.

The Tochs moved to Santa Monica a few weeks before Pearl Harbor. When America entered the war, communication was cut off and the heartbreak intensified. Lilly, whose sister died in a concentration camp, later observed in her UCLA oral history, *A Composer's Life,* " . . . there were really two worlds living here together: those who knew and those who didn't know. And we just were among those who knew. It was really a somber time." Even Villa Majestic was lost when the war began, first due to blackout regulations and gas rationing, then the building itself was washed away by the tides.

The arrival of Marta and Lion Feuchtwanger in 1941 and of Katia and Thomas Mann later that year brought added prestige to Pacific Palisades. Mann was known as the giant of German literature — author of *The Magic Mountain* and recipient of the Nobel Prize for literature in 1929. Although Thomas Mann was not Jewish, he had spoken out fearlessly against the Nazi regime; his books were being burned and he was marked for reprisal.

The Manns were on a three-week lecture tour in 1933 when the Nazis took over. Warned not to return to their home in Munich, they sought sanctuary in Switzerland and France. In 1938 Mann received an honorary doctorate at Harvard, and in the fall he accepted a guest professorship at Princeton.

At the conclusion of the Princeton appointment in April, 1941, the Manns came to Pacific Palisades and purchased a "beautiful, relatively inexpensive piece of property" on San Remo Drive. In Katia Mann's biography, *Unwritten Memories,* she remarks, "The location was beautiful, with a magnificent view of the sea and of Catalina Island, and with palm, orange, and lemon trees on a large plot." The Manns chose Bauhaus-trained J.R. Davidson to design their home, a functional structure in the modern mode, and rented a house on Amalfi Drive until the work was completed. Mann regarded the area's "Pacific Palisades" post office designation with some astonishment and wrote in one of his letters: "I did not consider that a town name at all —and in fact it probably isn't a township but a

landscape with a few colonial homes and ocean view."

Mann was busy and successful, with a full schedule of lecture tours, publication of his *Joseph* series, and a new novel, *Dr. Faustus,* in progress. When he was at home the neighbors often saw him on his solitary walks, lost in thought, planning his next day's work. Katia observed: " . . . usually all of the dogs would follow him. Americans don't walk much; in any case they didn't at that time."

As more refugees arrived, the Manns' circle of friends grew, leading Katia to write, "In the world of émigrés everyone has open house, and so in California we saw more German writers than we had in Munich." Accepting America as their new home, the Manns became citizens in 1944.

Although not strictly a Palisadian, the great Austrian composer Arnold Schoenberg lived on nearby Rockingham Drive and was an important member of the local refugee group. He arrived in Los Angeles in 1934, was appointed professor of music at UCLA in 1936, and moved to Brentwood at that time. Schoenberg steadfastly refused to compose music-to-order for the movies, but gave classes for other composers and arrangers and continued to write vocal and instrumental music in both the twelve-tone and traditional modes, much of it conveying his anguish and sadness over his homeland. In 1941 he and his wife both became citizens.

Schoenberg's passion for tennis was legendary. He played regularly at his friend George Gershwin's court where, Oscar Levant remarked, Schoenberg would arrive with an "entourage of string quartet players, conductors, and disciples." On one occasion, after two vigorous sets, he complained of being too tired to play well, then remembered, "That's right, I was up at five this morning. My wife gave birth to a boy."

Schoenberg was forced to retire from his UCLA post in 1944 at the age of seventy, and thereafter had a difficult time financially. Plagued by recurring heart trouble, Schoenberg died in 1951. Today he is recognized the world over for his musical achievements, and his name is honored locally by the presence of Schoenberg Hall at UCLA and the Schoenberg Institute at USC.

Of all the local refugees, Lion Feuchtwanger and his wife, Marta, seemed to adapt most readily to the American way and became true Palisadians. They liked the Americans — the camaraderie and the mixture of people — and felt comfortable here. Lion, a prolific and popular author who had been nominated for the Nobel Prize, was aptly characterized as a "German novelist whose heart was Jewish and whose mind was cosmopolitan."

According to Marta's lively and insightful UCLA oral history, *An Emigré Life,* the Feuchtwangers had been refugees virtually since 1925, when Hitler's growing influence in Bavaria led them to move from their home in Munich to Berlin. In 1933, when Hitler became chancellor of Germany, they were forced to flee and to abandon everything in their Berlin home to the Nazis, who killed their pets, trampled their gardens, and destroyed Lion's magnificent library. They sought refuge first in Austria, then Switzerland, and finally at Sanary on the French Riviera, where they were joined by an ever-changing group of friends — among them the Thomas Manns, Berthold Brecht, and Aldous Huxley, all of whom, like the Feuchtwangers, later made their homes in or near Pacific Palisades.

When war broke out in 1940, Lion and Marta were interned by the French as "enemy aliens," and after France was defeated were in danger of being handed over to the Nazis. The situation for Lion was desperate, since he had been sentenced to death by the Germans for his books against Hitler, and posters with his likeness were on display everywhere. Managing to escape from their captors, the Feucht-

Lion and Marta Feuchtwanger in the library of their home in Pacific Palisades. *Courtesy Marta Feuchtwanger*

wangers crossed the Pyrenees on foot, reached Portugal safely, and departed — each on a separate ship — for New York.

The Feuchtwangers came to Los Angeles, attracted by the climate and the ocean, and with the help of friends moved into a succession of rented homes — in Mandeville Canyon, on Sunset Boulevard, and on Amalfi Drive. Each had a special appeal, but for their own home, the Feuchtwangers preferred a house by the sea. Their search eventually led them to Paseo Miramar, where virtually all of the nine existing houses were for sale, and all in varying stages of disrepair. The steep, brush-covered ridge was considered too remote from schools, markets, and medical care, especially under gas rationing. Even so, the Feuchtwangers were pleased. The picturesque site reminded them of Italy.

The house they chose was the *Los Angeles Times* Demonstration Home, which had belonged to Judge Arthur A. Weber, one of the owners and developers of Miramar Estates. According to Marta, the Webers had patterned the house after a small castle they had seen near Seville. They returned from Spain with the authentic blueprints and wood for a ceiling and brought the patio fountain from Italy.* Before they could move in, however, the judge died in court. His widow, Sophie, found the house too large and isolated for herself and their two sons, and employed a caretaker who had occupied the home for the past eight years. At this point he too wished to leave.

The task that confronted the Feuchtwangers was monumental: the windows were broken; there was a foot of dirt in the house, spider webs in the basement, and a tangle of weeds and shrubbery in the garden. Lion had just sold his novel *Lautensacks* to *Colliers* magazine, providing funds for a down payment on the house, but not enough for furniture.

At first they had only sleeping bags, which were placed out in the garden and served as beds. Sympathizing with their plight, Pacific Palisades lawyer Eric Scudder, who had read and admired Lion's books, sent a workman to help Marta shovel the dirt, dead lizards, and mice out of the rooms. Gradually the Feuchtwangers furnished the house with interesting antique pieces from second-hand stores and bought a huge Oriental rug from titled neighbors farther up the hill.

They purchased more lots for privacy, built paths down the hillside and bridges over the ravines; Marta planted trees and designed flower beds, with roses and seasonal varieties. The garden was a delight to them both. Lion worked in the library,

*A version of the story that does not completely dovetail with the newspaper account presented in an earlier chapter.

where he dictated in German to a secretary, but the garden was his relaxation. Lion's generous income from book sales and movie rights permitted them both to indulge their hobbies — Marta to buy trees and Lion to begin again the pleasurable task of locating rare books and assembling a new library.

Friends and compatriots came to call. Charles Chaplin, Lewis Browne, and playwright Berthold Brecht were frequent guests at their home, as was Charles Laughton, who gave Shakespearean readings in the garden. The Feuchtwangers and Manns also took turns hosting large dinner parties at which the men read from their latest manuscripts. When they met at the Feuchtwangers' — for both English and German language sessions — the guests feasted on Greek and Italian salads and Marta's famous hot apple strudel.

Lion brought Brecht and his family to the United States in 1941. Although Brecht had a great talent, he was radical in politics and a skeptic in his point of view. He had no use for the Feuchtwangers' house and remarked, "Pacific Palisades doesn't exist; it's just trees and hills. When someone is sick there is no doctor; when you need a pharmacy, there's nothing to buy. You cannot live so far away from civilization."

Nevertheless, Lion and Brecht worked amicably together on a play, *Simone.* Later it was published by Lion as a novel, and in that form was chosen by the Literary Guild. The screen rights were sold to Goldwyn, Brecht's share of the proceeds enabling

him to buy a house in Santa Monica and to continue his writing. Many plays from this period, including *Mother Courage* and *The Good Person of Setzuan,* were eventually world famous, but only a new version of an earlier work, *Galileo,* was performed while he was here.

The English translation of *Galileo* was the result of a two-year collaboration with Charles Laughton, who was intrigued with playing the title role. To complicate the creative process, Brecht spoke little English and Laughton no German, but both men knew French. They met at Laughton's home on the bluff overlooking the sea in Huntington Palisades, often working in the garden, which was decorated with pre-Columbian ceramics and statuary and was Laughton's pride.

In his article in the *Reader,* "Artists in Paradise," Lawrence Weschler describes the scene as, " . . . day after day, the two convened — the small [slim] playwright in his leather jacket, chewing on the proverbial stub of his cigar; the huge actor in his bulging robe, the Bible and Shakespeare in opposite pockets — and through a special language of gesture and empathy, the two spun out the English translation." Laughton's wife, actress Elsa Lanchester, was less charitable. She loathed Brecht's jacket and objected to the smell of his cigars. The play, produced locally by John Houseman at the Coronet Theatre in August, 1947, with Laughton playing Galileo, drew standing-room-only crowds, but received mixed reviews in the press.

Berthold Brecht and Lion Feuchtwanger on the day of Brecht's departure from the United States. Photograph by Ruth Berlau. *Courtesy Marta Feuchtwanger*

Soon after the joint writing venture ended, the Laughtons moved. Laughton had always feared the prospect of landslides along the sheer cliff at the rear of his home — a fear that was confirmed in 1943 when a slide came to within ten feet of the adjacent Klepetko home, and again a short time later when a large chunk of the Laughtons' garden — walls, trees, and all — fell down on the coast highway. Dismayed, they left for safer pastures in Palos Verdes. Here it should be noted that the dramatically situated house on the point overlooking Santa Monica Canyon is often erroneously identified as the Laughton home, whereas theirs was, in fact, farther west on Corona del Mar.

Living next door to the Laughtons was Max Reinhardt, the world-famous stage and screen director whose Hollywood drama school launched many great acting careers. Also living in Pacific Palisades during the war years were composer Hanns Eisler, who wrote the music for *Galileo,* and two eminent social philosophers, Felix Weil and Professor Max Horkheimer. After the war Horkheimer became president of Frankfort University and exerted an important influence on European scholarship.

Yet another set of notables revolved around a trio of English émigré writers — Aldous Huxley, Gerald Heard, and Christopher Isherwood, all of whom were interested in Far Eastern philosophy and religion. Huxley came to California for his health in 1938 — accompanied by his Belgian wife, Maria, and their son, Matthew — and settled first in Hollywood. In April, 1939, the family moved to a rambling house (since demolished) at 701 Amalfi Drive.

The Huxleys were sociable and fun loving, with a wide array of friends, and were as delighted as children over the prospect of a picnic. Anita Loos, who lived nearby in Santa Monica Canyon, tells of one particularly madcap affair in which she and the Huxleys participated, joined by Christopher Isherwood, Greta Garbo, Charlie Chaplin, Paulette Goddard, Lord Bertrand Russell, the Indian mystic Krishnamurti, and a group of his friends. All came dressed in shabby, exotic, or merely casual clothing, and in looking for a safe place to build a cooking fire, unwittingly breezed by the "No Trespassing" sign and gathered on the dry, sandy bed of the Los Angeles River near Glendale.

Krishnamurti brought out vegetarian foods and prepared them in his own pots and vessels, kept free of contamination by animal products. Garbo, who was in a vegetarian phase, ate only carrots, which she plucked from a supply dangling from her waist;

The Kress house, overlooking the Uplifters Ranch, which attained world-wide recognition as the home of Aldous Huxley and his family and was the subject of good-natured banter by his friends. *Courtesy UCLA Special Collections*

The famous bar in the cellar of the Kress house. *Courtesy Allen and Gerry Beall*

Maria laid out an array of sandwiches for those with more conventional appetites; and Paulette unpacked champagne and caviar. At this point, the sheriff arrived. Failing to recognize any of the assembled celebrities, he ignored their story and bundled them off to finish their repast in the Huxleys' garden.

The Huxleys' house on Amalfi Drive was a source of wonderment to them all. It stood on the rim of Rustic Canyon, above the Uplifters Ranch, and belonged to the same Dr. Kress who, since 1922, had presided over the annual Uplifters' Circus. In addition to this jovial task, he made frequent trips to Europe with his wife and liked to surprise her by having a carpenter add a new room to the house while they were away. This resulted in a heterogeneous assortment of living spaces — with a barroom taste in decor.

Anita Loos and Christopher Isherwood both wrote about the house with horror, Isherwood calling it "log cabin decadent," but the Huxleys loved it. For them it was a peaceful island — five acres of gardens planted with citrus trees, avocados, and flowers, overlooking the polo field and the hills beyond. Maria described the house in a letter:

...And the man was German and collected horrors in European "kitsch" and specialized in women's bosoms. Pictures of women...all over the place..and statues of bronze.. Some we hid and when I got tired of hiding I hoped to get used to it and we did. Aldous turned the statues

around when he preferred bottoms to breasts. But there are three sitting rooms and a study for Aldous and a little bed and bathroom separate for Matthew....

Then there is a bar in the cellar.. Covered with more bozomed women and clocks which tick up and down a fan on a naked lady and luminous dogs as lamps and.. a full-sized painting of a gorilla carrying a woman in a chemise to a very easily guessed purpose; there also stands a harmonium next to the gorilla. But the house we can laugh at and it is the garden which is the paradise.

Except for their mounting anxiety over the war, the Huxleys' stay on Amalfi Drive was a good one for Aldous. His health, always precarious, improved, enabling him to write the major part of two books, *After Many a Summer Dies the Swan* and *Grey Eminence,* as well as screen adaptations for *Pride and Prejudice* and *Jane Eyre.* After three years Aldous and Maria moved to a dryer climate in the desert, and another refugee writer, Emil Ludwig, and his family moved into the house.

Huxley's British compatriot, Christopher Isherwood, joined the refugee colony in 1939, when war on the continent seemed imminent. He had lived in Berlin for several years, wrote his famous *Berlin Diaries* there and collaborated with Berthold Viertel on the film adaptation of a play, *Little Friend,* which was produced in Berlin. In coming to the West Coast, he knew that through Berthold he had an introduction to Salka Viertel and the circle of Hollywood celebrities who frequented her salon. He also looked forward to meeting Aldous Huxley and Gerald Heard and hoped that their philosophical pursuits might help him find a spiritual basis for his developing belief in pacifism.

Soon after his arrival Isherwood began his studies with the Swami Prabhavananda and became a dedicated follower of the Vedanta movement. During the war he worked with the Quakers in Pennsylvania and at the Vedanta Center in Hollywood, where he found time to write a new novel, *Prater Violet,* based on his film-making experience with Berthold Viertel.

Pearl Harbor and the involvement of the United States in the war compounded the tension in the lives of the émigrés. The Japanese were sent to internment camps, and the Germans, who were designated "enemy aliens," were placed under an eight o'clock curfew. Curiously, this ruling did not apply to Austrians and was not imposed in the East.

Thomas Mann and Albert Einstein both made a plea on behalf of those affected, but the curfew remained in force, and although it was humiliating to those who had resisted the Nazi regime, it was observed with good-natured acceptance. Several of the writers even managed to use the long evenings and the enforced isolation to their advantage and put in long hours of work on their writing. Salka Viertel's three sons, the Thomas Manns' son Klaus, and others from the refugee colony joined the armed forces and served their new country. All now had to watch and wait until the war came to an end.

The drama and tragedy of the refugees did not cease with the celebrations of V-E Day, but continued on through the painful months of hearing, one by one, the tales of friends and relatives who had perished in the Nazi holocaust. There were sad footnotes during and after the war, as many of the refugees themselves died. Several old friends were missing from Salka Viertel's famous soirees, but in their place were such talented newcomers as Norman Mailer, James Agee, John Huston, Norman Lloyd, and Jean Renoir. Christopher Isherwood lived in Salka's garage apartment for a time, and John Houseman rented the main house when Salka no longer needed it for her family.

The era of the Cold War and the House Un-American Activities Committee investigations cast a chill over the émigrés who remained. Berthold Brecht, whose radical views were well known, was called before the committee on October 30, 1947, and after one day of testimony boarded a plane and left for Europe.

The charge generally leveled against the émigrés was an ironic one — "premature antifascism." Even Salka Viertel, when she applied for a passport to visit family and friends in Germany, was repeatedly and rigorously questioned by the immigration authorities, and although her application was ultimately granted, she thereafter found it difficult to obtain employment. Objecting to a variety of such arbitrary actions and again protesting what he perceived to be injustice, Thomas Mann returned to Europe in 1949 and died in Switzerland in 1955.

Lion Feuchtwanger, whose postwar works included *The Widow Capet* and *Goya,* chose the life of Benjamin Franklin as the subject of a new novel, *Proud Destiny.* Envisioning the book as his gift to America, he postponed applying for his second citizenship papers until the manuscript was finished — in retrospect, a mistake in timing. He was called to testify in the McCarthy hearings, accused of premature antifascism, and action on his application repeatedly delayed.

Lion's next play, *The Devil in Boston,* was a commentary on the mood of the times. Its theme was Cotton Mather and the New England witch hunts, a dramatization that predated by several years Arthur Miller's famous stage success *The Crucible.* To no apparent purpose, the committee's badgering continued. Lion appeared before them less than a week before he died in December, 1958. In a final vindication, Marta was told the day after his death that her citizenship had been granted, and that, had he lived, Lion would have become an American citizen as well.

Marta's life had always been so interwoven with Lion's that without him even their garden brought painful memories. She let the weeds and flowers grow rampant as she sought a physical outlet for her grief and loneliness — walking in the mountains, scrambling up the ridges, and plunging into the surf. Deer and raccoons that came to her doorstep provided welcome distractions, and, with time, the ministrations of friends and the inspiration of music helped to heal the wounds.

In Lion's honor his friend Ernst Toch composed an impressive new work, *The Fifth Symphony,* based on the Old Testament theme of Lion's last book, *Jephta and his Daughter.* When completed in 1963, it was given its first performance by the Boston Symphony Orchestra.

Marta's tribute to Lion was twofold. In his memory, she made it possible for USC to establish the Feuchtwanger Institute for the Study of Exile Literature under the direction of Dr. Harold von Hofe. She also donated Lion's magnificent library, their house, and the surrounding gardens to USC, with the understanding that she could remain in the home during her lifetime. In recognition of Marta's own contributions to scholarship and learning, she herself was awarded an honorary Doctor of Humane Letters degree by USC in 1980.

Aerial photograph taken by Clifford Clearwater in 1947. Founders' Tract II, at the bottom of the picture, is sparsely settled; the business section, *center,* has not yet expanded; there is a small square of development at Charm Acres; and Founders' Tract I, *upper right,* is densely populated. The towers of the Methodist Church, *left,* and the elementary school, *right,* stand out clearly, while the Business Block, *above the church,* has retained its parklike setting.

16

POSTWAR BOOM

The unmistakable signs of prosperity that had bolstered the spirits and fattened the pocketbooks of Palisadians in the late 1930s returned with fresh energy as soon as the last battle of World War II had been fought. New homes appeared everywhere — along the hillsides, up the ridges, in the canyons, on the fringe of the mesas — defying risks of future slides, floods, and fires.

According to John H. Kennedy's UCLA master's thesis, there were 365 homes (many of them unoccupied) in the main tracts in January, 1930; ten years later there were 754. In 1941 a "house a day" was started — a record-breaking 268 new homes — before wartime restrictions halted all building. By 1950 there were 2,529 housing units. In terms of population, a nose-count tallied 400 residents in 1939; 796 in 1940; 957 in 1941; 6,387 in 1950; 16,289 in 1960; 18,231 in 1970; and an estimated 38,000 in 1980.

Property sales rose sharply in 1942 when the Palisades Corporation decided to liquidate all of its remaining landholdings and offered to sell unimproved lots in exchange for stock at $100 a share. As a result, lots in the heart of town sold for $500 and others for even less. Eric Scudder purchased several acres immediately north of the business district and, in spite of wartime regulations, developed the Charm Acres tract.

The community's concern over the fate of upper Temescal Canyon was happily resolved in April, 1943, when the seventy-seven-acre Assembly Grounds was sold to the Los Angeles Presbytery. The new owners announced that the camp would be available to Protestant groups on a year-round basis and that the Summer Assemblies would be resumed. An editorial in *The Palisadian* expressed the sentiment of the entire community:

It comes as a tremendous relief from a burden of suspense that has hung over the community during these nine years, during which fear has been expressed that the beautiful canyon spot would be bought privately and developed for residential purposes or in a commercial way that would be harmful to the moral and physical values established here in the past two decades . . . .

With the property in the hands of the Presbyterians, we need have no further worry on that score.

Two other historic parcels were bought by former Congressman Leland M. Ford, each measuring thirty-four acres — the mesa east of Temescal Canyon (which included Peace Hill) and the western mesa (which included Harmony Hall). The American Legion moved to new quarters on Swarthmore, and Ford converted the two-story building into his own private residence.

By August, 1943, the Palisades Corporation had disposed of 375 parcels of land and the campground and moved its records to Los Angeles. A year later the community lost another tie with the past when the Rimmer tract at the northern end of Monument Street was being graded, and workmen operating bulldozers on Peace Hill unceremoniously pushed over the cross, which for many years had been the focal point of Easter sunrise services. Carlisle Manaugh tells the story of the subterfuge by which he and his young friends retrieved the sturdy metal piece and installed it atop the tower of the local community Methodist church, where the cross remains today and is illuminated nightly.

With the Palisades Corporation no longer functioning, the Pacific Palisades Civic League moved in to fill the gap. It set up a new corporation in 1943 which assumed from the Santa Monica Land and Water Company sole ownership of the reversionary rights and took over the Palisades Corporation's responsibility of enforcing the deed restrictions pertaining to most of the lots in Tract 9300. This action gave the League a measure of control over building restrictions and community development. Exceptions to the League's jurisdiction were Charm Acres, Huntington Palisades, the Leland Ford tracts, the Business Block, and Ray Schafer's property in Potrero Canyon. The Civic League also outlined sixteen major community objectives, ranging from completion of sewers to the establishment

Above, the dedication of Will Rogers State Beach in 1942. Geoffrey Morgan is the speaker. Note the cross-section of a redwood log which for many years was a local landmark. Adelbert Bartlett, photographer. *Courtesy Carolyn Bartlett Farnham*

Below, the north wing of the enlarged Will Rogers home, with Will's favorite roping pony, Soapsuds, tied to the rail. *Young Collection*

of a new junior high school and local hospital facilities.

Progress on some programs, particularly park acquisition, had continued even during World War II. In 1942 the disputed Will Rogers beach, located between Pacific Palisades State Beach and Santa Monica Canyon State Beach, became state property when the Rogers family exchanged its beach frontage for a piece of property in Los Angeles, and on July 26, Will Rogers State Beach was dedicated to the public and the armed forces. The Lighthouse, where the ceremonies were held, was even then being operated as a recreational center by the USO. Subsequently, the state acquired the remaining beach frontage extending west to Castellammare, and in 1947 the Huntington Palisades property owners sold their 300-foot strip of private beach to the state for $82,500, completing the chain of public holdings.

After Will's death Betty Rogers continued to make her home in the east wing of the ranch house, and from 1938 to 1943 permitted visitors to tour the living room and the grounds for the benefit of the Salvation Army and the Red Cross. In 1943 she began making plans to donate the ranch house and the original acreage to the state for a park. With her approval, Emil Sandmeier arranged the interiors so the original furnishings and memorabilia would be seen by the public as they were in Will's time.

Mrs. Rogers also offered to give seventy acres of land in Rustic Canyon for a park. Designs drawn by landscape architect Ralph Cornell of UCLA showed an entrance on Sunset Boulevard, a natural garden bordering the stream, and a wide variety of recreational facilities on the flatland. Farther up the canyon, Mrs. Rogers proposed that Will's hideaway cabin be preserved and made the focus of a memorial shrine, surrounded by walks, lawns, and terraces. She also suggested building a Girl Scout camp nearby, with a dormitory and various other structures.

Betty Rogers died at home on June 21, 1943, and the same week the state reached an agreement to accept the ranch house and the original 242 acres as a memorial to Will Rogers — land which at that time was valued at $350,000. The dedication was held on August 19, 1944, with Will's favorite horse, Soapsuds, tied to the hitching rack. Will's close friend Leo Carrillo acted as master of ceremonies, introducing John Charles Thomas who sang "Home on the Range," Jimmy Rogers who spoke for the family, and Governor Warren who accepted the park on behalf of the state.

Today the ranch is operated as Will Rogers State Historical Park, with rangers, guides, and a volunteer docent organization to provide protective, interpretive, and educational services. A few horses are maintained on the premises, and polo matches are still held on the playing field, in accordance with Betty Rogers' wishes.

When continued efforts to convert the remaining acreage into parkland failed, the individual properties were sold as estates or subdivided. In 1945 the Villa Grove and Ravoli Drive mesas were sold for subdivision, and twenty-one acres on the floor of Rustic Canyon, formerly occupied by a pasture and stables, were taken over by four members of the Evans family. Following in the footsteps of their father, pioneer nurseryman Hugh Evans, they planted lush tropical foliage, flowering shrubs, and various exotic specimens around their homes, thereby enhancing the natural beauty of the setting.

Liz Whitney Tippett purchased the burned and vandalized remains of Will Rogers' hideaway log cabin and the accompanying acreage in 1960, enlarging the cabin and making it liveable. She named the property Llangollen Farms and brought her stable of thoroughbreds to the canyon during racing season. Between seasons her manager-in-residence, Archie Sparrow, trained prize-winning cutting horses.

The matter of a cross-mountain road surfaced again after the war when the Rogers family offered to dedicate a two-mile right-of-way for a highway from the San Fernando Valley. Simultaneously, the Los Angeles City Engineer again proposed a pair of bridges over Rustic and Santa Monica canyons — both plans bringing forth fresh opposition from civic groups. Dr. Rufus B. von KleinSmid, president of USC, and other prominent Santa Monica Canyon homeowners allegedly used their influence at City Hall to stave off the threat, while, at the same time, the public was reminded of the grisly record of the Pasadena Arroyo Seco bridge — a notorious launching pad for suicides.

The matter of an offshore breakwater was revived in grandiose fashion in 1962, when rapid expansion of the freeway system was in vogue. Herb Murray, Jr., writing in *Westways,* predicted that the projected Santa Monica freeway would shoot out to sea on a high-speed, eight-lane highway, and, according to the "Tower Island plan," would proceed along a series of islands for fourteen miles, returning to the shoreline at Malibu. The islands would be devoted to residences and businesses and the intervening lagoon to water sports — thereby meeting burgeoning transportation, housing, and recreational needs. An alternative plan envisioned a shorter "Sunset Seaway" with a single island reaching to Topanga. Both plans fell victim to rising construction costs and a growing concern for the impact of such a scheme on the environment.

Trouble for Palisadians persisted on yet another

The Villa Leon, as it appears from the coast highway in 1983. The gardens are gone, and a large section of the circular terrace has eroded away. The hillside is covered with plastic to prevent further slippage. Photograph by Thomas R. Young.

front as the state continued widening the coast highway, cutting into the cliffs and removing the last remnant of Castle Rock to accommodate new lanes of traffic. Even before the improved highway was officially opened in 1948, the state was being blamed for slides and erosion which repeatedly buried the highway and undermined homes on the hillside above.

The Bernheimer Gardens was one of the first areas to be affected. The enterprise had been in financial trouble since 1942 when wartime losses led Bernheimer to appeal to the courts for aid. In February, 1944, the state acknowledged that work on the coast highway had caused slippage and agreed to spend $50,000 for restoration. To no avail. On March 18, Bernheimer died, and six days later a major landslide covered the highway and created a huge gash in the hillside. The next month a second slide took more land, buried the highway, and obscured the mouth of Burning Canyon. To stabilize the earth, state crews cut back the cliffs, obliterating the canyon and all traces of its legendary Evil Spirit — fumes, smoke, and glow.

Thereafter the public was offered an opportunity to purchase $60,000 worth of preferred stock in the Gardens to liquidate the trust deed, pay taxes and other expenses, and leave $10,000 in working capital to renew the Gardens. Despite Civic League backing, the move failed, and Joseph M. Schenck (who held the note) bought the Gardens for $25,000 at a trustees' sale. Plans to build large apartment houses on the site were scaled down when much of the property proved unstable. Remnants of the Gardens still remain — bits of walk, hedge, walls, and an assortment of unwatered shrubs and trees — but its grandeur is only a memory.

Nearby Castellammare, with its concrete walks and walls, was equally vulnerable. Like the Bernheimer Gardens, the Kauffmans' Villa Leon lost its oceanfront Chinese garden to slide action in the mid-forties — even the birds in their cages. The Villa also had a brief brush with fame when Aly Khan considered buying the mansion for his wife, actress Rita Hayworth, but the deal was never made.

On June 10, 1952, the million-dollar Villa Leon was sold at auction for $71,000 to the Walter Osbornes, and the furnishings were auctioned off as well. In subsequent years, slides have cut deeply into the bank and have consumed a large portion of the circular terrace. In a belated effort to protect the main structure, drains have recently been installed and at times a plastic covering is stretched over the bare earth.

Fiction writer Gavin Lambert took note of this typically Southern California phenomenon in his 1959 book, *The Slide Area:*

. . . I find myself remembering how the summer began. The cliffs weakened under heavy spring rains, rocks and stones rolled away, then whole sections crumbled and fell. Houses skidded down with them. There were some deaths. For several miles the coast highway was closed. The newspapers rumored that a long geological survey would be undertaken. Had the highway been cut too deep into the cliffs? Would the land go on falling? Perhaps the area would have to be abandoned and a causeway built out over the ocean. Meanwhile, the ruins were shovelled away, FOR RENT signs went up on beach houses, a few bars and restaurants closed. After three months, the highway was opened again without explanation. Driving along, you saw jagged hollows and craters scarring the cliffs. They looked almost volcanic. WATCH FOR ROCKS. The sun grew stronger. Cars massed along the highway, the long pale stretch of pleasure beaches became filled with people. And the slides were forgotten, nobody talked about them any more.

The Thelma Todd Cafe went through a less visible metamorphosis. After Thelma's death Roland West changed the name of his restaurant to the Chez Roland and married movie actress Lola Lane. Although the couple continued to occupy West's hillside villa, the Castello del Mar, they also remodeled the second-floor apartment over the cafe, placing their bed on the semi-circular bandstand and surrounding it with draperies — a Hollywood touch that delighted prim and proper Palisadians.

When West died, Lola Lane inherited the cafe and married a Mr. Hanlon who took over its management. Lola became a Catholic, and after Hanlon's death, she presented the building to the Paulist order. The former cafe served for several years as the home of Paulist Productions, which produced the television program "Insight," and of Paulist Communications, which prepared taped radio messages of hope and inspiration for worldwide transmission. Recently it has been occupied exclusively by Paulist Productions, its plain white facade concealing its Art Deco interior and such architectural delights as the frosted glass swinging doors etched with the single word *Joyeux*.

It was inevitable that, as Pacific Palisades grew and changed, other denominations would follow the Methodists. Thus, in 1941, six ladies petitioned the Episcopal bishop to permit them to organize a mission, and October 5 the Episcopalians held their first service in Temescal Canyon. A simple redwood church, designed by Carleton M. Winslow, was built at the corner of Swarthmore and La Cruz Drive, and was formally dedicated as St. Matthew's Episcopal Mission on July 26, 1942.

Father Kenneth Cary came to the parish as full-time vicar in February, 1944, and served as rector until 1978. St. Matthew's sponsored the community's first nursery school in 1949, opened an elementary school the following year, and in 1951 purchased the upper portion of the Hamilton Garland estate in Las Pulgas Canyon. Forty-four acres were sold for subdivision to provide funds to develop the remaining thirty acres for the church.

The main house was remodeled and designated Founders Hall, while the old farm buildings were moved and converted into the first classrooms for the parish school. The original church was cut into

St. Matthew's Church, at its first location on Swarthmore and La Cruz Drive. It was first dedicated as a mission in 1942. *Swarzwald-Patterson Collection*

One of the versions of the proposed causeway, this one from Santa Monica to Topanga.

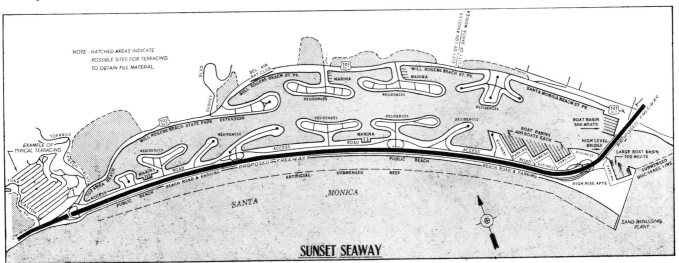

A lake was formed in Santa Ynez Canyon as a result of Alphonzo Bell's earth-moving activities, sometime after 1927. The Barham home may be seen on the hill to the right. *Swarzwald/Patterson Collection*

two pieces, moved to the canyon, and redesigned by architects A. Quincy Jones and Frederick E. Emmons. Today, facilities at St. Matthew's include a recreational building and swimming pool which are used for summer camp activities and serve the entire community

Other religious groups followed: Christian Science, Presbyterian, two Lutheran congregations, Calvary Church, Corpus Christi Catholic Church and School, the Self-Realization Fellowship, Jewish Congregation, and Latter Day Saints. Meanwhile, the United Community Methodist Church has continued to grow and in 1948 added a new $75,000 sanctuary.

Two of these religious groups today occupy significant historical sites. The Presbyterians held their first services in Temescal Canyon in 1949, purchased Harmony Hall in 1951, razed it, and built Janes Hall there on the mesa, overlooking Temescal Canyon and the Presbyterian Conference Grounds.

In Santa Ynez Canyon the parklike grounds of the Self-Realization Fellowship Lake Shrine have transformed the site of the old Inceville movie studio. The lake itself was created in 1927 when Alphonzo Bell reshaped the lower canyon to prepare it for future development. The buildings came later. According to Katherine La Hue's *Pacific Palisades Sketchbook,* the picturesque 16th Century Dutch windmill, now a familiar landmark, is a brick reproduction built in the 1940s by W.E. McElroy, assistant superintendent of set construction for 20th

Century Fox Studios. The windmill was used as a private home by the McElroys and is functional, although the sails remain tied down. When the property was given to the Fellowship in 1949, the ground floor of the windmill became a chapel, which has since been enlarged, and the second floor was adapted for use as living quarters by resident ministers and monks.

Construction of the Lake Shrine was personally supervised by the founder of the Self-Realization movement, the Parmahansa Yogananda. During this period he lived on a houseboat that had been built in the nearby hills and moved to the lake. Although the Yogananda's religious teachings are Indian and Hindu in origin, the shrine's location near the Pacific shore is symbolic of the meeting of East and West and of the universality of their doctrines.

Another portion of the Inceville movie lot is currently occupied by the National Center for the Transcendental Meditation Program, which was founded by Maharishi Mahesh Yogi and inspired by the Vedic traditions of India. The center's attractive white ranch-style buildings, with spacious public rooms and a patio swimming pool, formerly housed the Santa Ynez Inn, built after World War II as the largest hotel-restaurant complex in Pacific Palisades. Today a sign at the entrance reads "Capital of the Age of Enlightenment of California."

The center's facilities are used for classes in

Lower left, a Dutch windmill was built on the lakeshore in the 1940s by W.E. McElroy and used as a home. *Above,* the site was given to the Self-Realization Fellowship in 1949 and transformed into a garden. Here the Golden Lotus Archway is pictured as it appeared in the 1950s, framing the windmill (used as a chapel), a Chinese junk, and a houseboat. *Both, Swarzwald/Patterson Collection*

Lower right, the Gandhi World Peace Memorial. A brass coffer within the stone sarcophagus enshrines a portion of Gandhi's ashes. Photograph by Thomas R. Young.

transcendental meditation (TM) techniques and to provide accommodations for a residential program of instruction. The center also sponsors various activities and celebrations involving the group's eighteen thousand members throughout the Southland.

Like the housing market, the business community also had a brief pre-war resurgence. A street festival in July, 1942, celebrated the paving of Antioch Street and the construction of new business buildings there, and the following year John Pixley opened a new real estate office on Sunset, anticipating a future bonanza in property sales.

The community's only bank, however, closed in December, 1942, when executives of the California Bank decided to close several small branches, including Pacific Palisades. *The Palisadian* observed correctly that the bank left too soon: the community's rough times were over, and prosperity lay just over the hill. After the war, in 1947, Security Bank opened a branch in the same Business Block location and added a one-story wing to house its enlarged facilities. Today, some half-dozen banks and savings institutions are located in Pacific Palisades.

It was in 1947, too, that pioneer landholder Robert C. Gillis died, having seen his predictions for the growth of Los Angeles and the Santa Monica Bay Area come true. His son-in-law, Arthur Loomis, succeeded him as president of the Santa Monica Land and Water Company and moved the firm's offices to the second floor of the Business Block.

The Pattersons' truncated B-16 bomber, which was to have been converted into a motor home. Photograph by Thomas R. Young.

Zoning restrictions were changed in 1948 and again in 1950-53 to permit extension of the business district along Via de la Paz, Swarthmore, and Sunset. Thus, the New Horizons legitimate theater (today's YMCA) was built on Via de la Paz and the Bay Theatre opened on Sunset Boulevard in February, 1949. The latter event was a big Hollywood splash, with a band, bouquets in the lobby, and three famous Palisadians — Esther Williams, Deborah Kerr, and silent film star Francis X. Bushman — on hand to wish them luck. Recently, in 1979, lack of patronage caused the theater to close.

The first chain store operation came to town in 1950, when the Mayfair Market was built on the edge of Temescal Canyon, necessitating the removal of the venerable old "Bishop's Cottage," last used as an electrical and plumbing shop. Given the building on the condition that it be moved away and the site left clean, Martha and Charles Patterson transported the cottage to their property in Potrero Canyon, where they used it as a residence.

The Pattersons, who had three children, had purchased thirty acres in Potrero Canyon in 1949 — a plot extending from La Cruz Drive almost to the coast. Buying used equipment from Leland Ford, they built their own road, cleared the property, planted trees, and maintained a small farm. When they outgrew the cottage, they purchased two sections of the old Thomas May mansion in Beverly Hills, moved them to the canyon, and tied them together with new construction.

The grounds around the house accommodated the Pattersons' collection of vintage cars and exotic motor homes, the most unusual of which was to be assembled from a truncated B-16 bomber. In 1964 the city, through its Department of Recreation and Parks, acquired the lower 24 acres from the Pattersons under the power of eminent domain. The same year, the northernmost portion of the property was also sold and the cottage torn down. Today a business and professional building occupies the site, and the remaining 3.75 acres are being planned for single-family residential development.

As the community grew, organizations multiplied. The Men's Club was founded in 1943 and the Lions Club in 1948. The Garden Club grew out of interest in wartime Victory Gardens in 1944, and the Art Association came into being under the sponsorship of Mrs. E.F. Kennedy in 1947. The Pacific Palisades History and Landmarks Society — also under Mrs. Kennedy's chairmanship — was formed in connection with California's centennial celebrations, which were held from 1948 to 1950. The society performed a valuable service by focussing attention on the community's rapidly fading past and drew concerned citizens together by placing landmark plaques on various historic sites.

Pacific Palisades Playground today. Photograph by Thomas R. Young.

Continuing the cultural legacy of the summer chautauquas, drama enthusiasts organized the Palisades Players after the war and presented rompingly good plays in the 1940s and 1950s under the direction of Ray Verity. A subsequent group, Theatre Palisades, founded in 1963, currently gives thirty-two performances a year at Rustic Canyon Park, presenting a variety of popular twentieth century plays. Recently, Palisadians Lelah and J. Townley Pierson gave Theatre Palisades a strip of land adjacent to Founders' Oak, and funds are being raised to build a new 125-seat community theater, with space included for the use of the Pacific Palisades Historical Society.

In the realm of music, the Methodist church choir carries on in Nancy Kendall Robinson's tradition, with Ina Andrews Bitting and her brother, Howard Andrews, still contributing their talent and leadership. A secular musical group, the Brentwood-Palisades Chorale, was founded in 1963 by Francis Cain, and the Palisades Symphony Orchestra by Joel Lish in 1965.

The Chamber of Commerce, representing the business community, was formed in 1949 and promptly introduced two new annual traditions, the "Miss Pacific Palisades" beauty pageant and the selection of an honorary mayor. The first Palisadian to be named mayor was Esther Williams, followed by Virginia Bruce. Since then, a succession of public-spirited motion picture and television luminaries have assumed their ceremonial tasks graciously — each with a special flair.

The Palisadian inaugurated its "Citizen of the Year" contest in 1948, based on outstanding community service and achievement, and presented the first award to John Pixley. The American Legion continued to prosper, built a handsome new meeting room on land acquired with the aid of Dr. Clarence F. Ott, and sponsored the first official Fourth of July Americanism parade in 1961, an event which has grown steadily in size and scope. The list of honorary marshals today includes military heroes, film and television stars, and community leaders.

A more recent civic group, the Community Council, initiated the Sparkplug Award in 1974 to honor men and women who have given impetus to community betterment. Other active service groups include the Rotary Club, founded in 1952, and the Optimist Club, chartered in 1956.

Concern over parks and open space has involved several properties in the heart of town. Civic groups attempted to purchase the "triangle" at the corner of Antioch and Sunset in 1945 for a small park, but were outbid by an oil company which established a gas station there. In the end, patience paid off. Sparked by various civic groups, a subscription drive made possible the purchase of the plot in 1972 and paid for its conversion into an attractively landscaped "pocket park" — the first of three in the business center. Today its lawns and benches are enjoyed by sun-lovers, and maintenance chores are assumed on a volunteer basis by community organizations under the supervision of the Pocket Park Association.

Interest was also revived in buying the Jack Conway property in lower Temescal Canyon for a park and recreation area, with a roadway connection to the coast. However, attention shifted to Potrero Canyon in 1948, when the Los Angeles Department

201

Crowds lined the fairways at Riviera Country Club in 1929 for the fourth Los Angeles $10,000 Open Golf Tournament. This dramatic photograph appeared in *Pictorial California. Swarzwald/Patterson Collection*

of Recreation and Parks purchased seventeen acres on the eastern rim at a cost of $95,330 and installed a multi-purpose recreational building and tennis courts. Credit for the acquisition went to the Civic League and to the chairman of the parks committee, Jack Sauer, who had personally campaigned for park space for over fifteen years. A modern library was built by the city on property adjacent to the park, and contributions from private individuals were obtained to enhance the book collection and finance the addition of a community room.

The Civic League pursued its other goals with varying success. Sewer connections were finally completed in Tract 9300 and streets were repaved. Fire and police protection, however, remained ongoing concerns. A new fire station was built in the mid-sixties and the old structure torn down, despite efforts to retain it as a youth center. As for the police, residents continued to complain that a single patrol car provided insufficient protection for the entire Pacific Palisades area.

During World War II, in fact, Pacific Palisades provided the unlikely setting for a sensational crime.

The perpetrator was Mrs. Louise Peete, described by neighbors as a sweet, motherly little woman, but who had actually been sentenced to life imprisonment in 1920 for murdering her wealthy landlord, shooting him in the head and burying his body in the basement. Paroled in April, 1943, she changed her name to Anna Lee and six months later took a position as housekeeper with Arthur and Margaret Logan, who had befriended her during the trial.

Mrs. Peete moved into the Logan home on Hampden Place, ostensibly to care for Arthur Logan, who was elderly and allegedly senile, while his wife worked in real estate. The two women had a disagreement over an ill-advised joint business venture, and on May 2, 1944, Louise went off to Glendale, where she was secretly married to an unsuspecting widower, Lee Jordan. Louise continued to visit the Logans and began circulating stories of Arthur Logan's violent behavior. Also, she forged an endorsement on one of Mrs. Logan's checks and kept the cash.

On May 29 Louise came to the Logan home, and on the same date Margaret disappeared. Louise and

Lee moved into the house, Louise explaining to callers that Margaret had been severely beaten by her husband and was in seclusion. Meanwhile, Louise had Arthur committed to Patton State Hospital where he died on June 6, and was herself in the process of taking over the Logans' assets when forged parole papers and banking irregularities aroused the suspicion of the authorities. On December 20 the police arrived and found Margaret Logan's body. She had been shot in the head, beaten, and buried in a shallow grave under an avocado tree behind the Logan home. Without hesitation a jury found Louise guilty.

The chain of tragedies continued. Lee Judson, who was innocent of any wrongdoing but was plagued by guilt, plunged to his death down a stairwell in a Los Angeles hotel. And Louise, who was responsible for it all, was sentenced to death and died in the gas chamber in April, 1947.

A happier task that confronted the Civic League was the issue of schools. As the number of school-age children increased, the League appointed a special schools committee to cooperate with Brentwood and Pacific Palisades citizens' advisory groups in making plans for a new junior high and senior high school.

The search for a junior high school site in the bay area, where land was becoming scarce and prices were rising, soon focussed on the Riviera Country Club polo and equestrian center — an activity which was no longer of prime concern to the Los Angeles Athletic Club management. The new LAAC president, Charles Hathaway, Sr., Frank Garbutt's son-in-law, had been forced by the Depression and the war to reduce the parent club's losses, and the equestrian operation had never been a profitable one.

Thus, it was more of a shock to horse-lovers than to club executives when the Los Angeles Board of Education chose the northernmost polo field for the school and, pursuant to condemnation proceedings, paid $142,000 plus $15,000 in severance fees for the nineteen-acre parcel. On September 12, 1955, Paul Revere Junior High School, designed by architect Stiles Clements, admitted its first students, and the same year Marquez Elementary School opened on the west side of town.

Apprehensive lest the remaining land be similarly preempted for a senior high school, LAAC officials decided to sell it for subdivision. The first portion had already been sold in 1952, when a citizens' group intervened, determined to preserve the remaining property for a park or for continued equestrian use. During a public hearing, one of the neighbors who made a plea for the park was motion picture actor Ronald Reagan, who had recently moved into a ranch-style home on North Amalfi Drive with his new bride, Nancy. Despite his verbal efforts, the site was sold to developers and subdivided.

The Riviera Country Club golf course, which was never threatened by Hathaway's economy measures, survived the strictures of wartime intact and was restored to prime condition in time to host the Los Angeles Open Golf Tournament in 1945. Since then, except for a twenty-year hiatus, this event has been held annually at Riviera, attracting national press and television coverage.

An even more prestigious championship, the U.S. Open, was held at Riviera in 1948 — its first visit to the Pacific Coast — and the coveted PGA (Professional Golfers' Association) Tournament is due to be held on the Riviera links in August, 1983. As a further tribute to its challenging and scenic layout, Riviera is consistently included on the *Golf Digest* magazine list of the one hundred outstanding golf courses in the United States, ranking in the top twenty.

Rising land values also affected the secluded Uplifters Ranch in Rustic Canyon. The polo field was subdivided by realtor George Read in 1945, and the lower area, including the clubhouse, was sold in 1947 to Greek shipping magnate George Embiracos, who operated the former Uplifter facilities as a posh racquet club.

In 1953, when Embiracos put the club on the market, the Santa Monica Canyon Civic Association began soliciting funds and obtained a gift of $200,000 from Maybell Machris, a resident of Santa Monica Canyon, to purchase the eight-acre site. This included the clubhouse, swimming pool, and tennis courts — all donated to the Los Angeles City Department of Recreation and Parks by Mrs. Machris in memory of her husband. In addition, the SMCCA, aided by canyon realtor Al Edmundson, raised funds to help the city purchase the adjacent Hilltree Road eucalyptus grove — the site of the old Forestry Station and of the 1921 Methodist campground.

In the upper reaches of Rustic Canyon, other major changes were brewing. The Josepho family sold their ranch in 1946 to Felix and Helen Chappellet, who remodeled the buildings and added new stables and corrals for their quarter horses. Two years later the heir to the A&P food chain fortune, Huntington Hartford, Jr., arrived on the scene, and through Dr. John Vincent of the music department at UCLA negotiated the purchase of the Josepho and Murphy ranches to provide a 140-acre site for an artists' colony.

Hartford, whose interest in the arts was well known, had been inspired by the MacDowell Colony in New Hampshire and the Yaddo in New York to sponsor a similar venture here. Thus, he engaged architect Lloyd Wright to prepare the site plan and

Above, resident Fellows at the Huntington Hartford Foundation shown gathered on the terrace of the Community House (formerly the Josepho home) for informal conversation.

Below, Dr. John Vincent, director of the Foundation, at work in his apartment in the Community House. *Both, courtesy Dr. John Vincent*

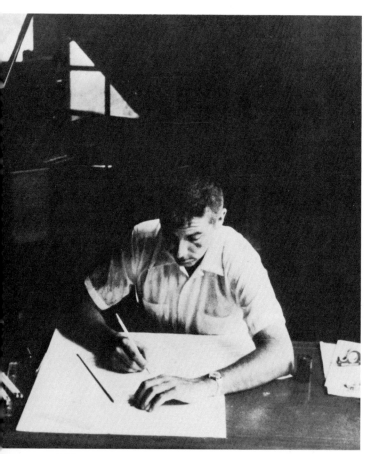

design such additions, alterations, and new structures as might be required. Wright combined the two properties, using the stone portals and iron gates of the Murphy Ranch to provide an impressive entrance. He enlarged the Josepho home to provide a Community House, with a dining room and lounge for the Fellows-in-residence, and expanded the existing cottages. Wright himself designed and built two new studio-duplexes; more units were added later by another architect.

The Foundation's doors opened in 1950 when the first Fellow-in-residence, wood engraver Viktor Podoski, arrived. Gradually the enrollment was increased until fifteen or sixteen artists were accommodated simultaneously. By the time the Foundation closed fifteen years later, five hundred artists — writers, painters, printmakers, sculptors, and composers — had lived and worked in Rustic Canyon. The first director, a Polish nobleman named Michael Gaszynski who ran a cheesecake concession at the Farmers' Market, was replaced in 1953 by Dr. Vincent, an eminent music scholar whose wife Ruth also filled an important role as hostess.

Artists-in-residence received grants of from one to six months, during which time they were housed in the cottages, provided with meals, and given the opportunity to work without interruption. In their leisure time, they enjoyed the swimming pool, the beauty of the canyon setting, and informal association with other artists. Recognized artists were invited to come as special award winners to give inspiration and guidance to the novices. Ultimately this group included such famous names as writers Christopher Isherwood, Van Wyck Brooks, Jean Starr Untermeyer, Mark and Dorothy Van Doren, and Max Eastman; painters Andrew Wyeth, George Biddle, and Edward Hopper; composers Walter Piston, Ralph Vaughan Williams, Roy Harris, and Lukas Foss.

Emigré composer Ernst Toch, who spent time at the Foundation on three different occasions, wrote his Pulitzer Prize-winning Third Symphony there. Lines from "The Sorrows of Young Werther" by Goethe provided the inspiration: "Indeed I am a wanderer, a pilgrim on earth — but what else are you?"

By 1965 it became apparent to Huntington Hartford's financial advisors that he was no longer able to afford the expense of the Foundation. When last-ditch efforts to find alternative funding failed, developer John Morehart purchased the entire property as a residence for his large family, and in 1969 sold the Murphy Ranch portion to Charles Lick. Growing public interest in establishing a major park in the Santa Monica Mountains led the state to purchase the Liz Whitney Tippett property (including Will Rogers' hideaway cabin) in 1966, and the Morehart property in 1973. Lick's portion, on the other hand, was not included. After his death in 1973, his heirs sold the property to the Los Angeles City Department of Recreation and Parks.

Meanwhile, in Temescal Canyon, the school board put an end to the latest civic brouhaha by choosing All Hollows Farm as a site for the new high school. Although closed to the public, the canyon had remained a rural paradise in the heart of town. The Conways used the grounds to raise Aberdeen Angus cattle, and Virginia Conway kept antiques in a portion of the old Lodge as an adjunct to her Westside antique shop.

Concerned architects and members of the community recommended plans for the proposed school that would retain the old oaks and the scenic values of the canyon, but to no avail. Efficiency was the keynote of school administrators. After the site was scraped clear of structures and vegetation, the canyon was filled to a depth of ninety feet with dirt, and Palisades High School (designed by Adrian Wilson and Associates) was built on two level pads. The newly widened canyon floor also made room for a major highway from Sunset Boulevard to the coast, giving the community a long-sought escape route.

The new school — affectionately known as Palihi — opened in September, 1961, and graduated its first senior class in February, 1963. Scholastic and athletic honors soon followed, as did notoriety — in the form of a 1965 *Time* magazine cover story, "Today's Teen-Agers." Spotlighting a select group of high schools across the country, *Time* described Palihi's new "$7 million red brick campus," interviewed a handful of its bright and breezy young people, and commented on the students' obvious affluence. Summing it up, *Time* observed, "smarter, subtler and more sophisticated kids are pouring into and out of more expert, exacting, and experimental schools."

A sobering followup appeared ten years later, in 1975, when Michael Medved and David Wallechinsky interviewed a number of their classmates and wrote the runaway best-seller, *What Really Happened to the Class of '65?* — a series of

Palisades High surrounded by the streaking lights of Sunset Blvd. and Temescal Drive. Photo by Thomas R. Young.

biographical vignettes that reflected the moral and social turmoil of that uneasy decade.

Competition in reporting local news appeared in 1950, when *The Palisadian* was joined on the local scene by a second newspaper, the *Pacific Palisades Post,* founded by Paul D. Weaver, Jr. Three years later the *Post* was purchased by Charles B. Brown and his brother, William W. Brown, two newspapermen from Minnesota who successfully guided the paper through twenty-eight years of rapid civic growth.

The whole community was shocked in 1956 when Clifford Clearwater died, with little warning, at his beloved cabin at Mammoth Lakes. His many friends who attended the funeral ceremony heard him eulogized as "the first citizen of Pacific Palisades" — a tribute to the quality of his public service. With advice and encouragement from Telford Work, Cliff's widow, Zola, took over as editor and publisher of *The Palisadian,* changing over from the traditional method of typesetting to the newer and more economical offset process — the first newspaper in Southern California to do so.

In May, 1960, Zola sold *The Palisadian* to the Browns, who consolidated both papers into one operation. During the ensuing years the *Palisadian-Post* played an effective role as a catalyst in community affairs and won a series of national newspaper merit awards. On August 18, 1981, the business was sold to Jean Alice Small, president of Small Newspapers of Kankakee, Illinois — a privately held, family-owned organization with several papers in the upper Midwest. The new ownership has chosen to retain the *Palisadian-Post's* experienced staff and to continue in the same vein, with an emphasis on local news and a community-oriented editorial policy.

By the mid-1950s the trend in Pacific Palisades toward a station wagon suburbia was unmistakable. Christopher Isherwood observed the transition in his Santa Monica Canyon neighborhood with an author's eye and recorded his impression in his novel, *A Single Man.*

The change began in the late forties when the World War Two vets came swarming out of the East with their just-married wives, in search of new and better breeding grounds in the sunny Southland, which had been their last nostalgic glimpse of home before they shipped out to the Pacific. And what better breeding ground than a hillside neighborhood like this one, only five minutes' walk from the beach and with no through traffic to decimate the future tots? So, one by one, the cottages which used to reek of bathtub gin and reverberate with the poetry of Hart Crane have fallen to the occupying army of Coke-drinking television watchers.

In 1958 a massive slide at the foot of Via de la Paz took the life of a state highway department supervisor who was overseeing cleanup operations from a previous slide. Subsequently the coast highway was routed farther out to sea, around the mass of earth. This is the same area where Occidental Petroleum is seeking to establish a drilling site. *Ernest Marquez Collection*

Most of the new suburbanites had business and professional ties outside of Pacific Palisades and were active in a variety of area-wide volunteer groups and social organizations. Many sent their children away to private schools and traveled to Westwood and Beverly Hills for their shopping. Yet, the average Palisadian felt a commitment to the local schools, his neighborhood church, and the limited variety of hometown business establishments.

As homes enveloped the open spaces, lots began to sell in the abandoned tracts of the thirties and in locations that were more scenic than secure. Eager homeseekers often ignored the evidence available in a 1959 geological survey map of Pacific Palisades that clearly outlined the unstable and slide-prone areas along the bluffs and the margins of the canyons. Similarly, the 1938 flood and fire had issued clear warning as to the hazards of canyon and hillside building sites.

Most notorious of the slippages was the massive "killer slide" of March 31, 1958, in which Vaughn O. Sheff, a state Department of Highways supervisor was buried under a hundred feet of dirt and rock at the foot of Via de la Paz. He had just overseen the cleanup of a slide which had occurred a few days earlier when, according to the *Santa Monica Evening Outlook,* a chunk of earth "the size of a six-story building a block long" fell without warning down onto the highway and overtook Sheff, who, with other workmen, was running to safety. Thereafter, the highway was reinforced with groins and routed farther out to sea, around the slide.

Fast-moving fires continued to plague the Malibu area, generally in the fall when dry brush and hot Santa Ana winds combined to create perilous conditions. On several occasions such blazes turned the evening skies to an angry red, but succumbed to changes in the wind or firefighting measures before reaching Pacific Palisades.

One of the most menacing was the Bel-Air fire of 1961, which broke out on Monday morning, November 6, on Stone Canyon Road and swept rapidly along the mountains, through expensive hillside residential areas, toward the sea. Around noon, a second fire started in upper Topanga Canyon, the two blazes threatening to converge on Pacific Palisades.

Early Tuesday morning, flames from the Topanga fire swept up the ridge toward Miramar Estates. Fearing for the safety of the Feuchtwanger home and library, Marta Feuchtwanger summoned aid from USC and shipped off as many rare volumes as possible, then stayed behind to fight the fire. At noon, just when her efforts seemed hopeless, a damp sea breeze blew back the flames. Pacific Palisades had been spared, but more than five hundred homes in Bel-Air and Brentwood lay in ruins, and 15,000 acres had been burned.

Palisadians weren't so lucky seven years later. What everyone remembers as "the big one" started mid-morning on Monday, October 23, 1978, when fallen high-tension wires ignited brush near Mulholland Drive and Sepulveda Boulevard. Late in the afternoon, as radio reports still focussed on the battle being fought to save Mandeville Canyon, a wall of flame swept through upper Rustic and Temescal canyons, descended without warning on Marquez Knolls and the Las Pulgas tracts and endangered the entire northern fringe of Pacific Palisades.

Sunset Boulevard was cordoned off to all but emergency vehicles, while firefighting helicopters landed on the Will Rogers polo field to fill their water tanks. Rangers evacuated the contents of the Rogers home and fought the fire on the periphery of the grounds, as horse owners led their animals from the upper corrals and from nearby canyons to holding areas and the Paul Revere playground. All along the front, residents and volunteers manned garden hoses, bracing themselves for the nighttime fury of the fire storm.

By Tuesday morning moist ocean air had moved in and aided the firefighters in quelling the flames. A survey of the area disclosed that six thousand acres had been burned and forty-three homes destroyed or damaged. Hardest hit were Lachman Lane, Las Pulgas Road, and the Las Lomas ridge. In Las Pulgas Canyon itself, St. Matthew's Church and the familiar windmill building went up in smoke before help could be summoned, and the roof of Founders' Hall was damaged.

Several homes occupied by state park rangers in upper Rustic Canyon were destroyed. At the neighboring Boy Scout camp, ranger Don Welch and his wife, Victoria, stayed behind to fight the fire and worked feverishly to protect what they could, saving two Scout structures, but losing their own home. Finally, when they saw their car explode and their escape route cut off, the Welches submerged themselves in the algae-covered waters of the swimming pool and spent the next two hours breathing the smoke-filled air through Don's baseball cap and fending off panic-stricken rats. When the worst had passed, they boarded a truck and drove at breakneck speed through "tunnels of fire" down the narrow road to safety, the heat so intense the tires exploded.

Predictably, floods followed the fire. Heavy rains in January, 1979, sent torrents of water down the canyons and buried the fire-ravaged remains of the Hartford Foundation buildings under mud and rock. A year later, in February, 1980, a nine-day storm dropped more than fourteen inches of rain on Pacific Palisades. Flood waters poured down the barren slopes of Mandeville Canyon, choked Rustic Creek with debris, and surged chest-high through businesses at the mouth of Santa Monica Canyon. Residents and merchants took it in stride as they filled sandbags, shoveled mud and debris out of their homes and shops, and shored up the sagging walls of their crumpled buildings.

Just as Palisadians band together when disaster strikes, they also express themselves on the problems of the day through broad-based community associations and single-issue citizens' groups, such as the Friends of the Santa Monica Mountain Parks and Seashore, which has chalked up a remarkable record of achievement since its formation in the 1960s. Through the efforts of the Friends, homeowners' associations, and environmental groups, large tracts of mountain land adjoining Pacific Palisades have been purchased and incorporated into Topanga State Park, and other parcels are in the process of, or being considered for, acquisition.

Another local group, No Oil, has for years fought a running battle with the major oil companies — reminiscent of the cement plant controversy of the 1920s and 1930s. No Oil and various homeowners' associations have generally represented those opposed to drilling and have pointed out the geological risks and safety factors involved in placing rigs at such proposed sites as the mouth of Santa Monica Canyon, the Riviera Country Club, and the coast highway at the base of the "killer slide." A subsequent group has been formed to support drilling, pleading the rights of oil companies and property owners to develop existing natural resources and turn a profit under specified environmental safeguards.

Currently, plans for the future growth and development of Pacific Palisades are controlled to some degree by the Brentwood-Palisades District Plan, which was drawn up by the Los Angeles City Planning Department and passed by the city council in 1977. The seaward edge of the community is also subject to the actions of the California Coastal Commission, which was mandated by state voters in 1972 under Proposition 20. A Local Coastal Plan is now under advisement and will be adopted at some future date.

Large developments and subdivisions come under the provisions of the California Environmental Quality Act of 1970, which requires that Environmental Impact Reports be submitted early in the planning process to the city planning department. At the present time, homeowners' groups are battling with city agencies over the size and impact of projected subdivisions and the location of access roads — particularly in and around upper Santa Ynez Canyon, which is the current focus of major new development.

The 1978 fire as it approaches the Palisades. *Palisadian-Post*

17

PRESERVING OUR HERITAGE

What of Pacific Palisades today? A community that is sure of itself, proud of its past, and seeking to have a voice in its future. There's a different flavor to the business district than a decade or two ago: less space given to real estate firms, more to professional offices, trendy clothing shops, boutiques, gourmet and specialty restaurants — even a long-forbidden cocktail lounge.

In an area where the price of an average home soared to $385,000 in 1980, Pacific Palisades is no longer a haven for retired missionaries and penny-pinching young couples; rather it attracts financially secure doctors and lawyers, business executives, and entertainment people — often two-income families with fewer children and a larger appetite for comfort and luxuries. Yet there is an intense interest in keeping Pacific Palisades the way it was — quiet and low-key — as well as in maintaining its unique scenic advantages.

It has become a place where old-timers and newcomers accept each other as friends and neighbors, where privacy is respected — a community where captains of industry, artists and writers, aerospace engineers, college professors, movie and television performers, and Academy Award winners visit the supermarkets, wait in line at the bank, serve on PTA boards, and take an active interest in local issues.

The spectrum of residents is uniquely broad and varied, ranging from world-class athletes to "think-tank" geniuses. One of the old log cabins in Rustic Canyon has for many years been the home of Dorothy "Dodo" Bundy Cheney, recently honored in *Sports Illustrated* as the winner of 114 national tennis titles, twice as many as were earned by her nearest competitor, Gardnar Mulloy . . . and it's only the beginning. Also hailing from Rustic Canyon was mountaineer Norman Dyrenfurth, who in 1963 led the first American expedition to climb the world's highest peak, Mount Everest.

Nearby, on a tree-shaded plateau at the mouth of Santa Monica Canyon, is the home of industrial designer Charles Eames and his wife, Ray, who collaborated with him on a variety of ventures and is an artist and designer in her own right. Charles Eames, who died in 1978, not only gave his name to the distinctive "Eames chair," but created his own home out of glass and standard steel building components in such an innovative fashion that it became a place of pilgrimage for young architects.

Humorously apropos was the decision of the controversial writer Henry Miller to leave his bohemian neighbors at Big Sur and spend the last years of his life in the conservative enclave of Huntington Palisades. At the age of eighty he was pictured in *Playboy* magazine, riding his bicycle down the placid, tree-lined street, and it was here, in 1978, that he wrote his last book, *My Bike and Other Friends.* Another octogenarian and highly visible Palisadian is Buckminster Fuller, renowned as an inventor, author, engineer, and social theorist. Today, over 200,000 versions of his famous geodesic dome have been built at locations around the world.

By all odds the most famous ex-residents of Pacific Palisades are Nancy and Ronald Reagan, who moved to Amalfi Drive in 1953, shortly after their marriage. In her autobiography, Nancy Reagan wrote, "A lot of our friends felt we were foolish to move so far from the heart of Hollywood, but we wanted to be farther out of town and have never regretted it."

Ronald Reagan became the host on television's General Electric Theater in 1954; two years later the Reagans built their own home on San Onofre Drive, "surrounded by the Santa Monica Mountains and greenery." For the Reagans, Pacific Palisades was a retreat — a place where the family, including their daughter Patti and son Ron, could live undisturbed. The path to fame and fortune for them both, however, lay in Beverly Hills and Hollywood and the political world beyond.

A new way of life was in store for the family when Ronald Reagan was elected governor in 1966 and spent the following eight years in Sacramento. Trips to Pacific Palisades were infrequent, but each election day turned into a ceremonial occasion, as

Above, the Reagan home on San Onofre Drive. *Courtesy Palisadian-Post*

Below, Nancy and Ronald Reagan voting at their neighborhood polling place in the 1980 Presidential election. *Courtesy Palisadian-Post*

photographers and reporters recorded the couple's presence at the neighborhood polling place. Reagan also made three appearances on the Palihi campus — crowning the homecoming queen in 1967 and addressing the student body in June, 1971, and December, 1976.

In 1980 Pacific Palisades and the nation gave Ronald Reagan a resounding victory in the presidential race, and the community began adjusting itself to a new place in the public eye. San Onofre Drive was cordoned off, only residents of the immediate block being permitted to pass through — an inconvenience that was cheerfully borne. On and after election day one television network rented a neighbor's tree and used its branches as an observation post. The Reagans' comings and goings were scarcely a secret, as helicopters circled overhead and long entourages of limousines, police cars, motorcycles, and vans traveled to and fro on Sunset Boulevard.

A rash of T-shirts proclaiming "Ronald Reagan Country" appeared in the shops, as did suitably emblazoned bumper stickers and drinking glasses. Discussion among the merchants centered around the probable needs and desires of the hordes of sightseers that would surely descend on the modest streets of Pacific Palisades.

People magazine generated a small traffic jam in the heart of town when they decided to photograph

Today, residential developments are reaching deep into the wilderness areas of the Santa Monica Mountains. Photograph by Thomas R. Young.

all of the residents of Pacific Palisades en masse, and two thousand men, women, and children crowded into Swarthmore Drive, just off Sunset Boulevard, under a banner reading, "Home of our 40th President."

Palisadians held their own hail-and-farewell party on December 21 at the Riviera Country Club, where Ronald and Nancy Reagan were greeted by five hundred invited guests, representing the various groups and organizations in the community. Sportscaster Vin Scully served as master of ceremonies, and the commander of the American Legion presented Reagan with a Legion cap as a token of the President-elect's life membership in Pacific Palisades Post 283.

On departure day, prior to the inauguration, the Reagans waved goodbye to their neighbors, paused briefly to greet students at Paul Revere Junior High School, and at the airport were saluted by the Palisades High School band and drill team. Already the news was out. The decision had been made to move the Western White House to the Reagans' Santa Barbara ranch. Their three-bedroom, all-electric home on San Onofre Drive, with its swimming pool and view of the coastline, went on the market for $1.9 million; contingency plans for tourists were scuttled and Pacific Palisades returned to normal.

Today, newcomers to Pacific Palisades, like religious converts, are apt to defend the natural beauty and historic values of their community with even more zeal than old-time residents, who give higher priority to individual property rights. Concerned over perpetuating the community's historic legacy in a positive fashion, a small group of Palisadians formed the Pacific Palisades Historical Society in 1972. Unfortunately, the road to preservation has been a long and rocky one, and the litany of lost causes continues to grow.

Known sites containing valuable prehistoric archaeological data have been the least honored, falling prey at an early date to "pot hunters," highway construction work, and land development. Similarly, all of the old adobes have passed into oblivion, as the land has been converted into modern neighborhoods. The last to go was the Pascual Marquez adobe on Entrada Drive, which succumbed to damages sustained in the 1933 earthquake. Today, only the Marquez cemetery, on the site of Francisco's original adobe, remains as tangible evidence of the rancho period.

Most of the early Methodist structures are gone as well, though the Presbyterian Conference Grounds in upper Temescal Canyon still harbors the first grocery store and the meat market (both combined into one unit), the cafeteria, and several of the casitas, which have been modernized.

Currently, first on the list of civic concerns is the

211

fate of the old Business Block. The building's long-time owners, the Santa Monica Land and Water Company (controlled by its stockholders, Robert L. Loomis, Dorothy Loomis, and Frederick P. Lee) had been aware that the 1981 earthquake safety code would demand extensive measures to strengthen the unreinforced masonry structure. The Loomises therefore, in 1979, employed an architectural firm specializing in restoration to propose plans for renovation and prepare a nomination for listing on the National Register of Historic Places, which would yield a measure of protection and provide tax credits. The effort failed. As a result of past alterations, the building was judged to have lost its "historical architectural integrity" and was rejected. An application to the city Cultural Heritage Board was similarly denied.

When, in the stockholders' opinion, estimated renovation costs proved excessive for the amount of space involved, the Business Block was put on the market and sold to a developer. The new owner announced that the building would be demolished and that the new structure would put the site to more efficient use, providing ample room for the existing bank, a small branch of a major department store, shops, restaurants, fast-food facilities, theaters, and four levels of underground parking.

The artist's rendering, however, created shock waves among Palisadians, who perceived it as a three-story, glass and concrete Beverly Hills-style mall which bore little resemblance to the familiar Business Block. Cries of alarm over losing the community's most visible landmark resulted in a major campaign with rallies, petitions, a slogan ("Don't Mall the Palisades"), and impassioned pleas from new and old residents of the community.

The building's fate was ultimately decided in court, when the bank and other lease-holders brought suit over cancellation of their long-term agreements. The judge's decision upheld the owner's contention that the earthquake ordinance and the expense of compliance altered the lease arrangement. He also affirmed a new owner's right to remove the building, but granted tenants a delay until September 18, 1985.

The original sale was never consummated. A second buyer recently announced that he hopes either to save the building or to plan a replacement in harmony with its surroundings. Meanwhile, a citizens' advisory committee has been appointed by Los Angeles City Councilman Marvin Braude to present recommendations to the city planning department on overall issues affecting the business district, such as land use and review of new structural designs.

Less publicized was the campaign undertaken by the Historical Society to preserve the isolated and little-known Huntington Hartford-Josepho Ranch complex for the enjoyment and use of the public. The Society became aware in 1975 that the state Department of Parks and Recreation had no effective plan for the buildings and understood that the property's bureaucratic guardian, the state Department of General Services, was empowered to allocate funds for demolition, but not for preservation.

The predictions came true, as tenants of the main house and several of the studios were evicted; upkeep was neglected; and the site was ignored on the general plan for Topanga State Park, even though the Historical Society and other groups made vocal appeals for consideration. Before long, vandals had broken holes in the windows and shattered the walls of the vacated structures, leaving the ravaged interiors to wood rats and bees. Still, five of the residences were occupied by park rangers.

It was an encouraging sign to preservationists, therefore, when feasibility studies were undertaken, and by August, 1978, plans were announced to use the complex as a base for a California Conservation Corps work force. Acting on the advice of experts in historical preservation, the Society appealed to the Los Angeles Cultural Heritage Board to designate the area as an historical landmark and began nomination proceedings for the National Register. At this point, the 1979 fire swept through the canyon, destroying the main house and several outlying structures; floods followed a few months later, further diminishing the Society's hopes.

On the basis of a revised application submitted by the Society in July, 1980, the California Historic Resources Commission approved the Josepho Barn and Murphy Power Station for nomination to the National Register. The commission also urged the state to retain the existing structures, foundations, fireplaces, and walls to enhance "the historic flavor of the Canyon."

Here, however, preservation efforts were stalled. The state park administration announced that the Josepho Ranch would be abandoned, citing problems of access, hazards from future fires, increased erosion, and lack of funds. Demolition notices followed. Crews began the bulldozing in the spring of 1982, specifically ignoring requests that the process be selective, on the basis that the ruins constituted attractive hazards and might lead to injuries. Instead, virtually all evidences of habitation, except for a few retaining walls, were obliterated and the swimming pool was buried. Today, it is a melancholy place — a rubble-strewn series of building pads, overgrown with weeds — marked by the broken remnants of a wishing well.

Only the barn was left standing, its tile roof and sturdy construction having withstood vandalism and the elements. Currently, the California State

Fire and flood took their toll in upper Rustic Canyon. *Above,* a view across the swimming pool toward the ruins of the Josepho home. *Below right,* the terraces and chimneys seen in this picture have now been leveled. Only a fragment of the wishing well remains. *Below left,* the chimney of the Will Rogers hideaway cabin. All photographs by Thomas R. Young.

Parks Foundation is endeavoring to finance removal of the barn to the proposed site of White Oaks Farm on the Hope Ranch at Malibu Creek State Park, where it would serve as a museum and have a featured place at the entrance.

The Will Rogers hideaway cabin and the Murphy Ranch structures also were burned in the fire and remain in ruins. Farther up the canyon, the Boy Scout Council has begun its program of restoration at Camp Josepho, bringing in utilities, improving the narrow access road, and shaping plans to rebuild the facilities. For its part, the state has begun work on trails radiating out from the Will Rogers ranch to make wilderness areas more readily accessible to hikers.

In this context, the preservation of Temescal Canyon as a convenient and natural gateway to the state park has been given a high priority. The land bordering the highway in the lower canyon was withheld from development and dedicated on May 19, 1974, as a city park. Immediately north of Sunset Boulevard, the 20.3-acre portion which had been purchased by the city for a junior high school in 1971 has been released by the school board and has been acquired for parkland by the Santa Monica Mountains Conservancy at its original cost of $845,000.

The northernmost parcel of 144 acres, still under the ownership of the Presbyterian synod, was abandoned in 1981 as a conference site and, despite an expression of interest by the Conservancy, was put up for sale at a high price to developers. Recently, however, other opinions have prevailed. The historically significant grounds and the conference buildings have been improved and renovated by the Presbyterians with the help of the CCC and local volunteers and are again open for use by non-profit groups. The fate of the outlying acreage has not yet been determined.

The Historical Society also recounts a few successes. Through a gift of land in 1973 from Lelah and J. Townley Pierson in memory of their parents, Founders' Oak Island has been preserved and is maintained by the Society as a small park, marking the oak-shaded spot where the Founders met in 1922 and established Pacific Palisades.

Attention was drawn to the site in 1955 when the surrounding streets were being widened and paved. The History and Landmarks Society under the leadership of Mrs. E. J. Kennedy selected one large tree to be spared and named it "Founders' Oak." Dr. Mildred Matthias, professor of botany at UCLA, was called upon to verify the age of the venerable old patriarch and judged it to be three hundred years old.

Eleven years later, when street-widening again threatened the tree, two members of the hastily formed "Save-the-Oak" Committee, June Blum and Edna Oleson, joined by Councilman Marvin Braude, successfully pled their case before the Los Angeles Cultural Heritage Board. They obtained the designation of the tree as Historic Cultural Monument No. 368 and averted the proposed expansion of Haverford Avenue.

Unfortunately, the oak's days were numbered. Despite the attentions of horticulturalist Irving Sherlock, the tree was found to be dying and in 1975 had to be removed. The local Garden Club and the Hortists West Society financed its replacement with a young coastal oak, which today provides the center of interest for a landscaped garden. Four rustic benches have been built and installed by Historical Society members Arvin "Pete" Ahrens and Victor Brucher — with funding and plaques provided by the Clearwater family (in honor of C.D. Clearwater), the Garden Club (honoring Mr. and Mrs. Irving Sherlock), the Norris family (honoring their parents, Mr. and Mrs. Robert Norris), and Mr. and Mrs. Florian "Jack" Sauer (in memory of their son, Lt. John Douglas Sauer).

Zola Clearwater on the site where it all began — Founders' Oak Island. Photograph by Thomas R. Young.

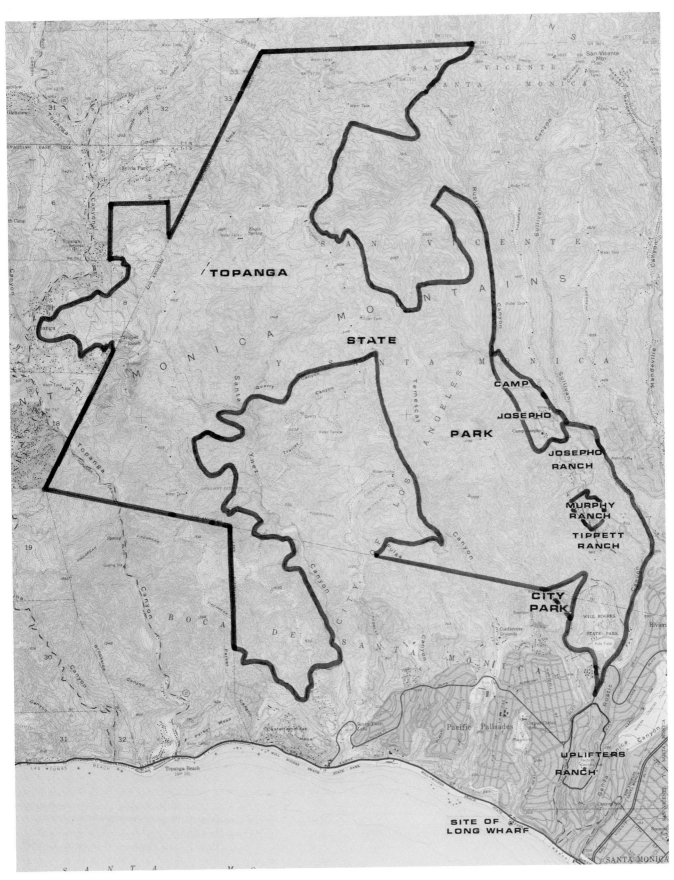

Map showing the present boundaries of Topanga State Park and the Will Rogers State Historic Park. It is historically significant that the lower portion of Temescal Canyon has been acquired by the city for a park, and the portion immediately north of Sunset Boulevard has been purchased by the Santa Monica Mountains Conservancy as an addition to the state park system. *Map prepared by Thomas R. Young.*

Bill Folsom's store at the mouth of the Cañon de Sentimiento, with Haystack Rock dimly visible in the background. *Courtesy Angelina Marquez Olivera*

Thanks to the diligence of Ernest Marquez, the site of Port Los Angeles was accepted as California Registered Historical Landmark No. 881 and dedicated by the state Department of Parks and Recreation, in cooperation with the Pacific Palisades Historical Society, on July 18, 1976. Marquez also designed a symbolic setting for the landmark, using original rails from the line which had led to the Long Wharf.

The most recent landmark was installed at the entrance of a new residential development on Elder Street by members of the Marquez family and the developer, Canyon Homes. Dedicated at a program sponsored by the Pacific Palisades Historical Society on August 16, 1979, the plaque noted that:

This land was part of the Mexican Land Grant Rancho Boca de Santa Monica, given to Francisco Marquez and Ysidro Reyes in 1839 . . . Since that year it has been owned and lived on continuously by members of the Marquez family . . . until the land was sold by them in 1979.

Today the jewel of the Pacific Palisades coastline is the J. Paul Getty Museum, though its address is erroneously given in the literature as Malibu. This designation was Getty's wish. Actually, the entire museum property, except for a small triangle of land to the west of the entrance gate, is in the city of Los Angeles and the postal zone of Pacific Palisades. Furthermore, it lies entirely within the boundaries of the old Rancho Boca de Santa Monica land grant, rather than within the Rancho Malibu.

The site is a special one historically — the narrow Cañon de Sentimiento, which was so precious to Pascual Marquez that he saved a 17.75-acre portion of it for his own use when the rest of his large

allotment was sold. After Pascual's death in 1916, his son Perfecto administered the property for the estate and moved his family to the canyon in 1920.

Perfecto's daughter, Angelina Marquez Olivera, recalls that Pascual's ranch house was located on a knoll west of the museum's herb garden, and that the sunny hillside was a favorite rallying ground for rattlesnakes. The family obtained water from a spring which is visible beside the entrance road today, and a second spring was located behind the Getty home. Near the museum's lower parking lot was an orchard, with a cookshack where Angie's mother prepared meals for the workmen. The plateau to the east was farmed by members of the Marquez family, who raised bumper crops of corn, tomatoes, watermelon, and squashes on the future site of Castellammare.

The other occupants of the property included an elderly Russian who lived in the cookshack, a merchant named Bill Folsom who had a small store at the mouth of the canyon, and a resourceful lady named Mrs. Hall who lived in a tent on a hilltop with her two children and taught ballet dancing to Angie and a handful of other pupils.

Occasionally Perfecto permitted organized groups to hold picnics on the property, hosting such events in an open area near the orchard. According to J. Paul Getty's biography, *Collector's Choice,* one such "Charro party" was in progress in 1921 when Claude I. Parker, who had long been interested in the ranch, arrived on the scene, learned that the property was for sale, and promptly agreed to pay a thousand dollars an acre for the "forty-acre" parcel — an over-simplified version of the transaction. Perfecto's records indicate that the estate received

$15,000 for Pascual's portion. The remaining acreage was owned by the Santa Monica Mountain Park Company.

Parker, a former collector of internal revenue for the sixth California district, was at this time a highly respected Los Angeles attorney who specialized in federal taxes, probate, and wills, and had a large clientele from the film industry. His wife, Blanche Irwin Parker, was the daughter of a prominent Santa Monica family.

For their home, the Parkers chose a site at the head of the canyon, near the upper spring. Here they built a six-bedroom, Mediterranean-style ranch house with a theater which they used for private screenings and previews of new motion pictures. This was appropriate, since the Parkers entertained large groups, including many movie people.

The grounds were equally spacious. Beyond the home were stables, a guest house, and cottages for the workmen. In the canyon and on the western ridge, Parker planted avocado and citrus trees and built trails for horseback riding. He transformed a gully behind the main house into a rock garden and planted a large grove of ornamental trees on the hillside. A stream, flanked by paths, ran down the rocky watercourse in a series of cascades and into a pool with a waterwheel. Around the house were formal gardens and beds of prize-winning roses. Halfway down the canyon, near Perfecto's old picnic area, was an adobe-walled barbecue where five hundred guests could be served.

In 1946 oil billionaire J. Paul Getty purchased the property for a price quoted at $250,000 by the *Los Angeles Times*. Mrs. Parker had died several years earlier; their son was grown; and Parker was living at the Los Angeles Country Club. Getty was familiar with the area. His home was on the oceanfront in Santa Monica, next door to William Randolph Hearst's palatial establishment; he had also visited Hearst's San Simeon ranch and openly admired the publisher's extravagant tastes.

On Getty's orders the house was remodeled, an extensive new wing and a more formal entrance were added on, and the name of the property was changed from "Canada Sentimenta" [sic] to the "Getty Ranch." Although Getty never lived in the

A view (ca. 1923) of the Claude I. Parker Ranch, at the head of the canyon. To the right of the main house are the garages, stables, and guest house. *Courtesy J. Paul Getty Museum*

Above, When J. Paul Getty purchased the Parker Ranch in 1947, he remodeled and extended the main house, creating a museum wing to house his collection of art works. *Left,* Getty also installed a small zoo on the property. Here, staff members are feeding the bears. *Both, courtesy J. Paul Getty Museum*

house, it was meticulously maintained by servants as if Getty might arrive at any moment, and, in fact, he is said to have spent three nights there.

Perhaps to compete with Hearst, who had wild animals roaming the range at San Simeon, Getty assembled a small zoo — a pair of brown bears, two bison, two white wolves, aoudads, gazelles, and a pet lioness named Teresa. To house them he installed rows of cages, prepared concrete dens, and fenced off a pasture where the parking lot is today. There were domestic animals as well — two large dogs, a pair of saddle horses, two cows, and a steer.

Getty seems to have been genuinely proud of his ranch and fond of his animals. Even after moving to Europe in 1951 to be near his Middle Eastern oil interests, he entertained thoughts of returning to California and called the ranch his permanent home. In 1959, however, he purchased a large estate in England named Sutton Place and lived there until his death in 1976 at the age of eighty-three.

Getty began collecting art objects in the 1930s and in 1953 established the Getty Museum in five rooms of the house. It was opened to the public on a limited basis, free of charge, and was expanded to nine rooms in 1970. Needing more space to accommodate his growing collection, Getty decided to build a completely new museum and chose, in cooperation with the trustees, to recreate a classical building as a suitable setting for his Greek and Roman antiquities.

The present museum building is patterned after the Villa dei Papiri, using detailed floor plans which were made when the first-century Roman villa was explored by means of tunnels in 1750. The site was located near Herculaneum, overlooking the Bay of Naples, and was buried in 79 A.D. in the same devastating eruption of Vesuvius that destroyed the nearby town of Castellammare di Stabia. The plan for the main and west peristyles was drawn from the Villa di San Marco at Stabiae. For today's visitors, therefore, the view looking seaward from the south porch of the museum incorporates not only the formal gardens below and the blue of the ocean beyond, but includes the western fringe of our own Southland version of Castellammare.

The museum itself was designed by the architectural firm of Langdon and Wilson, with Dr. Norman Neuerburg as historical consultant and London architect Stephen Garrett (who became the museum's first director) as consultant to Mr. Getty and the trustees. The resulting structure, which is built around a central garden and an atrium, is elaborately decorated with frescoes and Italian marble of rich and varied hues. It contains thirty-eight galleries and is particularly noted for its classical antiquities, Renaissance and Baroque paintings, and European decorative arts.

The gardens, designed by landscape architects Emmet Wemple and Associates, with Denis Kurutz as project director, are in the formal style of the day and feature plants characteristic of the Villa dei Papiri. A separate herb and kitchen garden, laid out along the same geometric lines, contains trees and other plants similar to those used by the Romans for household and medicinal purposes and religious rites.

The official opening of the museum — built at an estimated cost of $16 million — was held on January 16, 1974. The main building, grounds, and entryway occupy approximately ten acres; the remaining fifty-five acres are held for the benefit of the museum. The old home, which contained the original collection, is still called the "Getty Ranch" and is used for staff purposes. In Getty's will, he left the museum a handsome endowment which will permit a generous yearly expenditure in a manner to be determined by the trustees.

Recently a new director was appointed — John Walsh of the Boston Fine Arts Museum, who will lead the Getty through its future period of growth and change. A second complex, containing a major library and research facility and a new museum, is to be built at some as-yet-undetermined site, while the present villa will remain the Center for Antiquities.

When the museum opened, there were some harsh words from critics who pronounced it a "plastic paradise." The public, however, has embraced it warmly, finding it a place of ever-changing beauty, as well as a showcase for a burgeoning collection of art works.

Side-by-side with their appreciation of the Getty Museum, Palisadians continue to honor their own community origins and to wax nostalgic over the egalitarian cultural pleasures of the early Chautauqua assemblies. In this mood, the Pacific Palisades Historical Society celebrated the sixtieth anniversary of Founders' Day on January 14, 1981, holding a family-style birthday party at the United Community Methodist Church.

There were greetings from the Society's president, Harriet Axelrad, followed by a slide show, songs, and reminiscences. At the conclusion, Pacific Palisades' honorary mayor, Ted Knight, cut the huge anniversary cake, modeled after a float entered by Pacific Palisades in the 1928 Rose Parade. It was an evening that recalled the dreams of the pioneers and the old spirit of Beulah Land. In the words of the familiar gospel hymn:

I'm living on the mountain, underneath a cloudless
   sky, Praise God!
I'm drinking at the fountain that never shall run dry;
   O yes!
I'm feasting on the manna from a bountiful supply,
For I am dwelling in Beulah Land.

APPENDIX

CITIZEN OF THE YEAR AWARDS

1947	John Pixley	1966	Coline Wade
1948	Ethel Wilson	1967	Michael Martini
1949	Alta Swanson	1968	Ralph McKee
1950	Mrs. E.J. Kennedy	1969	Vahe Simonian
1951	Robert Wilson	1970	Vivian Braun
1952	Phyllis Genovese	1971	Tom McKiernan
1953	Robert Norris	1972	Robert Abernethy
1954	Gertrude McBride	1973	John Gabrielson
1955	Sylvia Morrison	1974	Ray Logue
1956	Arthur Loomis	1975	Robert McMillin
1957	Betty Linton	1976	Carlisle Manaugh
1958	Ah Wing Young	1977	Joseph Raymond
1959	Dottie Larson	1978	Jim and Gloria Stout
1960	William Hinchliff	1979	Wally Miller
1961	Anna Priolo Cool	1980	Jay Kuilee
1962	Edna Oleson	1981	Eva Holberg
1963	Russell Q. Olsen	1982	Herb Furth
1964	Albert Smith		Joe Jelikovsky
1965	Paul Spring		

HONORARY MAYORS

1949-53	Virginia Bruce	1967-69	Nanette Fabray
1953-55	Jerry Lewis	1969-71	Peter Graves
1955-57	Jack Owens	1971-73	Bob Abernethy
1957-59	Vivian Vance	1973-75	Edward Andrews
1959-61	Mel Blanc	1975-77	Adam West
1961-63	Doug McClure	1977-79	Walter Matthau
1963-65	Bob Rockwell	1979-81	Bert Convy
1965-67	Jerry Paris	1981-83	Ted Knight

Opposite, the J. Paul Getty Museum, located in the historic Cañon de Sentimiento, brings pleasure to thousands of visitors each year and is a source of pride to Palisadians. Photograph by Thomas R. Young

LANDMARKS

Site of Ysidro Reyes adobe (erected 1839)
   The first permanent residence built in Pacific Palisades.
   Pacific Palisades History and Landmarks Society
September 14, 1952
Pampas Ricas Drive, at Sunset Boulevard

Marquez and Reyes Landmark
   Honoring Don Francisco Marquez and Don Ysidro Reyes,
   grantees of the Rancho Boca de Santa Monica.
   September 14, 1953
   Jacon Way, between Marquez Terrace and Marquez Way

Indian Landmark
   "In Commemoration and Appreciation of the Indians who
   were first to live here."
   Pacific Palisades History and Landmarks Society
   January 11, 1959
   Santa Ynez Canyon, at Los Liones Street and Sunset
   Boulevard

Old Canyon School
   Second oldest remaining school in Los Angeles County,
   built in 1894 on Sycamore Road, moved to Channel Road
   in 1913, and later to Elder Street.
   Native Daughters of the Golden West
   November 11, 1965
   Elder Street, midway between Entrada Drive and East
   Channel Road

Founders' Oak Island
   Site where the founders gathered on January 14, 1922 and
   established the new community.
   July 16, 1955
   Pacific Palisades History and Landmarks Society
   also:
   Los Angeles Cultural Heritage Board, Los Angeles Historical

Landmark No. 38
March 25, 1966
Haverford Avenue, between Antioch Street and Temescal
   Canyon Road

Site of the Santa Monica Forestry Station
   "The nation's first experimental forestry station," established
   in 1887 at the instigation of Abbot Kinney, on land
   donated by Arcadia Bandini de Baker and Senator John P.
   Jones
   California State Department of Parks and Recreation, the
   California Division of Forestry, and the City and County
   of Los Angeles
   California State Historical Landmark No. 840
   August 18, 1971
   Rustic Canyon, opposite 574 Latimer Road

Site of Port Los Angeles: "The Long Wharf"
   At 4,720' the longest wooden pier in the world, completed in
   1893 by Collis Huntington and the Southern Pacific
   Railroad to serve as a deep-water port for Los Angeles.
   California State Department of Parks and Recreation and
   the Pacific Palisades Historical Society
   July 18, 1976
   Adjacent to the lifeguard station on Pacific Coast Highway at
   the foot of Temescal Canyon

Rancho Boca de Santa Monica Landmark
   Commemorating the continuous occupancy of this land by
   members of the Marquez family from 1839 until the
   present day.
   Sponsored by the Marquez family, Canyon Homes, and the
   Pacific Palisades Historical Society
   August 16, 1979
   Elder Street, opposite the old Canyon School

Palisades Basketball team c.1924. Left to right standing: Clarence Vore, Max Curtis, Noel
Rust. Kneeling: Lyle Addison, Rube Stadler, Dave Stadler.

BIBLIOGRAPHY

BOOKS

Ahrens, Katherine K. *Landmarks: Pacific Palisades, California.* Pacific Palisades: Privately printed, 1979.

Banham, Reyner. *Los Angeles: The Architecture of Four Ecologies.* New York: Harper & Row, 1971.

Bayless, Dan. *Riviera's Fifty Golden Years.* Los Angeles: Los Angeles Athletic Club, 1976.

Bedford, Sybille. *Aldous Huxley.* New York: Alfred A. Knopf/ Harper & Row, 1974.

Bowman, Lynn. *Los Angeles: Epic of a City.* Berkeley: Howell-North Books, 1974.

Case, Robert Ormond. *We Called it Culture: The Story of Chautauqua.* Garden City, N.Y.: Doubleday & Co., 1948.

Chandler, Raymond. *Farewell, My Lovely.* New York: Ballantine Books, 1940.

Crump, Spencer. *Ride the Big Red Cars.* Costa Mesa, Calif.: Trans-Anglo Books, 1962.

Fink, Augusta. *Time and the Terraced Land.* Berkeley: Howell-North Books, 1966.

Fryer, Jonathan. *Isherwood.* Garden City, N.Y.: Doubleday & Co., 1978.

Gabrielson, John. *The Town a Church Started.* Pacific Palisades: John Gabrielson, 1972.

Gebhard, David, and Winter, Robert. *A Guide to Architecture in Los Angeles and Southern California.* Santa Barbara: Peregrine Smith, 1977.

Getty, J. Paul. *As I See It.* Englewood Cliffs, N.J.: Prentice-Hall, 1976.

Harrison, Harry P., as told to Karl Detzer. *Culture under Canvas: The Story of Tent Chautauqua.* New York: Hastings House, 1958.

Huxley, Julian, ed. *Aldous Huxley: 1894-1963.* New York: Harper & Row, 1965.

Ingersoll, Luther A. *Santa Monica Bay Cities.* Los Angeles, 1908.

Isherwood, Christopher. *Exhumations.* New York: Simon & Schuster, 1966.

_____. *A Single Man.* New York: Simon & Schuster, 1964.

Jacobs, Lewis. *The Rise of the American Film.* New York: Columbia University, Teachers College Press, 1968.

[Jennings, Dean Southern.] *The Man Who Killed Hitler.* Hollywood: George Palmer Putnam, 1939.

Lambert, Gavin. *The Slide Area: Scenes of Hollywood Life.* New York: The Viking Press, 1959.

Le Vane, Ethel, and Getty, J. Paul. *Collector's Choice.* London: W.H. Allen, 1955.

Levant, Oscar. *A Smattering of Ignorance.* Garden City, N.Y.: Garden City Publishing Co., 1942.

Ludwig Salvator, Archduke of Austria. *Los Angeles in the Sunny Seventies: A Flower from the Golden Land.* Translated by Marguerite Eyer Wilbur. Los Angeles: B. McAllister, J. Zeitlin, 1929.

Lutjiens, Helen, and LaHue, Katherine. *A Sketch Book of Pacific Palisades, California.* Pacific Palisades: Phyllis Genovese, 1975.

Macgowan, Kenneth. *Behind the Screen.* New York: Delacourt, 1965.

Mann, Katia. *Unwritten Memories.* Edited by Elisabeth Plessen and Michael Mann. Translated by Hunter and Hildegarde Hannum. New York: Alfred A. Knopf, 1975.

Mann, Thomas. *The Letters of Thomas Mann: 1889-1955.* Translated by Richard and Clara Winston. New York: Alfred A. Knopf, 1971.

Marquez, Ernest. *Port Los Angeles: A Phenomenon of the Railroad Era.* San Marino, Calif.: Golden West Books, 1975.

Medved, Michael and Wallenchinsky, David. *What Really Happened to the Class of '65?* New York: Random House, 1976.

Miller, Henry. *My Bike and Other Friends.* Santa Barbara: Capra Press, 1978.

Nadeau, Remi. *City-Makers: The Story of Southern California's First Boom.* Los Angeles: Trans-Anglo Books, 1965.

O'Day, Edward F. *Bel-Air Bay: A Country Place by the Sea.* Los Angeles: Privately published for Alphonzo Bell. Young & McCallister, 1927.

Reagan, Nancy. *Nancy.* New York: William Morrow, 1980.

Rice, Craig, ed. *Los Angeles Murders.* New York: Duell, Sloan & Pearce, 1947.

Rindge, Frederick Hastings. *Happy Days in Southern California.* Los Angeles: Privately published, 1898.

Robinson, David. *Hollywood in the Twenties.* London: Tantivy Press, 1968.

Robinson, W.W. *Los Angeles from the Days of the Pueblo.* Menlo Park: Lane Publishing Co. and the California Historical Society, 1959.

_____. *Ranchos Become Cities.* Pasadena: San Pascual Press, 1939.

Robinson, W.W. and Powell, Lawrence Clark. *The Malibu.* Los Angeles: Ward Ritchie Press, 1958.

Smith, Grover, ed. *Letters of Aldous Huxley.* New York: Harper & Row, 1969.

Swanberg, W.A. *Citizen Hearst.* New York: Scribner's, 1962.

Viertel, Peter. *The Canyon.* New York: Harcourt, Brace & Co., 1940.

Viertel, Salka. *Kindness of Strangers.* New York: Holt, Rinehart & Winston, 1969.

Volker, Klaus. *Brecht: A Biography.* New York: The Seabury Press, 1978.

Warren, Charles S. *History of the Santa Monica Bay Region.* Santa Monica: A.H. Cawston, 1934.

Young, Betty Lou. *Rustic Canyon and the Story of the Uplifters.* Santa Monica: Casa Vieja Press, 1975.

————. *Our First Century: The Los Angeles Athletic Club, 1880-1980.* Los Angeles: LAACO Press, 1979.

PERIODICALS

Bourne, Tom. "Isherwood: The Hollywood Stories." *Reader,* June 13, 1980, p. 1.

Duncan, Robert. "The Ince Studio." *Picture Play Magazine,* March, 1916, pp. 25-39.

Hordern, Nicholas. "The Death of Thelma Todd: Hollywood's Strangest Unsolved Case." *Los Angeles,* August, 1976, p. 102.

Houseman, John. "The 1940s Exile of Bertolt Brecht in Southern California." *West Magazine, Los Angeles Times,* March 23, 1980, p. 3.

"Inceville Ghost City of the Movies." *Motion Picture Classics,* August, 1927, p. 71.

Isherwood, Christopher. "California Story." *Harper's Bazaar,* January, 1952, pp. 126-29.

Lieber, Jill. "A Dodo in Name Only." *Sports Illustrated,* August 9, 1982, pp. 40-49.

Locke, Sam. "Exclusive! We Solve the Murder of Thomas Ince." *Los Angeles,* November, 1981, pp. 94-110.

Lyon, James K. "Bertold Brecht in America." As reviewed in *New York Review of Books,* February 5, 1981, pp. 8-9.

Murray, Herb, Jr. "Study for a Super Seaway." *Westways,* December, 1962, pp. 4-6.

Nepean, Edith. "Thomas Ince." *Silent Pictures,* Spring, 1972, pp. 4-7.

"News of Los Angeles and Vicinity." *Motion Picture World,* October 9, 1915, p. 110.

"On the Fringe of a Golden Era: the U.S. Student." *Time,* January 27, 1965, pp. 56-57.

Pohlmann, John O. "Alphonzo E. Bell." *Southern California Historical Society Quarterly,* Part I, September, 1964, pp. 197-222; Part II, December, 1964, pp. 315-350.

Pratt, George C. "Spellbound in Darkness." *Rochester University School of Liberal and Applied Studies,* 1966, p. 129.

Rubsamen, Walter H. "Schoenberg in America." *The Musical Quarterly,* October, 1951, pp. 469-489.

Sexton, R.W. "An Up-To-Date Ranch House in the California Hills." *Arts and Decoration,* 1935, p. 17.

Shaw, David. "J. Paul Getty's Dream Museum: Critics Pan It, Public Loves It." *Smithsonian.* May, 1974, pp. 28-43.

Simpson, Jeffrey. "Utopia by the Lake." *American Heritage,* August, 1972, pp. 76-88.

"The Villa Leon." *Architectural Digest,* 1928, pp. 51-61.

Weschler, Lawrence. "Exiles in Paradise." *Reader,* November 17, 1978, p. 1.

UNPUBLISHED SOURCES

Feuchtwanger, Marta. "An Emigré Life." 4 vols. *UCLA Oral History Program,* 1976.

Greenwood, Roberta S. "Cultural Resource Evaluation: Palisades Preparatory School." Report prepared for James E. Schreder, Palisades Middle School, September 25, 1981.

Kennedy, John Hanscom. "Historical Development and Present Composition of the Commercial District and Surrounding Residential Areas in Pacific Palisades, Ca." Master's Thesis, UCLA, 1973.

O'Connor, Craig. "Housing Location and Street/Tract Layout of a Planned Community: Pacific Palisades, 1920-1940." UCLA, 1974.

Olmsted Associates, Inc. Records. Pacific Palisades — Charles Scott materials, 1922-29. 115 pages. Microfilm. Library of Congress.

Toch, Lilly, "The Orchestration of a Composer's Life." 2 vols. *UCLA Oral History Program,* 1976.

Waco, David. "Pacific Palisades: A Community Unique in its Background." History paper, UCLA, 1960.

Wendt, George. "The Mesas Have Changed: A History of Pacific Palisades." History 199, UCLA, 1963.

Weschler, Lawrence. "Ernst Toch: 1887-1964. A biographical essay ten years after his passing," Toch Fund, October, 1974.

NEWSPAPERS

Pacific Palisades Progress, 1924-28.
The Palisadian, 1928-1960.
Palisadian-Post, 1960-1983.
Los Angeles Times, 1921-1983.
Santa Monica Evening Outlook, 1921-1983.
Los Angeles Herald, December, 1929.

INDEX